ANTONIN ARTAUD

Man of Vision

ANTONIN ARTAUD

ANTONIN ARTAUD
MAN OF VISION

by

Bettina L. Knapp

With a Preface By

Anaïs Nin

SWALLOW PRESS
Chicago   Athens, Ohio   London

ISBN 0-8040-0809-4
Library of Congress Catalog No. 79-9637

Originally published by
    David Lewis, Inc., New York, in 1969

Reprinted in 1980 by
    Ohio University Press/Swallow Press
        Chicago   Athens,Ohio   London

TO THE MEMORY OF MY FATHER
DAVID LIEBOVITZ

CONTENTS

PREFACE

THIS IS A BOOK which is essential to a deeper knowledge of Antonin Artaud's work. Too little has been available in translation from the seven volume anthology of his works. Too much emphasis has been placed on the sensational aspects of his own life dramatization, on his madness. At last Dr. Bettina Knapp has given us a balanced analysis, interpretation and biography of Artaud, blending her familiarity with French literature, French theatre with an acute psychological insight and a woman's natural gift for interrelating the work and the human being, thus bringing us closer to his inferno with more empathy.

The total work of Artaud is impressive. In ancient times insanity was considered a possession by the spirits, and was believed to give access to intuitions which were denied to ordinary men. How the madness influenced Artaud positively and negatively Bettina Knapp measures with sensitive scales. There is in this book the rare awareness that when a man is cut off from ordinary life he is more intensely connected with his subconscious forces. His vision into new forms, new poetry, new theatre, new cinema, was unhampered by restrictions, conventionalities, hypocrisies, the fear and pettiness of men concerned with their own survival in society. Artaud took all the risks, took a perilous journey for us, and added to this the contemporary gift of keen awareness:

"Artaud's understanding of his mental state, the accuracy and technical exactitude with which he described it, the objectivity in analyzing the genesis of his sickness, gave one the impression of a man working at an art and at the same time watching himself work at it through a mirror."

Dr. Otto Rank, who understood the artist so well, once said that the artist created not *because* of the neurosis but in spite of it. In spite of the physical and mental torments Artaud experienced, his vision, his imagination, his invention was keener than his contemporaries whose orderly cartesian ideas were more in harmony with tradition and the times.

Bettina Knapp is well equipped to interpret Artaud. She has lived in France, knows France, has written about French writers, French theatre, and studied the sources of occultism which inspired Artaud.

"He was not only an actor, a director, a writer, and an artist; he was also the father of a new brand of theatre known as the Theatre of Cruelty."

She does indeed fulfil her promise "to trace Artaud's intellectual, philosophical and psychological development through his own works, in order to understand the visions and perceptions of this man who lived ahead of his time."

He was, as Bettina Knapp realizes, misunderstood by most of his contemporaries. When a revolutionary spirit confronts his contemporaries, the violence of his contempt for banalities, for the dead weight of worn out traditions, for dead symbols as D. H. Lawrence called them, causes antagonism and resistance. Fear paralyzes understanding. Artaud caused fear by his own dramatizations of moods, inner states, angers and rebellions which he hoped would be contagious, and instead alienated those who witnessed them. When he first presented his poetry it was a break in traditional poetry. This fear and resistance only disappear with the death of the artist. When Artaud was no longer there to insult the fearful and the ordinary, the static and the mediocre, people began to hear him. But even then, in America at least, all they pursued was a theatrical concept expressed dramatically.

Very little was known of the beautiful prose of *L'Art et la*

Mort, of the construction, the sum total of his work. Bettina Knapp's book is indicative of her imaginative and sensitive approach.

This book places Artaud far above the current fascination with the outer gestures of madness; it stresses its significance, and the knowledge to be gained from it. For it is only in certain states of exaltation that the artist sees further and more clearly than others. The same love which was given to Rimbaud's eruptions should be given to Artaud who went much further and more courageously and more fruitfully into his inferno.

"Artaud was in essence constructing an entire metaphysical system around his sickness; or if you will, entering the realm of the mystic via his own disease."

Bettina Knapp studies Artaud's relation to surrealism, his reasons for severing his connection with it. She has an unusually lucid mind and a clear, sharp focus upon chaotic and diffuse material. She has a gift for extracting the essential, and clarifying the disorders of poetry which end ultimately in a new organic pattern, truer to emotional forces.

One of the most striking chapters is devoted to The Theatre and the Plague. The title Artaud chose later, of Theatre of Cruelty, is in itself ambiguous and gave rise to many misunderstandings. Dr. Knapp studies this in depth.

"Strangely enough, Artaud's innovation, for the most part, arose directly as a result of his malady. An inability to think in a cartesian manner and an overly sensitive and high strung nature, led him to opt for a theatre which worked on the nerves and the senses, and reject one which sought to speak to the intellect alone."

What follows is a study which everyone interested in Artaud should read. It not only clarifies his theatrical concepts and intentions, but also the fear which alienated people from them. His acting out of his inner states, despairs, angers, might have swept them all into his personal infernoes.

Bettina Knapp registers with infinite care and skill both the failures and the gains.

"The universe which Artaud succeeds in evoking is a universe where everything takes on meaning, mystery and soul. It is difficult to analyze the effects obtained, but they are breathtaking and truly concern the re-integration of the magic of poetry in the world," writes Benjamin Crémieux.

When the theatre failed (only in a conventional sense because unknowingly Artaud had changed forever the direction and atmosphere of theatre in France) he turned to film and there again made his daring contributions.

"Artaud had very definite ideas on the art of the cinema." He anticipated the large screen, and sound emanating from all directions. He realizes the immense value of cinema for the pursuit of images, of dreams and fantasies. He acted, directed, wrote scripts.

Bettina Knapp gives us meticulous descriptions of plays and films unavailable to us.

At one moment she states: "There seemed to be no common denominator between Artaud and the directors of his day."

Her understanding is unfailing, illumining the darkest passages.

The quality of this book is that it conforms to the concept Artaud pursued throughout:

"I call organic culture, a culture based on the mind in relationship to the organs, and the mind bathing in all the organs, and responding to each of them at the same time."

From this book he should emerge as he would have wished: as a human being who gave his whole self to be consumed by a creation, as a poet who suffered his poem and his vision, every word meaningful and not the stutterings of a nightmare, every word a gift to us.

Los Angeles.
September, 1968

ANAïS NIN

INTRODUCTION

ANTONIN ARTAUD (1896-1948) was not only an actor, a director, a writer, and an artist; he was also the father of a new brand of theatre known as "The Theatre of Cruelty." Though his own theatrical productions were not commercially successful, Artaud stands out today as one of the great seminal forces of this century in the creative arts. His greatest contribution lies in the theatrical field, which he helped revolutionize. In this connection he influenced such divergent playwrights as Jean Genet, Eugène Ionesco, Arthur Adamov, Harold Pinter, Günter Grass, and Peter Weiss, among others.

Antonin Artaud was both a visionary and a mystic. He saw the theatre as had the people of antiquity, a ritual able to give rise to a numinous or religious experience within the spectator. To achieve such experience theatrically, he expanded the spectator's reality by arousing the explosive and creative forces within man's unconscious, an area he considered more powerful than the rational conscious in determining man's actions. By means of a theatre based on *myths, symbols,* and *gestures,* the play, for Artaud, became a weapon to be used to whip up man's irrational forces, so that a collective theatrical event could be turned into a personal and living experience.

In this volume, I have tried to trace Artaud's intellectual, philosophical and psychological development through his own works, in order to understand the visions and perceptions of this man who lived ahead of his time. Artaud was misunderstood by most of his contemporaries: Anaïs Nin was one of those rare exceptions. Artaud was quick to respond to her extreme sensitivity and uncanny artistic sense. In fact, he confessed that Anaïs Nin was different from the rest . . . she truly understood him whereas the others rejected him and his work. Indeed, it is only now that his ideas concerning the theatre, motion pictures, music and the pictorial arts are being discovered and understood as revolutionary.

My profoundest gratitude goes to Mrs. Estelle Weinrib whose knowledge, guidance, and unstinting friendship, during those tortuous days when this manuscript was being written, were invaluable to me. Her sharp and penetrating mind, her grasp of things psychological and theatrical made Artaud and his ideas living realities for me. My deepest thanks go to Mr. Georges Chimes, whose conversance with philosophical and religious concepts helped me through the all too hazardous *ways* of mystic teachings; to Mr. Weyland Schmitt for his expert editorial help; and to Anaïs Nin, whose friendship with Antonin Artaud permitted me certain insights into his character and works.

I should also like to thank Dr. and Mrs. Ado Avrane, Colette and Claude Avrane, Denise Macagno, Professors René and Sidonia Taupin, Professor Alba della Fazia Amoia, Dr. Edward Edinger, Bianca Garufi, Jerry Frienman, and everyone else who helped in any way to make this work possible. The New York Public Library, the Bibliothèque Nationale and, particularly, Mme. M. F. Christout of the Arsenal Library in Paris, have my special gratitude for furnishing me with photostats and microfilms of material which would have otherwise been unavailable to me.

As always, I thank my family for their understanding and patience: my husband, Russell S. Knapp, my mother, Emily Gresser Liebovitz and my two little children.

Hunter College of the City University
of New York

BETTINA L. KNAPP

PART ONE

THE FRAGILITY OF
THE MIND
(1896-1926)

. .

I have only aimed at the clockmaking of the soul,
I've only transcribed the pain of blotched adjustment.[1]

CHAPTER I

THE LITTLE CELESTIAL POET

I

ANTOINE-MARIE-JOSEPH ARTAUD was born on the morning of September 4, 1896 at 4 Rue du Jardin des Plantes in Marseilles. He was the first of numerous children, most of whom died in infancy. His mother, Euphrasie Nalpas, had come from Smyrna and was of Greek origin. His father's family, of French Provençal stock, was well-to-do, having been in the ship-fitting business for over one hundred and fifty years.

Not much is known about Artaud's early years, and he himself spoke little of them.[2] It would seem, however, that he had a very special affinity for his grandmother; her warmth and understanding, that particular wisdom and gentleness which comes with old age, made him feel for her what he had never experienced before nor would, perhaps, ever again: a closeness and a calmness, a sense of belonging and an inner joy. He used to sit and watch her by the hour kneading the dough with her strong and sturdy fingers, for what would be delicious cakes dipped in honey.

Pleasant memories were in short supply, however. Marie-Ange Mallausséna, Artaud's sister, reported that at the age of five he suffered almost unbearable head pains which developed into meningitis. The young child was cured of this almost-always fatal sickness, but the after-effects were to last the rest of his life. Under constant medication and unblinking supervision, the intense young Artaud did manage to enjoy some of his days in Marseilles

(3)

and the occasional trips he took to Smyrna to visit his grandmother and her family.

Whenever he returned to his home, however, he was again
plunged into the tense atmosphere created by an over-solicitous
mother and an anxious father. Artaud's father was determined
that his son not only inherit, but make a success of the family
ship-fitting business. His mother, on the other hand, was forever
concerned about her son's health. She gave him no freedom to
develop, instead created, inadvertently of course, in the highly
sensitive youth a tremendous sense of dependency and guilt at
having been the cause of so much of his mother's suffering.
Though feelings of extreme tenderness were directed toward his
mother, he began to rebel at such a crippling situation as he grew
older; never overtly, however. His altered attitude manifested
itself rather in the increasingly important role his inner world
played in his life. Only in this realm, he reasoned, could he roam
entirely free. But sometimes his feelings of anger were uncontrollable and retorts which hurt his mother deeply burst forth.
Minutes later, however, the young Artaud could be seen knocking
frantically on his mother's door, begging for forgiveness.

Artaud studied at the *Collège du Sacré Coeur* in Marseilles and
was a good student. He loved to read and to draw and was pas-
sionately interested in the works of Baudelaire, Rollinat, and
particularly Poe. Indeed, the imagination of the sensitive youth
was so keenly stirred by the symbolist poets and by their American
"mystic brother" that he began writing poems of his own. Around
1910, he founded a small literary magazine of which he became
editor-in-chief, and for which he signed his works "Louis des
Attides." Artaud worked assiduously on this magazine which
lasted, it is believed, three or four years. It was at this period also
that a bent for the dramatic became noticeable. One afternoon,
Artaud created a stage set in his room which was so grotesque as
to frighten a cousin who had come to spend the afternoon.

Though Antonin Artaud's life was full and active, it was considerably saddened by his grandmother's death. Furthermore, he
was now repeatedly plagued by severe head pains, probably the

after-effects of the meningitis. By 1914, when he was about to take his baccalaureate in philosophy, and for no apparent reason, Artaud became despondent. He complained of "internal" discomfort and refused to see people. Shortly thereafter, attacked by an acute case of neurasthenia, he tore up all of his poems and short stories, and gave his books away. His parents, extremely concerned over such behavior, consulted the well known phychologist, Dr. Grasset of Montpellier. The prognosis, after lengthy examination, was bleak and Dr. Grasset suggested he be sent to a rest home, *La Rougière,* near Marseilles. Some months later, his health was so improved that he was returned to his family.

Artaud spent a relatively pleasant summer in the country with his family in 1916. During this time, however, he was drafted and left for Digne to join the 3rd Infantry Regiment. Nine months after his induction into the army, Artaud's mental stability had become so impaired that he was released and sent home.

Artaud had changed considerably during those months. He had grown more solitary than ever. In fact, he was going through a severe mystical crisis. Spending days on end fingering his rosary beads or in fervent prayer, he seemed to be desperately searching for *something.* By 1917 his moods had become stormy and totally incomprehensible. His mother took him to Divonne-les-Bains in the Vosges mountains, having heard that the air was beneficial for nervous ailments. But the young man's health did not improve. In fact, it grew worse and in the fall of 1917, mother and son went to Saint-Didier near Lyon, then to Lafoux-les-Bains in the Gard. Artaud's health by this time had so deteriorated that a male nurse had to be with him constantly. His head pains had become steadily more acute and apparently affected his entire behavior pattern. At times, during the periods of wracking pain, he would throw stones at the male nurse whose presence seemed unbearable to him during each crisis.

It became clear to his family that Antonin would have to be sent to another rest home. The talented and high-strung youth went to *Au Chanet,* an establishment for nervous ailments near Neufchâtel in Switzerland, headed by a Dr. Dardel. Here Artaud was encouraged to draw and to write, and, after two years of treatment, his condition was so improved that Dr. Dardel felt him ready to leave what had become his psychological home, and to strike out on his own. He suggested that the young man go to Paris where he could nurture his artistic bent and not return to Marseilles; the family atmosphere could only have a deleterious effect upon him. He further counseled that Artaud stay in Paris with Dr. and Mme. Toulouse who would provide him with suitable, still-necessary supervision.

Antonin Artaud arrived in Paris in 1920. He was twenty-four years old, intense, handsome, slim, with a straight nose, fine lips, and piercing eyes. His talents still undeveloped, his ideas not yet coalesced nor his magnetic personality tested, Artaud stood at the threshold of *his way: his search.*

He was particularly fortunate in being able to live with Dr. and Mme. Toulouse. Husband and wife seemed to understand Artaud's needs from the very outset of what was to become a profound and lasting friendship. A writer and a cultured human being as well, Dr. Toulouse encouraged Artaud in every possible way to express himself in words. He not only asked his pensionnaire to become his secretary and to write for the magazine he edited, *Demain,* but also to preface his anthology: "In the Course of Prejudice" (*Au fil des préjugés*) (1923).

During the formative years with the Toulouses, Artaud learned to express the rhythms, the sounds, and the ideas which lived within him. He crystallized them in poems, essays, and short stories. Whatever the form, his works manifested his inner anguish. Whatever the subject matter, it was always the unseen, the unknown, the intangible, the symbolic and metaphysical aspects which attracted Artaud.

But Artaud could not always dwell in his inner world. He was faced with a very real problem at this juncture: financial. If he was to become self-sufficient and no longer lean on his family for support, he would have to earn a living. But how? He was not even certain as to what his professional path in life should be. Would he write? He thought he might enjoy the acting career.

Perhaps he could become part of Paris' theatrical world and so bring poetry and new life to the stage.

It was Lugné-Poe, director of the symbolist Théâtre de l'Oeuvre, a man responsible for encouraging many young talents, who offered Artaud his first role, the part of a bourgeois awakened during the night, in Henri de Regnier's play *Sganarelle's Scrupules* (Feb. 17, 1921). But Lugné-Poe did not really have enough challenging roles to offer Artaud who was intent, at this point, upon pursuing a dramatic career. He therefore auditioned for the celebrated Firmin Gémier. Gémier detected Artaud's extraordinary presence, his insight and sensitivity and recommended him to Charles Dullin, the founder of the *Théâtre de l'Atelier*. It was at Dullin's school and theatre that Artaud learned the theatrical trade. He absorbed what material his "master" had to teach, and began to inject himself into the characters he portrayed.

Artaud's first months with Dullin were happy ones. In fact, it has been said that this period in which he was affiliated with Dullin was the happiest in Artaud's life. It was at this time that he met Génica Athanasiou, a hauntingly beautiful actress in Dullin's troupe. She was to be the only person with whom Artaud could live, even for a little while, and share some measure of warmth and love.[3]

Artaud was also enthusiastic about Dullin's way and his manner, and fascinated by his extraordinary craftsmanship.

> When listening to Dullin's teachings one has the impression of rediscovering old secrets and a whole forgotten mystique of the *mise en scène*. It is at once a theatre and a school.[4]

He believed in Dullin's training methods: rhythmic gymnastics, diction, discipline and improvisation, which forced the actor "to think out the movements of his soul instead of representing them. . . ."[5] Dullin wanted his actors to use their hands, their feet, their muscles, every inch of their bodies to express the essence of the work being performed. His theatre was not just "an enterprise", it was a "research laboratory".[6]

Artaud remained with Dullin for over a year interpreting such parts as Sottinet in Regnard's work "The Divorce" *(Le Divorce)*; creating the costumes and decors for several works, including the interlude "The Olives" *(Les Olives)* by Lope de Rueda. Though Dullin admired the integrity and fervor Artaud brought to his work, there were occasions when he found it more than trying to cope with Artaud's way of seeing things. When, for example, *Huon of Bordeaux* by Alexandre Arnoux was in rehearsal, Artaud as Charlemagne, with his long and curly beard, advanced toward his throne on all fours. Dullin tried his best to dissuade him from interpreting his role in this fashion. He looked like "an enraged French poodle", declared Dullin.[7] At this remark, Artaud shot up suddenly, brandished his arms and in a commanding tone stated flatly: "Oh! When you work in truth! Then! . . . ."[8]

Such divergencies of interpretation led to a break with Dullin. But their estrangement was brief. Indeed, a few months after Artaud had left Dullin's troupe, the two men, who had great admiration for each other, frequently spent long hours together, dining or discussing their work. In addition to their common theatrical interests, they shared a great admiration for things Oriental. Artaud had seen the Colonial Exhibit in 1922 in Marseilles and had watched the sacred Cambodian dancers perform before the reproduction of the Temple of Angkor Wat. The gestures, the masks, the stunning costumes, the exotic atmosphere, the strange and haunting lighting effects had made a profound impression upon Artaud.[9]

Though Dullin and Artaud were on friendly terms, they both realized they would be unable to work together. Artaud, more certain of himself in the theatre, had his own vision as to the interpretation of plays and roles. Furthermore, quixotic by nature, he did not seem to fit into the routine work of acting companies. In addition, it might be said that Artaud was not really a good actor because he was physically stiff and awkward on stage. Each time he moved, one of his acting companions Jean Hort later wrote, his various limbs seemed to be in total disarray. A simple movement, for any actor, turned into a complicated series of jerky and trembling motions or manoeuvers for Artaud. His muscles were taut, his body unbending, his face pale and hard, his eyes flashing and, as he advanced in zigzag formation, his hands seemed to wave about him in "crazy arabesques".[10]

Artaud, however, persevered in the acting profession and was soon engaged by the well-known Russian actor, Georges Pitoëff. But once again, only minor roles were dispensed to him. And even these shrank considerably as time went on, due to his inner turmoil, his overly personal, too-tense approach to certain roles. In fact, he was finding it increasingly difficult to work with people— with a group of actors, with a director.[11]

Artaud had sufficient insight into himself and others to realize that the performing phase of his theatrical career was passing. He would have to find a different way to express himself, and this would not be easy. Imprisoned in his subjective anguish, life was made endurable only by the fascination with his inner world which stirred and captivated his imagination. He tried to express these sentiments in his "Correspondence with Jacques Rivière" (*Correspondance avec Jacques Rivière*), one of the most crucial documents in modern literature and the most revealing that ever came from Artaud's pen.

II

It all happened in 1923. Artaud had sent a group of eight poems entitled "Backgammon in the Sky" (*Tric Trac du Ciel*)[12] to Rivière, the editor of the *Nouvelle Revue Française*. He had hoped that his verses would be accepted by this well known literary review to which Jacques Copeau, André Gide and Jean Schlumberger, among others, had furnished the sap back in 1909. Though Rivière rejected the poems, he was sufficiently taken with them to want to meet their author. In a letter dated May 1, 1923, Rivière asked Artaud to stop at his office some Friday between 4 to 6 o'clock, and Artaud did just that.

Artaud found a sensitive and discerning man in the editor of the *Nouvelle Revue Française*. Jacques Rivière discovered a talented, perhaps quixotic, but certainly fiery poet. Each man responded to the other and each seemed to answer some inner need in the other. Desperately seeking a kind and intelligent confidante, Artaud wrote to Rivière on the very evening of their first encounter. A correspondence developed.

Rivière had at first criticized Artaud's poems from a purely literary point of view, as was natural, since he was a magazine editor: the awkwardness of the verse, the oddness of the themes, the lack of focus. Indeed, in a letter dated June 23, 1923, he wrote Artaud stating:

> As I told you at the very beginning, there are awkward things and disconcerting oddities in your poems. But they seem to me to be due to a certain quest on your part rather than to lack of command over your thoughts.
>
> . . . . you do not in general, achieve sufficient unity of impression. But I have enough experience in reading manuscripts to sense that it is not your temperament that prevents you from focusing your abilities upon a simple poetic object and that with a little patience you will succeed, even if only by the simple elimination of divergent images or features, in writing perfectly coherent and harmonious poems.[13]

Artaud reacted instantly to Rivière's appraisal. He felt that the editor had merely skimmed surfaces; that he was absolutely unaware of his state of being, the profound turmoil which was his existence. Rivière was judging him as he would anyone else—any *normal* writer. And this was wrong. He was different. It was, therefore, imperative for Rivière to approach his work with a keener sensibility. A more profound reaction had to be solicited from the editor of the *Nouvelle Revue Française* and this could only be forthcoming after he had become better acquainted with Artaud's *real* problem.

In a letter dated June 5, 1923, extraordinary because of its precision and lucidity, Artaud described what he *knew* to be not purely a literary difficulty on his part, but rather a *physical* one. Only Artaud could really explain Artaud. He depicted himself as being overcome with frequent seizures of anguish and turmoil; so intense at times as to succeed in stifling *all* poetic inspiration.

At these moments, his physical energies froze; a paralysis of all creative activity ensued; and life became a horrendous experience.

> I suffer from a frightful disease of the mind. My thought abandons me at all stages. From the simple act of thinking to the external act of its materialization in words. Words, forms of phrases, inner directions of thinking, simple reactions of the mind—I am in constant pursuit of my intellectual being. Hence, *whenever I can seize upon a form,* however imperfect it may be, I hold it fast, lest I lose the entire thought.[14]

Artaud's understanding of his mental state, the accuracy and technical exactitude with which he described it, the objectivity in analyzing the genesis of his sickness, gave one the impression of a man working at an art and at the same time watching himself work at it through a mirror.

What tortured Artaud most acutely at this point, and what he wanted Rivière to understand, as fully as one being can comprehend another, was what he called the ineffectiveness of his thought processes. He described the ideas which flowed into his mind and which he believed he possessed at certain moments and then, for no reason at all, they would disappear, dissolve into *nothingness.* Gone was the train of thought; a lapse of memory followed. In fact, Artaud went so far as to declare his total inability to follow an idea through to the end, of sustaining his thought, both in his daily pursuits and in his literary endeavors. Each time he believed he was about to seize the amorphous content and transform it into the material word—it vanished before him, as in a dream. Yet, he felt compelled to continue. He tried valiantly to pursue his "intellectual being," which he described as his *thought clusters:* the content of his inner self which he could see and feel within him but which he could rarely if ever seize and imprint on the blank page. The struggle was unending.

To be plagued by such a physical disability made the difficult literary task Artaud had set up for himself an even more tormenting experience; to express in words the *idea,* the *sensation,* the *coloring* which lived within him in a dormant stage—that is, to transform the *non-material* into the *material,* the feeling into the syllable. Flaubert had also been obsessed with this problem, that is, to find the "mot juste", *the* word which would express the *exact* feeling, thought, and image. Flaubert's had been an uphill fight, as witnessed by *Madame Bovary*. What would be the outcome of Artaud's endeavor? Could dealing with a problem he was unable to resolve and over which he had little or no control bring forth anything positive?

It would have been impossible for Artaud to evaluate his chances of winning his battle at this point. Whatever the outcome, he wanted Rivière to know that the ineptitudes, platitudes, and failures which appeared in his poems, resulted from his disease. These deficiencies, he wrote to Rivière in his letter dated January 29, 1924, stem from "the profound uncertainty of my thought . . ." they are the product of a man who is "a mental case, an actual psychic anomaly . . ." [15] It is not merely a matter of practice or of literary discipline. Had he all the experience in the world, Artaud declared, the outcome of his efforts could not possibly be any different. Yet, paradoxically, he was fully aware of the fact that he possessed great talent and that he was bursting with ideas. But he also knew, and this worked on him, that he would need *heroic* strength to continue the battle—because his thoughts blurred and scattered like birds in flight during any protracted effort. Artaud described the physical breakdown and the ensuing disintegration of his ideas visually, in plastic images; already giving a clue to what would become his *concrete* metaphysical concepts. He stated that his agonizing situation was due

> . . . . to a central collapse of the mind, to a kind of erosion both essential and fleeting, of my thinking, to the passing nonpossession of the material gains of my development, to the abnormal separation of the elements of thought (the impulse to think, at each of the terminal stratifications of thought, including all the states, all the bifurcations of thought and form.[16]

But this destructive force which Artaud felt so keenly had its constructive aspect. It forced him to attempt some expression of his inner rage and frustration, thereby urging a creative effort. It also resulted in his trying to destroy that force within his own being which prevented him from following his idea-cluster to its logical conclusion. A victim, therefore, of his own psychic energies and conflicts, he tried valiantly to gain control over his inner dynamism, and thereby know himself as Creator and Destroyer.

As both Creator and Destroyer, Artaud knew times of extreme terror. When he peered within himself, he saw a large and gaping *void*. This void, as described by Artaud in his letter dated June 5, 1923, was not to be understood as a feeling which came upon him only during moments of creativity, but rather as an awesome, almost supernatural force during which time he saw *total emptiness,* and *total absence* of feeling.

Like Parmenides of Elea, Artaud believed in the existence of the void. Indeed, he considered himself to be forever situated on the edge of a gaping abyss. The void has been a symbol used by man in one form or another since time began. It can be linked psychologically and philosophically, to the Creation Myths. In *Genesis* (I, 1-2) there is mention of void:

> In the beginning God created the heaven and the earth.
> And the earth was without form, and void; and darkness was upon the face of the deep.

Hesiod, relating the Greek Creation Myth, tells us that *Chaos* arose first. In Greek "chaos" signifies an empty "yawning" or a void. Within Artaud then, this unlimited void also existed; to be feared, as is the unknown, to be longed for, since it is the source of creation.

Artaud's terror of the void then parallels his fright of creation; for to create means opening oneself up to new experiences and with them, dangers. Each creator must go *down* into the depths of his unconscious and dredge up from this limitless and awesome region of his being what is of import to him. Going down into these depths is in effect an initiation process, the price one pays for entrance into a new realm. Dangers are forever present; balance can be lost; vertigo and drowning can ensue. The initiate may never surface again; the poet might be so fascinated by the unconscious realm, as was Narcissus when looking at his own image in the pool, that he might never be able to see the light of reason or deal with his conscious or rational mind. The great danger of not returning from the deep always faced Artaud. He feared, and with reason, the dissolution of his ego or the loss of his identity—a lapse into insanity.

In his letter of January 29, 1924 to Rivière, Artaud inserted a poem entitled *Cri,* indicating in poetic imagery the forces which lived within him and which were tearing him apart.

> The little celestial poet
> Opens the shutters of his heart.
> The heavens clash. Oblivion
> Uproots the symphony.
>
> Stableman the wild house
> That has you guard wolves
> Does not suspect the wraths
> Smouldering beneath the big alcove
> Of the vault that hangs above us . . .[17]

In this nine stanza poem, Artaud is transformed into that "little celestial poet" who has opened his heart. He describes his emotions during those moments when he is seized by the forces of *creation.* However, once his tender adolescent feelings are exposed, they will percipitously take control of his being: "The heavens clash." The inner struggle for ego-control increases, his emotions become more violent, and a counterforce—"oblivion"— develops within him and "uproots the symphony" or the poem. The "alcove" or "vault" that covers and protects the poet hides the extreme upheavals within his breast, which are expressed in such words as "wolves" and "wraths". "Silence" and "night" follow. There ensues an extreme effort for control of what is by now a cataclysmic turmoil. The poet must "muzzle" all "impurity" which arises from within him, the mind must clarify and transform the unchannelled instincts writhing within him. The "star", the "sky", the "night", all outer forces (reflecting his inner world), feed on the repast brought forth from within, that is, the poet saps and eats of his own being, and "a strange dream" which is "nevertheless clear", emerges from the "uprooted earth", a fragment dredged up from the poet's tormented being.

> The lost little poet
> Leaves his heavenly post
> With an unearthly idea
> Pressed upon his hairy heart.[18]

So Artaud described his personal "creative act": to seize one idea from the maze of emotions, to clutch it, before it falls back into oblivion—the void.

In Rivière's letter to Artaud on March 25, 1924, he indicated what seemed to him to be a paradox: the extraordinary precision of Artaud's self-diagnosis, his remarkable insight into himself, as opposed to his complaint of being unable to control his thought processes, of suffering from lapses of memory and concentration, symptoms which by their very nature should make impossible the clarity in Artaud's letters. Rivière was so struck by this dichotomy, this lesion within Artaud's personality, the unique problems besetting this individual mind, that in a letter dated May 24, 1924, he asked him for permission to publish their correspondence. The "writer and the recipient" would of course be given "invented names" and identities would remain carefully hidden. Artaud was delighted with the idea, but made the proviso that the entire correspondence be printed as is and signed by the parties involved. There should be no anonymity. Artaud wanted the readers to have the impression of being part of "a true story," of a living agony.

> Why lie, why try to place on the literary level a thing which is the very cry of life?. . . . The reader must believe that it is a matter of an actual sickness and not a phenomenon of the age, of a sickness which is related to the essence of the human being and his central possibilities of expression and which is involved in an entire life.[19]

The readers would be told of a man's inner existence as revealed to him in sporadic fragments. Artaud insisted he possessed no sense of continuity, and saw himself and his works only in spasmodic flashes during moments of creativity,[20] he could experience his total existence only in fleeting fragments. His inability to pursue his own thought to its conclusion, to concentrate on an object for any length of time destroyed whatever sense of balance he might possess.

> I am quite aware of the jerkiness of my poems, a jerkiness which derives from the very essence of inspiration and which is due to my incorrigible inability to concentrate upon an object.[21]

Artaud's problem had become such an obsession that it was reflected in all of his work; in his attitude of dissatisfaction toward himself; and society, in general. His feelings of discontent seemed to mirror those of certain of his contemporaries. But there was, however, a vast gulf which separated them. And Rivière, as well as the subscribers to the *Nouvelle Revue Française* who would read his *Correspondance* must be informed of these differences. Tristan Tzara, the founder of the Dadaist movement (1916), could be likened to him by strangers because the Romanian-born poet was one of those rebellious young men intent upon bringing about a change. Similarities, however, end here. Though he had sunk into a kind of nihilist depression, Tzara's mind was clear even when he used the irrational to mock the rational. André Breton, the founder of Surrealism (1924), also possessed a fine instrument. With his mind he explored the unconscious, that autonomous region which he felt was the source of truth and beauty. Pierre Reverdy, another defiant writer whom Artaud included in his list, employed fantastic, illogical, and disturbing images in his work, but again, in a rational manner. At all periods there are those who seek to change things—to discover new theories and philosophies to replace the old. They are humanity's innovators. With a tinge of envy, Artaud pointed out the *wholesome* nature of Tzara's, Breton's, and Reverdy's rejection of contemporary society and their search for something more satisfying, a personal *raison d'être*. But Artaud, unlike his friends, possessed a soul which was "physically impaired," and which brought him excruciating emotional and physical suffering.

> . . . . the fact is that they do not suffer and that I do, not only in my mind, but in my flesh, and in my everyday soul. The unrelatedness to the object which characterizes all literature is in my case an unrelatedness to life. I can truly say that I am not in the world, and this is not a mere mental attitude.[22]

Artaud was unable to adapt to life; he could not relate to others; he was not even certain of his own identity.

Such an attitude of "rootlessness" or of "suspension", was by no means a façade or a pose; it was rather the direct result of a smouldering and festering disease which was slowly eating away at Artaud's very being.

> A sickness that affects the soul in its deepest reality and that infects its manifestations. The poison of being. A veritable *paralysis*. A sickness that deprives you of speech, of memory, that uproots your thinking.[23]

Indeed, this sickness was destroying his ability to *speak,* to *recall,* and to *uncover* his thought. To see such destruction occurring and to be unable to arrest it was terrifying. What had caused all this suffering? Why had *he* been singled out by destiny to experience such anguish?

Artaud had his own answers to these questions. It must be recalled that he had gone through a deeply religious phase. This stage of his life, however, had passed. Artaud no longer considered himself a practising Catholic. In fact, he had, for all intents and purposes, renounced the trappings of his faith. What remained— and this is of utmost importance—was a profoundly spiritual orientation toward life's forces: an unusual capacity to experience the *numinosem*. The intensity of his religious feelings affected him so suddenly and so totally at certain moments, that his entire body quivered; and he felt himself to be inhabited by some unknown physical presence. He was convinced that the force which was corroding his body and mind stemmed from a "superior and malevolent will" which had arrived from the *outside* to wreak havoc upon his thoughts, his inner being. This outer force was of mysterious origin, and like "vitriol," was corroding the poet's very vitals.

Rivière now understood Artaud *plain*. And in an outburst of great empathy and sympathy, tried to encourage him to keep fighting. He explained to him the benefits which could accrue to such a person as he: familiar with depression, experienced in the pain of a "soul being broken by the body" and "invaded by its weaknesses."[24] Only the being with a great capacity for suffering, he maintained, possessed the *vision* required to see beneath surfaces. *Sight*, however, is concomitant with agony. To struggle fiercely against pain; to try to overcome the difficulties which bar the enlightened path is to participate fully in life's flow. "There is no absolute peril," Rivière assured Artaud, "except for him who acquires a taste for dying."[25] And Artaud wanted to live— desperately.

CHAPTER II

LEFTOVER ICICLES OF THE MIND

I

"... the shreds that I have managed to snatch from complete nothingness",[1] referred to the eight poems Artaud had sent to Jacques Rivière for publication and which the editor of the *Nouvelle Revue Française* had rejected. It was these verses that had led to their correspondence and had aroused Rivière's interest in the young poet. He was caught up in them for some strange reason, fascinated by a certain mystical and haunting quality which they possessed. Though much of the coloring, images, rhythms, and symbols in these poems are reminiscent of the works of Baudelaire, Rimbaud, Poe, Mallarmé, Laforgue, there is a very personal clement—Artaud's own agony—present in these finely chiseled quatrains which makes them unique.

Even the title *Tric Trac du Ciel* which Artaud gave to the slim volume published in May of 1923 by the Galerie Simon,[2] is significant in itself. "Trictrac" means backgammon, a game played with dice. Though this game has its rules, its guiding element is chance. The "sky" indicates the limitless spiritual possibilities offered to the dice player who tries to wind his game or to the poet creating a poem. Before the dice are cast, both player and poet have infinite possibilities; afterward, all choice has been eliminated. The player's number appears before him as does the poet's work.

Artaud was not alone in his torment. To be able to express the infinite by means of the finite, the non-material by means of the material had also preoccupied Mallarmé. While Mallarmé's efforts ended finally in the sterile blank page, Artaud's attitude at this point was positive. He was young and a fighter, and though he was the victim of enormous physical and psychological infirmities, he would continue the struggle to the end.

The poems in *Tric Trac du Ciel* focus around several themes: the genesis of the creative process, the conflict between inner and outer reality, and the fear of the void.

The violence of the imagery as well as the auditory qualities of these verses can be used as a barometer to measure the highs and the lows of the author's emotional state. Fire and flames (hot images) express activity, the fervent onrush of ideas as in the poem "Organ Grinder" and "Romance"; ice and snow (cold images) denote passivity and sterility as in "Snow" and "The Organ and the Vitriol." The almost constant juxtaposition of images takes on metaphysical significance: it indicates eternal flux and by extension the perpetual metamorphosis of all elements within the universe. Therefore, "blankness" or "whiteness" does not necessarily mean the end of the creative forces within the individual, it signifies only a change in direction. "The Trappist," for example, shows that what was once unfit food for poetry can in time turn into a delectable dish. A haunting cosmic quality is achieved by a depletion of imagery and a slowing down of pace as in "Moon," an exquisite little poem in which the author ponders the question of reality and its mirror image. The auditory sense frequently assumes greater importance in these verses than does the visual. *Prière,* which depicts the author's fright of the void, is accompanied by a whole series of tumultuous sounds.

Artaud's style is so personal, and the qualities inherent in his verses so unusual, that it might be fitting here to analyze four of them in detail: "Organ Grinder," "Snow," "Prayer," "Moon."

A close-up of an "Organ Grinder" (*Orgue allemand*) and his monkey looms into view; they are entertaining at a fair. Like the poet, they excite a crowd around them. The music emanating from the organ grinder's box is like an echo or answer to "the noise of the heaven's organs," combining thereby the spiritual (heaven) and physical (earth), the inner and the outer world. The entire city is waltzing under the spell of the organ grinder's music and the poet too is dazzled by his swirling emotions as he begins creating his work. But within the organ grinder's "stomach", no one divines what "rocket" explodes, just as no one understands the poet or what he feels when those "flaming" moments of creation engulf him. The "music" to which the city reacts, but which it has not really absorbed, is comparable to "marble," it is hard and cutting, and though a thing of beauty, it has the power to crush. The spirit, because of it, has been transformed into a "frozen sky." The poet, agitated by his own ideas and emotions, can be so possessed by them as to transmute the heat of energy into a frigid ice: creation becomes sterility.

The coldness, the whiteness, the purity, and the feeling of fruitlessness of the image "Snow" (*Neige*) seemed to preoccupy and tantalize Artaud as it had Mallarmé. "Obsession of snow, pearl," he wrote, "Whirlwind of souls white atoms . . . Burning silver wise men's souls. . . ." But where there is frigidity, there is the possibility of its opposite, fire. To make the feeling of sterility more terrifying, Artaud introduces his reader to a series of antithetical images, rhythms, and colors, thereby reflecting and at the same time contributing to the conflict raging within him. In swift succession, emotions swirl about, first destroying each other, then blending into one-another, building up, toppling over and rebuilding *ad infinitum*. And as "this wheel turns into ecstasy," the poet experiences, as had Faust, the heights of jubilation and the depths of despair. He sees everything, from the spiritual or Godly aspect of man down to the very "sperm," beyond the rational, to that eternal circle where opposites unite. The poet is a visionary, as Rimbaud said he was, a man who sees what no mortal can see.

In "Prayer" (*Prière*), the poet prays and beseeches. He wants to experience not the terror of the void, that gaping abyss, but those moments of lucidity, of fiery creativity, of intense suffering and extreme joy, which only a creator *knows*. The burning coals, the thunder, the chasms, the vertigo, the inner turmoil that rends him, the division that grows wider within him and which causes such searing wounds—in short, the totality is what the poet longs for. Though it is an excruciating feeling, it is proof that the poet is alive, that he has not been swallowed up in that immense yawning abyss.

> Make our mind vacillate
> In the heart of its own science
> And ravish our intelligence
> With claws of a new Typhoon

In "Moon" (*Lune*), the poet, like the astral body, can express himself only as a result of the experiences which he has *known* in another world, that limitless realm of eternal riches, the unconscious. The surface of the moon which shines only by reflected light can be bitter and sullen; in the same way, man's image is affected and distorted by reflection from his inner fire or light, that is, his inner world.

> In the fabulous obscurity
> Where the moon had risen
> The placidity of summer
> Extended its smoking branches.

The moon is a mysterious being as it wanders through space, reflecting and extending its white rays of light, veiling its essence from humanity. Similarly, the poet creates a maze about his inner world, never disclosing it to the outsider except through the medium of words. The poem, cold and inanimate like the moon, also derives its force and light from another realm.

II

Tric Trac du Ciel was published through the efforts of the art dealer Kahnweiler and was printed with woodcuts by Elie Lascaux. Though Artaud could take some satisfaction in the fact that his literary career was progressing, and that he was earning the admiration and recognition of a small group of artists and poets, his physical condition was deteriorating. In 1915, a doctor had advised him to take opium to alleviate the terrible head pains he suffered. As time progressed, however, Artaud found himself taking more and more of the drug until he became addicted to it. Such reliance on a drug increased rather than diminished his fears forever crystallizing about insanity.

Artaud's anxieties concerning his mental state, so directly and incisively analyzed in his "Correspondence with Jacques Rivière," aesthetically in his poems, are expressed in metaphysical terms in "The Umbilicus of Limbo" (*L'Ombilic des Limbes*). The title itself is an indication of the mood and meaning of the work. "Umbilicus" or navel is the scar on the abdomen where the umbilical cord binding infant and mother had once been attached. This "point of cleavage" is where energy and life is first infused into the human being by the mother. The Indians describe the entrance of psychic energy through the navel in the Vishnu myth: the time when "Vishnu sank into a profound trance" and Brahma emerged from his naval bringing the Vedas with him.[3] The navel is the point of creation and this scar or hole or abyss, by extension, is the only physical remembrance of that other life or of *primordial unity*. "Limbo" is the abode of souls barred from heaven through no fault of their own, souls of men who died before the coming of Christ or unbaptized infants. It is, therefore, a place of confinement, a state of neglect or of oblivion.

The umbilicus is a physical attribute; limbo, a condition existing in the mind, a spiritual concept. Artaud unites these opposites, the spiritual and the physical. He does so primarily because of his inability, at times, to differentiate between them. He *felt* acutely an intense power (physical or spiritual) within him, which he tried to seize hold of and which frequently became visible to him through concentration, introversion, or the drug. In such states, primordial images or archetypes were thrust up into his conscious mind, and through them he was permitted to sink into that world *within*. Like the mystics of old, Artaud wanted to seize, in one intense illumination, the total image, to come face to face with *Self* (identity, inner Deity, *Deus absconditus*). He wished to transform the visual or audible symbol or experience into the word, the unknowable into the knowable, but unfortunately Artaud was unsuccessful, as we learned in his "Correspondence with Jacques Rivière," in capturing and holding the word much of the time. Even if he found the "right" word, it still represented a mere fragment of what he had experienced. Meanwhile, his original thought or idea had vanished and despair suffocated him.

Artaud was in essence constructing an entire metaphysical system around his sickness, or, if you will, entering the realm of the mystic via his own disease. The focal point of his universe was himself and everything radiated from *him* outward. To explicate himself, he reasoned, would enable him to understand the collective, the spiritual, the physical, life, death, and so relate to them. For this reason, perhaps, although Artaud was essentially a secretive and introverted individual, he felt compelled to express himself in writings others would read. This might be his only means of holding his volatile personality together. It could also become a weapon to be used aggressively, against a society which could not understand him and individuals who mocked his quixotic ways. And "Umbilicus of Limbo" was all these things. It was intended to "derange man," to take people on a journey "where they would never have consented to go."[4] Artaud was going to open the door on to his *reality*, take his readers down the damp corridors of time, into recesses riddled with strange beasts and grotesque phantoms, display his inner world, the source of creative energy itself, where black suns sparkle and blue flames congeal.

What Artaud revealed during the course of his inner pilgrimage and how he described these discoveries makes for one of the most thrilling, horrifying, and absorbing documents since Dante's *Inferno*. By means of Artaud's peregrinations through the mystical *spheres* of his heavens and his hells of existence, or the various layers of his unconscious, he succeeds in contacting the most primitive elements within himself and within all men: the Beginning, Chaos, the Abyss—the source of all Creation—Reality. Artaud looked upon the Abyss or Chaos as *Nothingness* from which Creation or *Something* arises. This process of transformation from Nothing to Being has been illustrated by mystics linguistically, by means of two Hebrew words: *ain,* which means nothing, and *ani,* which means I. A mere rearrangement of the same letters totally alters the meaning of the words. Such a change implies, symbolically, the passage from "a gap in existence" or the Void or Nothingness, to existence. Artaud tried intensively to experience this process or instant of transformation when Nothing becomes Something.[5]

Artaud's journey brought him *self-knowledge* and with it, suffering; as a similar venture had brought it to Nietzsche—pain in the spirit and in the flesh, *that* agony of the man who sees. Artaud's voyage inward can be divided into three distinct phases: the journey itself, fraught with all sorts of hazards; the initiation, a painful rite; the partial attainment of his goal. The quest is accomplished on four different levels: the conscious, the unconscious dictated by the drug, the visual medium of painting, and the dramatic world.

During the first phase of Artaud's travels, he confronts his readers with a whole series of images which not only impose upon them the weight of his sensations, but take on metaphysical and psychological import: as witnessed by the following extract in which rootlets and wind are mentioned, among other images.

> And the tiniest rootlets peopled this wind like a network of veins, their intersections glowing. Space was measurable, rasping, but without penetrable form. And the center of it was a mosaic of explosions, a kind of merciless cosmic hammer of distorted heaviness, which fell again and again into the space like a forehead, but with a noise as if distilled. And the muffled enveloping of the noise had the dull urgency and penetration of a living look . . . But little by little, the mass turned into a slimy powerful nausea, a kind of immense flux of vegetal thundering blood. And the little roots trembling at the edge of my mental eye detached themselves with dizzying speed from the mass shriveled by the wind.[6]

The above mentioned images take on special meaning. They permit Artaud to deliberately repress the rational thinking function and allow the irrational (unconscious) contents of the human psyche to float into consciousness in the form of visual images. The images, in turn, are such potent factors of the human psyche that once recognized, they can bring about an alteration of the individual and also in his thinking process. Artaud did not, therefore, experience an idea as a rational phenomenon. First, there was the external visual image transmitted to him via the senses; there followed the powerful responding inner image which, fed by his *nerves* and *senses,* snowballed and gained momentum within his mind, turning into a massive avalanche and, finally, striking with the impact of a burning and overwhelming *idea.* Thus, an idea for Artaud became not merely an intellectual exercise but a numenous experience. For him, it is the impact of the image brought by the "irrational" *senses* that brings about a "sovereign reorganization" within him. At the moment of impact, the irrational plays a part in the creation of "a new Sense," a new way of experiencing and seeing. In this manner, Artaud could express through the image, metaphysical and philosophical concepts: as witnessed by the previous paragraph in which rootlets and wind are mentioned; in other passages, hammer, burning acid, and glass come into sharp focus.

What Artaud saw surrounding him, as revealed in the above passage, was a whirling mass. The speed and force of this infernal movement could engulf him at any time and it had to be stopped. Slowly, therefore, he forces his inner eye to focus on a more precise part of the whirling mass. The image of the wind looms in, symbolizing the spirit. But this blast was so intense and came at such a pace, that instead of the one root, "the root of all Roots," as it was referred to by XIIIth-century Spanish Kabbalists, meaning unity or beginning, Artaud encountered many uprooted rootlets.[7] Such an image indicated a lack of equilibrium. He had not yet discovered his identity (Self, inner Deity, *Deus Absconditus*); nor reached down into the *center* of his own depths to that focal point or primordial and dimensionless point which the Jewish mystic, Moses de Leon, in the *Zohar,* looked upon as the point within the circle, the "Origin of Being" or the "Beginning."[8]

Torrents of feelings are experienced during the poet's inward flight: a numbing sense of hopelessness, despair, and death in the poem "The Poets Raise their Hands"; depression, in "Black Poet." The wanderer has now become bitter, haunted by a virgin's breasts, tormented by burning, stormy internal forests, raging eyes, and searing tongues—all set in the poet's path to halt his progress. He likens these feelings and instincts to dogs and horses and although he knows them to be the source of creative force, he is tormented because he cannot transform the unchanneled mass of instinctuality into the work of art.

> Black poet, a virgin's breast
> haunts you,
> embittered poet, life boils
> and life burns,
> and the sky resorbs itself in rain,
> your pen scratches the heart of life.

Anger drenches the poet in "With me God-the-Dog, and his tongue. . . ." By means of a series of brutal and sensual images (tongue, crust, vault, triangle, burning coals, knife, water, ice, root, virgin), Artaud explains that he must hammer his way through, break down the crust and barriers of man's rational world with his tongue, if need be, until he reaches the very "breast of earth and gelid water," where all is in the process of change, of disintegration. As the poet feels himself to be transcending the barriers imposed upon rational man, and at the very instant of attaining the "dog-star," the paradoxical height in the depth which is the union of spirit and matter, he feels "levelled" by a paralyzing sense of the utter inadequacy of his aesthetic rendition of the experience.

Artaud was like a man possessed and pursued. The immense treasure within himself which he wanted to *see* and to *seize* and to drive out of him like an evil spirit, was surrounded by sparks and flames, His visions are reminiscent of certain images in the Kabbala—for example, Enoch's transformation into the Angel Metatron, during which time flesh becomes like "fiery torches";

veins, fire; eye-lashes, flashes of lightning. Artaud felt the same burning sensations Enoch had experienced, that is, the pain one must know as part of an initiation process which permits one to cross from one world to another.[9]

Such a crisis or initiation is referred to by certain mystics as a "break-through" from one aspect of life to another, from self consciousness to cosmic consciousness. When this "break-through" occurs, the inner Abyss or Nothingness, that gaping hole or void which Artaud so feared and at the same time so longed for, would be experienced. After such a confrontation, hopefully, the inner light would become apparent and would be absorbed into the conscious mind. When and if Artaud could make contact with that region, of "pure absolute Being" or of "inexpressible fullness" or of "Nothing," his initiation would be completed.[10]

Artaud did see the Abyss—but for seconds only. At these moments, he spoke in terms of "gel" and "clarity", implying that from these icy impersonal depths, the clarity and purity of absolute Being, or the Deity was revealed. To penetrate this new realm had its dangers. In this undifferentiated state or sphere of Being, one risked being sucked down into those limitless waters of the unconscious world, of never returning to a differentiated or conscious existence. Artaud, therefore, experienced ambivalent feelings toward his quest: fright and joy; love and hate.

The more deeply Artaud searched within himself, the more removed he became from society, and for long periods of time he felt cut off from the rest of the world, isolated and despairing. Added to his dolor was the terrifying reality of being severed from his *Self,* doomed to a state of oblivion in limbo, fully communing neither with his inner world nor with the world about him. Unlike Dante who succeeded in his goal of acquiring cosmic consciousness, Artaud could as yet only keep trying. He resorted to the drug to bring on visions artificially which he hoped would lead him to the discovery of his identity as well as enable him to understand and cope with his creative process. Artaud's description of those forces within him which break through from his unconscious to his conscious mind are of short duration, as they were with Baudelaire and Rimbaud, their violence and intensity being too great to be endured for any length of time.

In his essay "Description of a Physical State" (*Description d'un état physique*), Artaud provides his readers with sharp and brutal images that emerge from his murky depths and reveal the effects that opium or morphine had on him.

A sensation of burning acid in the limbs, twisted muscles as if skinned, the feeling of being in glass and breakable, a fright. . . .[11]

At these moments Artaud seems to be pinioned by disorder. Every gesture requires extreme effort. He feels disconnected by "a type of inner rupture between the connections of all his nerves." Each limb, each facet of his being—both physical and spiritual, inner and outer—seems to be separate and working against the other. Artaud will have to burrow still further to the point where "things no longer have an odor, no sex,"[12] if he is to reach the state of *unity,* and be able to "equilibriate what is falling, reassemble what is separate, recompose what is destroyed."[13]

There was still another way Artaud could descend into himself: by stirring his visual sense, through a painting. When looking at André Masson's canvas of a "Nude", for example, he did not remain detached, but rather felt co-mingled with the essence of the color and form that appeared before him. He saw himself wandering about in the circular stomach, the tongue of fire, the egg, the spire, the cells, the marble, the skies, the mountain, the Morgue, the burning sun, the air which was like congealed music, the abyss—images he used to describe the paintings and evoke his sensations and reactions to it. He felt he was communing with the matter figured on the canvas and becoming part of it (through psychological projection). Therefore, he reasoned, he had breached the gap between inert and active matter. Having achieved another dimension, he felt himself more able to commune fully with the forces within the universe. Such a feeling of relatedness made it possible for him to experience, if only momentarily, an inner balance and harmony. At these moments, he wrote: "I am returning to my source."[14]

Indeed, Artaud was so captivated by the visual—a painting in particular—that his "mental drama", "Paul the Birds or the Place of Love" (*Paul les Oiseaux ou la Place de l'Amour*) which revolved around the renewal and rediscovery of his inner world, featured three Florentine painters as the protagonists. These artists are projections of certain aspects of Artaud: Paolo Uccello ("Paul Bird") represents Artaud, the rationalist, the cerebral side of human endeavor; Donatello, the spiritual; Brunelleschi, the earthly and sensual side.

An understanding of this work is so vital in explaining Artaud's increasing fascination with the fine arts, the plastic image, and the philosophic, that a detailed explanation of "Paul the Birds or the Place of Love" is warranted here.

The drama begins as Paolo Uccello tries to find out ". . . where he lost the roads to his soul, even to the form and suspensions of his reality." A voice speaks out and tells him "Leave your tongue." He then tears his tongue out.[15] Such action means, in effect, that he destroyed his ability to communicate, his spirit. He had maimed himself and, therefore, could only work on surfaces, never reaching beyond them. If he felt or saw *within* he could express such sentiments only in the most rudimentary fashion since he had been deprived of his vocal organ. Furthermore, Uccello is described by Artaud as walking about like an insect, as speaking in a small voice, as being detached, unreal, and disembodied. Like the Florentine artist, then, who was preoccupied with problems of perspective and sought to draw on his canvas as many lines as possible which led the eye inward, Artaud's Uccello is more interested in intellectual concepts than in living experiences. As for sensuality, it holds no interest for Uccello, since "he sees it as glassed and mercurial, cold like ether."[16]

During the action of the play, Brunelleschi and Donatello tear each other apart while Artaud remains prostrate and helpless, like a woman about to give birth or one who has just given birth. Watching the drama unfold before him in which he is the *sole* (though divided) protagonist, he is both observer and observed: viewing elements of his own being act and react. He is impotent to change the course of events because, he explains, he is "on the other side of all mental glasses," that is, separated from what he sees by glass. These hard, cutting, mirror-like glass partitions prevent him from coming into contact with his other selves which are rootlets, propelled willy-nilly before him. But though the energy present is unchanneled and destructive, it also has its positive aspect: "The fire in which those glasses macerate has been translated into fine fabric." Hence, from agony and disorder, arises creation: from Chaos, the work of art.

Brunelleschi declares his annoyance with Uccello who is letting his wife die of starvation. Leaping across space and time into a dimensionless world, Brunelleschi's exasperation "lacerates the purely mental atmosphere of the drama . . ." But how, asks Artaud, can Selvaggia die of hunger? "Does one die of hunger in the Spirit?" After all, this drama is taking place "purely in the Spirit." The answer is in the affirmative. Though this is a mental drama, the spirit must be fed; if not, the renewing and restoring principle is lacking and the person in question will starve, *spiritually* and *mentally*.

"Paul the Birds" is remarkable because it reveals an Artaud beginning to detach himself from his writings: cutting them out, transforming them into the work of art, impersonalizing them— letting them live in the realm of the collective. Such an achievement marks enormous strides over Artaud's early works in which he could only depict himself, within himself; and not yet project on to other forms.

Paradoxically, Artaud who was now turning outward in his writing was leaning inward in his daily existence. He was considered by his friends to be quixotic and bizarre, a "shadow" type not really of flesh and blood but evanescent, transparent, fluid almost. Artaud himself sensed the fact that he was *double,* if not *triple,* and that perhaps his struggle for harmony and unity was an impossible one. His nightmarish existence takes on dramatic form in "The Jet of Blood" (*Le Jet de sang*), a work in which he demonstrates an even greater ability than he had in "Paul the Birds" of abstracting himself from his work.

"The Jet of Blood" is a short play which attacks the political, social, sexual and religious attitudes of the day in a half-mocking, derisive manner; one which is suffused with a sense of dread and despair. Far more than a criticism of society, it is a revelation, of course, of Artaud's inner life: this time, the difficulties he had in making his adjustments as he grew from boy to man, and the bloody struggle to make some connection between inner and outer reality. What Artaud sets before his viewers, however, is anything but personal. It is, on the contrary, an anonymous collective world, detached and objective. Even the cast is impersonal, each character appearing as a function rather than by name: the young man, the young girl, the nurse, etc.

"The Jet of Blood" not only stands as a landmark in Artaud's development, but also as a bizarre and highly original theatrical concoction which has gone a long way in influencing the writers of the *absurd*. It is so important a document, in fact, that a meticulous explication of it is imperative if comprehension of Artaud's later theatrical world is to be realized.

The play opens as a young boy and girl say to each other, "I love you and all is beautiful." This statement is repeated by both boy and girl with variations in emphasis and on different tonal levels, like a litany or joyful refrain expressing the intensity and pitch of their emotions. The boy and girl represent youth and idealism, satisfaction with the *status quo,* the state of childhood contentment, reminiscent of Adam and Eve in paradise. Suddenly, there is silence. One hears the noise of an immense wheel turning as it releases air and a feeling of terror is aroused as a storm breaks. During the course of the storm stars collide, legs, living flesh, hands, columns, masks, scorpions, a frog, and a scarab and other items fall from heaven in slow motion, as if into a void.

The world is no longer beautiful. It had become ugly, sordid and dangerous. The differentiated world of the adult can now be seen, divided and disoriented. The triurnal aspect of the world is seen as a scorpion crawling upon the earth, ejecting its poison at will, as a frog living on land and in water, as a scarab worshipped as a spirit by the Egyptians. These represent three facets of existence—the will of the conscious mind, the amorphous material of the unconscious world, and the spiritual character of the upper regions. These aspects, once unified in the innocence of childhood, are now, in adulthood, divided and in conflict with each other, arousing hatred, lust, fanaticism—and disgust.

The young boy and girl are frightened when they see this new world and they leave it. A knight in shining armor appears on stage with his heavy-breasted Nurse. The Knight seems to symbolize past strength and grandeur. But the audience is in for a surprise. Instead of the sturdy and courageous knight, we see a ten pound emotional weakling. He asks his Nurse for the gruyère cheese which she is carrying wrapped in paper, implying that this adult-boy is still in need of that nourishing aspect (cheese) of his Nurse-Mother.

The Young Man now appears on the scene: "I saw, I knew, I understood. . . ." he declares. Then society's representatives come forward: a priest, a shoemaker, a procuress, a judge and others appear on stage. The priest puts his arm around the young man's neck and, in confessional tones, wonders to which part of the girl's body the Young Man most frequently will allude. Hoping for some kind of lewd answer, he is annoyed when the Young Man speaks in sincere and innocent tones and names God. The Priest now assumes a Swiss accent, implying that if one religion does not work another might. Switzerland, referred to by Rabelais as the Vatican of the Calvinists, is implied here.

Darkness suddenly engulfs everything; there is great thunder and flashes of lightning and then an enormous hand comes down and seizes the procuress by the hair. But she bites the hand of God and blood spurts from His wrist. Having *experienced* pain and anguish, she acts out her aggressions and blasphemes. Having overthrown old concepts and fables, she and the Young Man rush into each other's arms. At this moment, the Nurse returns carrying the dead Young Girl of the beginning of the play. When the Knight sees his Nurse, he shakes her; he wants more gruyère. He is in a rage and curses her, implying his ambivalent relationship to his Nurse-Mother. But the Young Man, the idealist, sincere and naïve speaks out: "Don't hurt mommy." The Knight, all brawn and no strength is covered with flashing armor that hides the infant who is still tied to the nourishing aspect of the mother. And, as he curses his Nurse, scorpions emerge from beneath her skirt.[17] The Young Man and the procuress flee. The Young Girl arises, almost as in a miracle play and dazzled, says: "The Virgin! ah! that's what they were looking for."

"The Jet of Blood" reveals youth's optimism and idealism, the desire for independence and the need to belong, the nostalgic world of the past and the pain to come.

III

Paris was rippling with new ideas in the 1920's and the publication of "Umbilicus of Limbo" did not even make a dent in the literary structure of the day. It was drowned out by the noisy demise of Dadaism, born in 1916, and the effulgent emergence of Surrealism, in 1924.

Dadaism was a movement which rebelled against society, language and literature; it sought to destroy all established values and replace logical reason with conscious madness. The early Surrealists had been, for the most part, Dadaists first: André Breton, Paul Éluard, Louis Aragon, Benjamin Péret, Philippe Soupault, Pierre Reverdy, Jean Cocteau. But since Dadaists had become destructive in their outlook and had offered nothing constructive to the young generation, the Surrealists felt they must break away. In 1921, therefore, Dada died when the students at the École des Quatz' Arts drowned its effigy in the Seine.

André Breton published his *Manifeste du Surréalisme* (Surrealist Manifesto) in 1924. It was in this work that he defined the Surrealistic movement which he saw as both a liberating and constructive force. It freed man from the grasping tentacles of an overly constricting moralistic bourgeois society as well as from literary and artistic conventions. It brought forth another world to be scrutinized, one not limited by man's rational vision, but unconscious and infinite.

The Surrealists wanted to expand man's conception of reality, to make it express or reflect the totality of the universe. To accomplish this, man must commit himself to his unconscious world, he must allow that inner realm to speak, unhampered by any preconceived thoughts and judgments concerning time, space, and motion. In painting, for example, the Surrealists created collages as introduced by Picasso and Braque. These creations flouted all previously held artistic conventions by introducing foreign matter into a picture, changing not only the possibilities of the image *per se,* but creating doubt as to the nature of the form itself. Marcel Duchamp painted on glass, Francis Picabia signed his work with an ink blot, Max Ernst in his "La Femme 100 Têtes" resorted to humour to attack established values. (Note the pun. The title can be interpreted as "The Woman Without a Head" or "The Woman of 100 Heads.")

While the Surrealists rejected everything that was fixed or regulated, they did lay the groundwork for something constructive. They wanted to become "the deaf receptacles of so many echoes, modest RECORDING INSTRUMENTS" of another world. The unconscious was as real for them as the material world was for the average person.

The magazine "The Surrealist Revolution" (*La Révolution surréaliste*) (1924-1929) was the chief voice for this group of energetic men. Pierre Naville and Benjamin Péret were its directors. In the magazine there appeared transcriptions of dreams which had been recounted: reports of sessions of automatic writing; answers to questions of suicide; love; surrealistic methods of investigation; philosophical questions; and attacks on Paul Claudel, Anatole France and the novel in general. Literary works, in poetry or prose, by Louis Aragon, Robert Desnos, Paul Éluard, Pierre Reverdy, Roger Vitrac, Michel Leiris were also printed at odd intervals, as were reproductions of drawings by de Chirico, Breton, Masson, Miro, Man Ray, Ernst, Magritte, Arp, and Tanguy.

"The Bureau for Surrealist Research" at 15 Rue de Grenelle was to be the center for Surrealist research. The Bureau issued communiqués to the press and became a laboratory in which experiments in the creation of a new type of "psychic" life were

carried out. The group welcomed all those who could not accept
or adapt to the established society: inventors, psychotics, dreamers,
etc. They would form the *prima materia* for a new alchemy.

To lay bare the treasures that the unconscious mind holds
buried within its folds, to expose these to society in a new ethic
and aesthetic, was the goal of the Surrealists and it would coincide
exactly with Artaud's own mode of survival and his artistic creed.
During the year 1925 Artaud became associated with the Surrealists. He published several articles in their journal "The Surrealist Revolution" and in others, the *Disque-Vert,* and the
Nouvelle Revue Française, in which he outlined his views concerning the various topics preoccupying him and his fellow
surrealists: the destruction of reason and logic first.

In an editorial "A Table",[18] Artaud derided everything that
was logical and suggested that a search be made to seek out just
the "marvelous," the hidden and the mysterious forces within
man and nature. "Beware of your logic, Sirs, beware of your
logic, you don't know to what ends our hatred for the logical can
lead us."[19] He attacked reason in "Manifesto in Clear Language"
(*Manifeste en Langage clair*) and demanded its suppression in the
field of education in "Letter to the Rectors of European Univer-
sities" (*Lettre aux recteurs des Universités Européennes*). Artaud's
attacks on reason reflected perfectly his mental deficiencies. What
was faulty within his own make-up—his reason or mind—he
sought to destroy in others. It was not merely a rejection of the
status quo, as it was for the Surrealists. Artaud wanted, unconsciously only perhaps, to destroy the normal. With the reign of
the illogical, he could find himself one of many, like the others:
no longer a recluse, tormented by the vast moat which existed
between himself and society. To be part of something; to relate
to others; and not always suffer the torments of the damned. . . .

And Artaud was able to communicate with the Surrealists to a
certain degree, particularly on such subjects as religion and death.

Both Artaud and the Surrealists had been disenchanted by
Christianity. They felt that it no longer served mankind's spiritual
needs. In an article "An Address to the Pope" (*Adresse au Pape*),

Artaud declares that everything in the Catholic dogma: confession, the Index, the meaning of sin, canons, anything connected with the "Roman masquerade," produced hatred and became a vehicle for torturing the spirit. Christianity had developed throughout the centuries into a crushing force, stifling all creative activity within man. Artaud and his fellow Surrealists believed in a modified form of Buddhism. They craved, and Artaud in particular, for a state of *non-being* or *nirvana,* in which suffering no longer exists. Such a state of non-being could be reached through the wisdom of the East. Oriental philosophy, alluded to by Robert Desnos as "the citadel of all hopes",[20] might serve to alleviate the occidental condition of alienation from true, inner reality. From the Surrealist's point of view, through Buddhism it was possible to achieve a condition of no conflict or duality—no longing. Man could enjoy perpetual communion with the core of life, with the spirit of the *all,* thereby experiencing total and absolute liberty and happiness.

As for death, a question which would occupy Artaud increasingly with the passing of time, it did not exist *per se,* as an end of everything. Death simply meant passing from one phase of existence to another. It is not a destructive power, but rather a vehicle for rebirth. Artaud covers the subject of Death philosophically and imagistically in "Art and Death" (*L'Art et la Mort*), a small anthology of articles he had published in periodicals: *La Révolution surréaliste, Feuilles libres, Cahiers d'art,* and *Nouvelle Revue Française,* between the years 1925-1928.

There was an urgency in Artaud's fascination for death: a frenzied and throbbing attraction, intimately connected with his disease. It is, therefore, described in many strange and frightening ways: as crushing, yet marvelous sensation; material as is a thought; alive, as is an object; "a kind of suction-cup placed upon the soul";[21] a "suspended breath"; a bad dream. Death, for Artaud, can be experienced on different levels and in various phases of existence: in childhood, linguistically, and with an imbalance in attitude.

Death appears to man in childhood or when experiencing certain terrible frights. At those moments, a veil seems to lift, ancestors are heard and seen, memories of past existences fly into focus, colors can be touched and sounds become visible. The world of appearances vanishes and one is introduced to the realm of essences—to the absolute. But this image of death is lost as the child grows to maturity, acquires identity and differentiates himself from his origin.

Death can be known linguistically and had been by Artaud. When writing, for example, he used *terms* to describe his feelings and ideas which acted by their very nature as limiting agents. The *term terminated* the thought, he maintained, rather than described or represented it; it paralyzed his efforts, confined, limited, "localized" and strangled his every action and breath. Bound and constrained, hemmed in and tied up like a "knot" by his mental and physical deficiencies, Artaud felt imprisoned and his only desire at these moments was to untie or unbind these "knots" which asphyxiated him: "A knot of central suffocation."[22] This "knot" is referred to in "Fragments of a Journal in Hell" (*Fragments d'un journal d'enfer*) an essay appearing in "The Nerve Scale" (*Le Pèse-Nerfs*) and which, in certain respects, is reminiscent of Rimbaud's "A Season in Hell." The "knot" is a mystical term and implies a "barrier", something which prevents man from enjoying complete freedom or from being liberated from the bonds that constrain him. When, as is mentioned in the Tibetan "The Book of Untying Knots," these knots have been untied, the soul is freed from the bonds of the flesh. These "knots" that the Tibetan, the Buddhist, and the Hebrew mystics refer to have a dual nature. They keep the soul a prisoner within the individual's body during his existence, but they also protect him against the "flood of the divine stream" or in psychological terms, the contents of the collective unconscious, which would crush or drown him.[23]

For the poet, the situation is paradoxical. If the stops or "knots" were to remain, he might find it increasingly difficult to perceive the archetypal images and would lose all numenous experience. On the other hand, if he risked untying the knots, whatever raw materials his conscious or rational mind might capture could be worked on by his judgment, which would discern and sift out what was not absolutely essential in the creation of his work of art.

Artaud's extreme conflict stemmed in part from his desire to perceive natural forms in their raw unconscious state without being overwhelmed by them, to merge with the Spiritual, Cosmic or Unconscious forces—and yet retain his identity. There were times when Artaud's "knots" did become untied. He describes such instances in "Fragments of a Journal in Hell",[24] when his unconscious surges forth with tornado-like speed. These are painful moments for him, when he feels "stigmatised", suffering from the blinding pain of *vision*. Unable to act to quell the "terrifying forms which advance" toward him, he lives without identity as "the roads to eternity open up" before him, and he becomes part of the cosmic flow—as an individual, he is dead.

Death can also be experienced as an imbalance in attitude which results in a withdrawal from life. Such was Artaud's case as far as sexuality was concerned. Artaud could *not* accept sexuality on a conscious level. The reason for this attitude can only be guessed. The fact remains that he considered sexuality harmful, ugly, and sordid. His own sexuality, therefore, emerged as eroticism in *all* of his works. To wish to live only through the spirit, as Artaud was determined to do, is to reject the physical aspect of the human personality which is tantamount to psychological dismemberment or death.

The conflict which raged within Artaud between spirituality and sexuality was objectified by him in essays such as "Héloise and Abélard", "The Clear Abélard" (*Le Clair Abélard*), "The Anvil of Forces" (*L'Enclume des forces*), "The Personal Automaton" (*L'Automate personnel*), and "The Love Pane" (*La Vitre d'amour*), included in "Art and Death."

Artaud projected on to Abélard. Like the castrated XIIth century monk, he felt that some vital and binding force within him was lacking or had been removed. Such a lacuna made for psychological imbalance, resulting in an inability to relate to women except on a spiritual level. The sexual is, therefore, described as something "tarnished", "moldy", as a decaying and unproductive act. In an image which resembles a scene from the *Danse macabre,* Artaud features Héloise opening up the covers of her tomb, pulling and tugging at Abélard (Artaud) with "ant-like knuckle bones." Sexuality is described also as a window pane— always alluring, bright, and shiny; but also as having its opposite side—cutting and death-dealing. To succumb to a woman phys- ically is, therefore, dangerous; Abélard had been named for his sexual appetite. Eroticism can be the outcome of a suppression of the physical aspect of the human species as witnessed by "The Personal Automaton," where Artaud focuses on the male sexual organ which he compares to a metal object, to a piece of uprooted flesh, to a part of a body suspended by cords and directed by the pulsation of the atmosphere and or the head.

Artaud's feelings toward the opposite sex were ambivalent. He was drawn to them spiritually, on the one hand, and repelled by them sexually. When considering Héloise ethereally, she is fea- tured as "being fair" and "light", and alluding to an Abélard who could have been chaste, as living in the "clear" and "rarified atmosphere" of heaven and spirit. When conflict arises between the two opposing emotions, juxtaposition of images ensues: "a paradise embedded in her nails," or beauty and ugliness.

That Artaud was torn by the conflict between the sexual and the spiritual, indicated an inner dissatisfaction with the status quo; a desire to heal the split within his personality. Such healing could take place through death, looked upon as an initiation rite, a passage into another world which brings with it renewal and rebirth. Such an experience is described in "The Anvil of Forces", where Artaud suffers through an immense combustive force which engulfs, crushes, and kills him, psychologically speaking. Death, looked upon in this manner, meant complete identification with the collective unconscious and a total loss of identity. When Artaud emerges from his depths, he is, hopefully, re-formed; his whole being re-activated and refurbished, fed by the universal flow of cosmic forces. Artaud chose the medium of fire and water to pursue his initiation and rebirth. What had formerly been dismembered he felt would become *one* with the right mixture of fire and energy needed to transmute *prima materia* into something real, and water, symbolizing the origin of all things.

Artaud still clung to a slim hope that all could be well. . . . .

The year was 1926. Artaud severed relations with the Surrealist group. It is always difficult to keep together such dynamic personalities as those involved in the Surrealist group for any length of time. With the Moroccan War and André Breton's adherence to the Communist cause, more specifically to Trotsky's point of view, many members of the Surrealist group, for political or literary reasons, severed relations with it.

In 1927 Breton, Aragon, Éluard, Peret, Unik joined with the Communist Party. Soon after, the Big Five, as they were known, wrote a pamphlet "In the Light of Day" (*Au Grand Jour*) in which they proclaimed their expulsion of Artaud and Soupault from their group and also made their political affiliations quite clear. They did not stop there, but proceeded to attack Artaud's Achilles' heel—the weak rational aspect of his mind. He could not leave an affront unanswered. Artaud counter-attacked in "In Broad Night or the Surrealist Bluff" (*A la grande nuit ou le Bluff Surréaliste*).

"In Broad Night" is a statement of Artaud's position. He accuses his former friends of treachery, declaring that Surrealism died the day Breton and his cohorts rallied to the Communist banner. To try to reconcile freedom with constriction is impossible. They are simply in favor of permitting "social armature" to pass from one form of power to another, whether the bourgeoisie or the proletariat hold power makes little difference to the artist who quests for the free, eternal aspects in man. Though Artaud harbors no hatred for the Surrealists as individuals, he condemns the group *en bloc* because they have betrayed their own cause. Artaud remains, he feels, true to the tenets of Surrealism.

In 1929, when Breton published his "Second Surrealist Manifesto," he made his political views even more precise and this time surrounded himself with a new group of poets and artists, including Luis Buñuel, René Char, George Hugnet, Salvador Dali, and Yves Tanguy. The ex-members of the Surrealist group, smarting because they had been publicly excluded from the Group by the Big Five, annoyed by the manner in which Breton had denounced them in his "Second Manifesto," published a virulent pamphlet against him, "A Cadaver" (*Un Cadavre*) and buried, though prematurely, Surrealism as they saw it.

Artaud's break with the Surrealists had perhaps a salutary effect on him since it forced him to strike out on his own. Crippled by head pains, unable to view life except through his own personal anguish, he had, through his association with the Surrealists, gained self assurance, both artistically and emotionally. He was more determined than ever to concretize his ideas at all costs. He wanted to found his own theatre, to be named the Théâtre Alfred Jarry. Although such an enterprise seemed impractical, if not foolhardy to many, for Artaud, it was a step in the right direction in his struggle for emotional and artistic fulfillment.

PART TWO

THE THEATRE AND
THE PLAGUE
(1927-1935)

∴

*The spectator who comes to us knows that he has agreed
to undergo a true operation, where not only his mind, but
his senses and his flesh are going to come into play. Henceforth, he will go to the theatre as he goes to the dentist.
In the same spirit with the thought that he will not die
from the ordeal, but that it is something serious and from
which he will not emerge intact. If we were not convinced
of being able to strike him in the most serious manner
possible, we would consider ourselves incapable of carrying
out our most absolute task. He must really be convinced
that we are capable of making him scream out.*[1]

CHAPTER III

A THEATRE-ABORTION

THE MONTHS devoted to the actual planning of the Alfred Jarry
Theatre were both exciting and moving for Artaud as well as for
the two co-founders of this venture: the ex-Surrealist, Roger
Vitrac, the playwright, and Robert Aron, the essayist. The year
was 1926. Artaud was thirty years old. Finally, on the threshold
of turning vague insights into concise realities, dreams into
actuality, life seemed to be looking up; verdent and exquisite in
all of its facets. Enthusiastic, filled with vigor, though still tortured by his own physical disabilities, Artaud was convinced that
he would succeed in imposing his theatrical conceptions on the
Paris of his day.

I

Strangely enough, Artaud's innovations, for the most part,
arose directly as a result of his malady. An inability to think in a
cartesian manner and an overly sensitive and high-strung nature,
had led him to opt for a theatre which worked on the nerves and
the senses, and reject one which sought to speak to the intellect
alone. Artaud's theatre, therefore, would be militantly anti-ra-
tional as well as hugely emotional; it would attempt to spew
forth venom—to scathe—all those with whom it would come into
contact.

Artaud's credo was simple: divest the theatre of *all* logic and
verisimilitude; touch and bruise the spectator, thereby forcing

(45)

involvement. Only through the irrational, evocative happenings, he reasoned, can the proper atmosphere be created, life be pared to its essentials and so be illuminated—and *reality* emerge.[2]

The theatre, therefore, cannot be considered as mere entertainment, nor as a game-like activity, but rather as a "reality", as "unique", and as unpredictable as life, and each production as "a kind of event", a totally unexpected event. The audience becomes an intrinsic part of the theatrical venture. The spectator must be shocked, react violently to the "unprecedented eruption of a world" on stage; he must feel that he is seeing the essence of his own being before him, that his life is unfolding within the bodies of others. If a theatrical production is to be considered effective, the spectator must experience anguish, be immensely and intensely involved; so deeply affected, in effect, that his whole organism is shaken into participation.[3]

Since Artaud's ideas concerning the dramatic arts were born from his sickness, he looked upon the theatre as a curative agent; a means whereby the individual could come to the theatre to be dissected, split and cut open first, and then healed. The healing ritual would proceed as follows: the stage happenings would elicit psychological projections from the spectator. As tension was developed on stage, as events moved toward a climax, there would ensue a corresponding tension in the audience that would eventually become so great as to force the spectator to recognize the nature of his projections and anxieties. Once having permitted his anxieties to come to the light of consciousness, the spectator would now see his various problems from a different point of view and would gain, thereby, greater perception and self-understanding. This new vision would allow the fragments of the spectator's personality, which had been projected onto the stage, to return to their source, the spectator's being—nourished and renewed by the added understanding.

No ordinary play could force such tremors as Artaud wished to inject into the hearts of his onlookers. It had to be something unusual, many things wrapped into one: "a synthesis of all desires and of all tortures"; a "crucible for revolt"; a "transubstantiation of life"; sufficiently dense so as to fuse "the maximum of expression with the maximum of audacity."[4] The piece would have to cause traumas in the spectators' psyche: create guilt, horror, and fright. New plays would have to be written to bring about the visceral reaction Artaud sought so desperately to conjure forth. The great writers of the past (Sophocles, Aeschylus, Euripides, Shakespeare, Racine, Molière) who had dealt with man's profound and eternal aspects, had succeeded in relieving him of his excruciating pressures because their works possessed "purgative" powers: they instilled fear and chilled audiences with terror and fervor. Modern dramatists, Artaud reasoned, must find their own *mystique*, their own vital and moving force—that special, particular power which will strike hard at man's very vitals.[5]

After much searching, Artaud felt he had discovered the perfect play-formula which would make for total audience involvement. It has been alluded to as Artaud's "police-raid theatre."

> What is more abject and at the same time more remarkably terrible than the spectacle of a police raid (on a brothel) . . . When the police prepare a raid, it looks like the performing of a ballet dancer's evolutions. . . .[6]

The spectators, Artaud was convinced, would watch the events on stage in breathless panic: the police coming and going outside of the brothel, planning their attack, listening to the sharp and ominous whistles. Caught up in the action before them, chilled by the air, benumbed as the net closes in on the frantic victims, the onlookers would feel for the three participating groups (police, prostitutes, clients); captivated by the strange rhythms and dynamism within the spectacle itself. What was important then to Artaud was not the verisimilitude of the action on stage, but rather "the communicative force of the reality of this action."[7]

Though the Alfred Jarry Theatre was an original theatrical enterprise, it stands to reason that the ideas and method of the man after whom it was named would come into sharp focus.

Artaud was drawn to Alfred Jarry's works because of their spontaneous irrationality, their satiric and grotesque qualities, as well as their mystical aspects. Jarry's approach to people and things was uninhibited, his humor biting, and because he rebelled against what he considered to be the stupidity, cowardliness, greed, and hypocrisy of his age, he was thought of by many as "eccentric."

The "pantophile" Jarry wrote about everything that interested him: art, music, sports, literature, the theatre, science, and the trades. All of his works are different, yet they share a common stamp: a corrosive way of looking at life that is somewhat mitigated by a powerful sense of humor. Monstrous beings emerge alive and grotesque from his pages as witnessed by his character Ubu ("King Ubu"), vengeful, gluttonous, brutal, avaricious, and egotistical. Sentimentality is banished and rational coherence totally disregarded. Jarry willfully shocks his audiences and readers alike with his provocative language, his use of strange word associations, harsh alliterations, neologisms, unusual rhythmic patterns, bizzarre analogies, and seemingly unrelated series of events. Jarry indicates his disdain for *appearances* by *dislocating* or *dissociating* what seems rational in the character or object at hand. Once the *façade* has been shattered he recomposes the remaining disparate elements into a new and startling picture to express the true nature of each thing as he sees it.

Jarry developed what has been called "a panoramic vision of the world and its problems". His interest in the metaphysical was as intense as his interest in the machine to which he felt modern man was attached. In fact, Jarry devised a new science: "Pataphysics", a science which went "beyond metaphysics", hypothesizing a "universe supplementary to this one", and a "science of imaginary solutions." Jarry burst on to the Parisian scene in 1896 with his play *Ubu Roi* like a meteor. His eccentricities and charm, his imagination and literary and theatrical inventiveness inspired not only the Futurists and Dadaists, but the Surrealists.

Artaud considered Jarry to be his spiritual ancestor. He was fascinated by Jarry's bubbling personality, his humor, brutality, and irrationality, the effulgence of his spirit; qualities which came through in such a viable manner in his writings. Blending

Jarry's strange concoctions with his own, Artaud was to emerge with a strikingly different brew from that offered by his contemporaries. Such a diversity of views becomes shockingly apparent after a brief examination of the Parisian theatre of the 1920's.

Outside of the Boulevard Theatres, where plays were designed to appeal to as many people as possible, and the Comédie-Française, which produced classical and traditional dramas, the Parisian theatrical scene was dominated by four innovators: Louis Jouvet, Charles Dullin, Gaston Baty and Georges and Ludmilla Pitoëff. They reacted against narrow realism that permeated French stage and sought to make their productions imaginative works of art.

Louis Jouvet, director and actor, for example, relied on his own judgment to assess the rhythms of the dialogue and the structures of the play. He did not hesitate to follow the dictates of his intuition when creating a *mise en scène*, for he realized that the truths of the theatre were not necessarily rational. It was Jouvet who had introduced Jean Giraudoux to Parisian audiences, a playwright about whom Artaud had written: "In matters of style, our period possesses only one inventor: *Jean Giraudoux.*"[8] It was Jouvet who freed Molière from the trappings of tradition and who introduced new verbal musicality and rich rhythmic effects into the dialogue of his productions of plays by Molière, Giraudoux, Romains, Vildrac, Archard and Passeur.

Charles Dullin fought with ardor and passion for a simple, artistic theatre, as opposed to naturalistic theatre, which he considered artificial and vulgar. Because Dullin refused to bow to commercial considerations he was always plagued by financial difficulties. He believed in producing only plays of *his* personal choice. He trained his actors in correct breathing and diction, trying to extend their voices and make them supple, without distorting them.

Georges Pitoëff and his wife Ludmilla, both Russian by birth, infused vitality and poetry into their astonishingly beautiful and profound productions of works by Gide, Cocteau, Shakespeare, Pirandello, Chekhov, and Molnar. As actor, director, and lighting technician, Georges Pitoëff's innovations were innumerable, his theatrical creations renowned for their aesthetic beauty, excitement, mystery, and symbolism.

Gaston Baty, a disciple of Max Reinhardt, professed tremendous admiration for the *mise en scène* and sought to create a theatre in which actors and writers would be used as mere instruments of the director's imagination. Baty defined the theatre in terms of "the total scenic image." When he directed "The Dibbouk" (1928) by An-Ski, his scenic inventiveness seemed to beget "the presence of the invisible." Baty aimed, through the use of visual means, to suggest what was beyond the visible, to fuse together costumes, decors, accessories, music, lighting into a poetic whole.

It was in this creatively charged atmosphere that Artaud sought to make his mark. Certainly, he was not a new-comer to the field, having acted bit parts for short periods of time with the finest theatrical companies of his day: namely, those of Lugné-Poe, Charles Dullin and Georges and Ludmilla Pitoëff. But Artaud had not made his mark as an actor. In fact, he had been a dismal failure whenever he tried to portray someone else's personality. He was far too subjective in his approach to roles to achieve the detachment necessary from his own tormented being, to beget another life. But, actually, there was much more to it than met the eye. Artaud *could not* act because he was terror-stricken each time he clothed himself in somebody-else's skin; fearful of losing his identity during the transaction. Such a Faustian exchange managed with ease by any other actor presented Artaud with a very real stumbling block though he may not have realized it at the time. The fear of the void, so vividly described in his *Correspondance avec Jacques Rivière,* the trauma caused by the facing of the collective unconscious, depicted so intensely in the "Umbilicus of Limbo," had overflowed the banks of the literary and drenched his work-a-day world, crippling his talent as an actor.

Writing, however, was different. In "The Jet of Blood," Artaud had dramatized the pain caused him by certain adjustments he had to make in life; from adolescence to manhood he was unable to communicate with others. In this short play, he had achieved the objectivity required to create a living piece of literature because he had succeeded in dissociating himself with the images which welled up from within him. In so doing, he had, perhaps inadvertently, struck upon a device, so ingenious, so novel, as to turn it into a directing and writing technique—in time.

Like the mystic, to a certain degree, Artaud sought to pursue the very images or fragments thereof which emerged alive from his inner world, and which he had always claimed, possessed their own fanciful way of eluding him.

> But one must relearn . . . . how to be a mystic, at least in a certain manner, by forgetting our own selves, forgetting the theatre, waiting and fixing images which will be born within us, nude, natural, excessive, and pursue these images to their conclusion.[9]

But to follow an image to its conclusion was no simple task for one whose temper was so quixotic, whose manner, so bizarre. In writing, in fact, in the midst of conversations with friends, it was not unusual for Artaud to suddenly strike a blank; to clench his lips, tightly, holding back whatever was in store for the listener; his eyes, staring like two glassy agates into the distance—Artaud had retreated into his personal domain. Moments later, however, he would return to the world of the living, seek to make contact with those about him, resume a "normal" way.

Though Artaud did suffer from these lapses, there was no reason to think that he could not function as a director, and produce works which would captivate audiences. The Alfred Jarry Theatre was, nevertheless, a gamble, as are all novel enterprises, and the stakes were high, but for one possessed of a vision, it turned into an urgent compulsion.

II

Artaud's belief in the use of any and all means, however grotesque, to achieve audience-involvement was indeed novel for a time when directors were, for the most part, looking toward artistic simplicity and aesthetic naturalism to achieve their visions of truth. To go to the theatre, not to be entertained or amused, but to be forced to confront one's own existence, to be torn by what takes place on stage, to go to the theatre as one goes to a dentist or to a surgeon in order to have the soul's unhealthy elements extracted was, at this time, a nearly incomprehensible phenomenon—shocking to say the least, as to a large extent it still is.

Accustomed to the smooth productions of the Boulevard Theatres, the aesthetic and natural creations of Jouvet, Dullin, Baty, and Pitoëff, Artaud's idea of a visceral theatre was to fall like a clap of thunder on deaf ears. But Artaud was a fighter. Despite almost insurmountable financial difficulties, he persisted; together with Vitrac and Aron, he solicited benefactors and friends to contribute funds to the founding of the Alfred Jarry Theatre.

Dr. and Mme. René Allendy were the kindest and most generous of the few benefactors. They not only contributed money to the Alfred Jarry Theatre, but also Mme. Allendy frequently assisted Robert Aron in his managership of this venture. Their relationship, however, went beyond the strictly commercial aspects; Dr. Allendy thought of Artaud as a son. Indeed, they had much in common. A psychoanalist, Dr. Allendy, was the founder of the *Société Française de Psychanalyse*. In fact, he was a mystic of sorts, convinced that destiny follows the dictates of man's unconscious will, that man's actions are so often repeated because there are profound desires within him that urge him to re-enact the same or similar events and actions. Man projects this inner force onto his environment and considers external reality rather than himself to be responsible if things do not turn out as he wishes. Dr. Allendy felt that man could, if he so wished, control fate. In order to do so, however, he would have to understand his inner motivations. To succeed in bringing the unconscious forces to the light of consciousness requires an almost Buddhist-like discipline, which permits man to free himself of his *karma* (Fate) by means of knowledge. Psychoanalysis, he felt, could bring about the required enlightenment that would permit man to escape from his misfortune.[10]

It is no wonder then that both Dr. and Mme. Allendy were interested in Artaud's kind of theatre and in Artaud himself who was, in certain ways, living proof of Dr. Allendy's theories.

By almost miraculous manipulation of funds, Artaud and his group put on the Alfred Jarry Theatre's first production. Since no theatre was available to them for permanent use, they were forced to rehearse wherever room was offered them. A theatre was rented *only* for the actual productions.

Opening night: June 1st and 2nd, 1927 at the *Théâtre de Grenelle*. A hushed silence hovered over the house, the atmosphere was charged with excitement. Just before curtain time, Artaud ran frantically here and there, back stage and on stage, attending to the minute details of what was to be a three-play evening. On the agenda were: Artaud's own one-act play "Burned Stomach or the Mad Mother" (*Ventre brûlé ou la mère folle*), a lyrical "sketch", with a musical score by Max Jacob, "which denounced humoristically the conflict between the movies and the theatre";[11] Roger Vitrac's "The Mysteries of Love" (*Les Mystères de l'amour*), a surrealistic drama which dealt with the anguish, loneliness, and sensual desire of two lovers; *Gigogne,* a one-acter credited to Max Robur, but in fact written by Robert Aron "with the systematic aim to provoke."

Despite Artaud's efforts, and those of the troupe as a whole, the first productions of the Alfred Jarry Theatre failed to please both audience and critics on the whole. The gamut of reaction experienced on the two nights given over to the performance of these three works ran, however, from shocked distaste to admiration— but only very few fell into the second category. Artaud and his troupe, therefore, were faced with a very serious problem: financial. Although the *Théâtre de Grenelle* had been filled to capacity and this, in part, thanks to the kind efforts of Dr. and Mrs. René Allendy who sold the seats before the date of the plays had been fixed, there was a deficit of 6 to 7000 francs which Robert Aron managed, somehow, to pay in full. Though deeply concerned by the lack of funds at his command, the trying conditions under which he was forced to work, despite the Surrealists' perpetual derision of his approach—Breton's in particular—the uninterested audiences, and the severe and frequently ruthless criticisms, Artaud persisted.

He was angered. He sought to provoke, to lash out at both audiences and society. For this reason he chose to show a film "The Mother," adapted by Poudovkine for the movies from the Maxim Gorki novel; and to direct one act from Paul Claudel's play "Break of Noon." Artaud was playing with fire and he knew it. The audience at the *Comédie des Champs-Élysées* thrilled with expectation at the opening matinee on January 14, 1928.

Artaud had wanted to show "The Mother," a film advocating revolution, not only because of the stunning realism of certain of its scenes, but particularly, because it had been banned by the censors. In this way, he could dramatize his opposition to any law which sought to bridle man's creative energies.

The production of "Break of Noon" was an even riskier affair. It could mean prison. Paul Claudel had not only *not* authorized a production of his play, but had strictly forbidden it. "Break of Noon" had a very special, even traumatic meaning for its author. The plot of this work had been drawn in many ways from his life. In 1901 when on board ship, returning from China where he had been sent in foreign service, he had fallen in love with a married woman. The liaison which ensued was in direct opposition to his Catholic faith, and Claudel came to consider it a "trap" of destiny. After the final break, Claudel re-created his obsessive love in the play "Break of Noon." After writing the work (1906) he permitted a limited edition of one hundred and fifty copies of this play to be published. The work was then withdrawn from the market and its performance stopped.

Since Artaud's production of Claudel's play was unauthorized, all rehearsals were carried on in the utmost of secrecy. Indeed, no one outside of the troupe knew what play was going to be given. The announcements simply stated than an unpublished act of a play by a "famous" author would be performed without his authorization and the title of the play would be made known to the audience only after the curtain went up.

Emotions ran high on what was a dangerous evening. The play itself, however, was performed without any major mishap. Artaud stepped out on stage after the curtain had come down and to add further spice to the affront, spoke the following words:

> The play we have just performed for you is by M. Paul Claudel, French Ambassador to the United States. . . . An infamous traitor![12]

Vehement applause arose from the anti-Claudel quarter, composed of those people who considered Claudel's Catholicism and politics constricting and hypocritical. Pro-Claudel factions were less favorably disposed. Jean Prévost, for example, writing in the *Nouvelle Revue Française,* stated:

> The interpretation appeared to have displeased the majority in the audience . . . But many spectators concluded from this that instead of giving a presentation of *Break of Noon* they were purposely giving a parody . . .[13]

Despite unfavorable criticisms, Artaud had, according to good Surrealist doctrine, upset the *status quo.*

The Alfred Jarry Theatre's third production was to première "A Dream Play" by Auguste Strindberg; presented at the *Théâtre de l'Avenue* on two matinees; June 2nd and June 29th, 1928.[14] What could have been a hugely successful affair turned out to be quite the opposite, a total disaster, and through no fault of Artaud.

Mme. Yvonne Allendy, Artaud's friend and benefactor, related the events leading up to a critical finale in the following manner. Two of Mme. Allendy's Swedish friends had seen Artaud's production of "Break of Noon" and had been very excited by it. They told Dr. and Mme. Allendy that if the Alfred Jarry Theatre undertook to produce a Strindberg play, the Swedish colony in Paris would most certainly buy many seats at fifty francs each and some at several thousand francs. Since Artaud had wanted to produce "A Dream Play" anyway, and had announced such plans back in 1926, he went ahead with the project.[15]

Things were not to be simple, however. Artaud had forgotten what to expect from his erstwhile friends, the Surrealists, now bitter enemies. When they heard of the financial aid being given Artaud and his troupe, they screamed betrayal and materialism. To accept financial aid for a theatrical venture was to be bound and tied artistically and the Surrealists would not permit what they considered to be a deceitful gesture. They threatened to act; to take matters into their own hands.

The first performance of "A Dream Play" took place on June 2, 1928 at the *Théâtre de l'Avenue*. Mme. Allendy had sold seats in advance, as had been agreed, to many Swedes in diplomatic, governmental, social, and artistic circles. Other nationalities were also present on opening night: Americans, Austrians, Belgians, Dutch; many notables likewise: La Duchesse de La Rochefoucauld, Paul Valéry, Princesse Edmond de Polignac, Prince George of Greece, François Mauriac, Countess Greffühle, Arthur Honegger. When they arrived at the theatre, to Mme. Allendy's shock and consternation and no less so to the spectators who had paid large sums of money for their seats, they learned that the seats had been "mysteriously" re-numbered at the last moment. Thirty persons who were supposed to sit in the orchestra were forced to sit in the balcony and their empty seats were immediately occupied by Surrealists. Tempers were high and the atmosphere crackled with jangled nerves. Dr. and Mme. Allendy, acting in good faith, reimbursed the "displaced" people.

Despite this unfortunate occurrence, however, the Swedish press was kindly disposed toward Artaud's interpretation of "A Dream Play." They even commented on the stunning *mise en scène* which they felt to be "superior to that of Reinhardt" in Stockholm. Certain French critics, though very few, also voiced their approval in Artaud's production:

> The least one can say of Antonin Artaud's *mise en scène* is that he has created a breathtaking work, with a sensitive and attentive understanding of the text's most subtle nuances.[16]

Benjamin Crémieux was also favorably disposed:

> The universe which M. Artaud succeeds in evoking is a universe where everything takes on meaning, mystery, and a soul. It is difficult to analyze the effects obtained, but they are breathtaking and truly concern the re-integration of the magic of poetry in the world.[17]

But the "affair" of "A Dream Play" was still smouldering. One more performance was scheduled: a Saturday matinee on June 9th. The Surrealists, now in a frenzy of anger, resorted to more direct methods: they simply forbad Artaud to go through with this second performance. Robert Aron and Artaud decided to ignore the threats, refusing to be "persecuted" by former friends. They decided to send a letter (a *pneumatique*) to André Breton the night before the scheduled performance, on June 8th. This letter informed André Breton that they did not fear his threats, that the performance would proceed as planned, and that they would forbid him and his friends to enter the theatre and would resort to any means available "even those which are most repugnant to us" to do so.[18]

June 9th, the day of the performance, arrived. When Breton and his friends reached the theatre they discovered to their dismay that policemen had been posted on both inside and outside of the theatre. A barrage of invectives ensued, accusing Artaud of having resorted to unforgivable and underhanded methods to keep him out. The performances, however, proceeded without further incident.

Though funds had reached a new low, Artaud ploughed ahead, unabashed. The new play would be Roger Vitrac's "Victor or Children Assume Power" (*Victor ou les enfants au pouvoir*), a three-act drama and was performed at the *Comédie des Champs-Élysées* on December 24th, 29th, and January 5th, 1929. Rehearsal time for *Victor* was minimal, as it had been for all the Alfred Jarry Theatre's productions. In fact, there was only one complete rehearsal on stage before opening night.[19] Perhaps this accounted for the jagged edges in the final production. Nevertheless, some critics, namely the one writing for *L'Ami du peuple*, were rather favorably disposed, though far from lavish in their praise.

> After a very amusing and well done first act, during which time the characters were well drawn, the play . . . . went astray along strange paths.[20]

Jean Prévost of the *Nouvelle Revue Française* stated: "This play gives proof of true liberation . . ." Most critics, however, voted "no" on the production. Few understood that Artaud and Vitrac had been aiming at the expression of *symbolic reality* in their theatre.

III

What were Artaud's *mises en scène* really like? What was his technique for directing? Rational? Did he think through certain problems, roles, etc? To what horrors or beauties was he exposing Parisian theatrical audiences?

Even in the capacity of a director, Artaud's psyche determined the path he was to take: a strictly non-rational approach. As a director, Artaud would follow no set rules, but rather be guided by intuition, inspiration, chance. He would discover during the course of the rehearsals "the element of disquietude necessary to cast the spectator into the sought-for doubt". In his article "The Evolution of Decors" (*L'évolution du décors*), Artaud suggested that modern directors had lost that certain *"mysticité"* so vital to the theatre, because they no longer looked within to create a *mise en scène* and consequently were incapable of experiencing the "purity" of their "initial reactions." Since they look about them, attaching importance to externals and so remain confused, they are not qualified to discover and generate what Artaud considered of utmost importance and what he tried to bring forth in all of his productions, "a magnetic inter-communication between the spirit of the actor and the spirit of the director."[22]

Artaud believed as an article of faith in the universal value of the theatre and in the need for its general renewal, which could only come about if man gains a new understanding of himself. On his stage, therefore, the amorphous contents of the protagonists' unconscious would be embodied and used in order to shock audiences into awareness: the awareness of the banalities of their conscious lives. Furthermore, the theatre for Artaud was to become a *magic ritual* with *mystical significance;* he would be the magician and the alchemist to wave the wand and mix the brew.

> We conceive of the theatre as a true operation in magic. We do not speak to the eyes, nor to the direct emotions of the soul; what we are trying to create is a certain psychological emotion where the most secret mainsprings of our heart will be laid bare.[23]

Every gesture and every word uttered on stage, therefore, had a secret meaning and significance that the director transmitted to his audience.

> The *mise en scène*, per se, the actors' evolution must be considered only as visible signs of an invisible or secret language.[24]

In Vitrac's "The Mysteries of Love," for example, Artaud emphasized the rhythmic and hypnotic effects within the drama by fusing lights, sets, and accessories. Such an effect was not easily accomplished because, perhaps, of the difficulties intrinsic to the play itself. "The Mysteries of Love," a biting and sardonic drama in which Jarry's influence is plainly visible makes use of Surrealistic techniques to satirize the traditional "well-made" play with its climaxes, suspense, plots, is in certain respects a prolonged lover's quarrel between Patrick and Leah. It is made up of seemingly incoherent recriminations, platitudes, repetitions and nonsequitors. Well-known personalities are also featured in this drama: Lloyd George, for example, is seen in a dismal light, while Mussolini is featured as weak, helpless, and stupid. The author himself appears as a character in this play covered with blood and laughing most heartily after his unsuccessful attempt to commit suicide. Characters appear and disappear on stage, bombarding the audience with corrosive humor, with attacks on the army, politics, religion, society, parents, marriage, logic, life, and death. Vitrac also hammers at the dramatic arts. One of his characters, the Author, speaks, suggesting, perhaps, a new type of theatrical production—"without words."

How did Artaud go about establishing "direct communication" between the audience and the bizarre machinations being enacted on stage? Technically, first of all, the action of this work begins in "A box overhanging the stage", which by its very location includes the audience within its fold. Other devices are also used to this end: asides, the author playing a role in his play, and the violent ending of the drama, when Leah fires a shot from the stage into the audience and "kills" a spectator.

Furthermore, the sets, inspired most probably from Apollinaire's "Breasts of Tiresias" (1917), were so conceived as to confuse or even obliterate in the audience any rational sense of time and space. The fourth tableau, for example, was composed in parts: a railroad station, the sea-shore, a dining car, a hotel lobby, a yard-goods shop and the main square in a town. Once the rational had been crushed, the audiences, Artaud was convinced, would approach the happenings on stage in a fresh and spontaneous manner—unburdened by the weight of preconceived judgments. The spectator would, therefore, be able to heave a sigh of relief and project fully on to the riotous concoctions before him.

Artaud's production of Vitrac's second play, "Victor," was, perhaps, more successful from an artistic point of view than was that of "The Mysteries of Love." Such an outcome can be attributed, in part, to Artaud's additional experience in this domain and also to the fact that *Victor* was a better play.

Victor, an ironic drama directed against bourgeois families, attacks the *status quo* and touches with candor upon such questions as adultery, incest, anger, patriotism, sanity, and death. In order to arouse his audiences, Artaud chooses to play up the "shocking" elements of this drama, thereby bedazzle the onlookers, rather than minimize them and so "cheat" audiences out of what they sorely deserve.

Two worlds arise from the domain of limbo in *Victor*, much to Artaud's delight, both conflicting and contorted: the adult world, consisting of stupidity, inanity, platitude and hypocrisy; and the children's world, which, though fantastic at times, is astonishingly real and sincere. Victor, a nine-year old boy, is seven feet tall and as intelligent as a grown-up. He and his six-year old girl friend, Esther, are the only "adults" and "rational" beings in this bourgeois family. When they learn that Victor's father is having an affair with Esther's mother, the "two adults" decide to reveal the relationship. A strangely beautiful and exotic looking character, Mme. Ida Mortemart, enters the picture now. She suffers, however, from a terribly embarrassing physical handicap, which symbolizes uninhibited sexual appetite. At the end of the piece Victor dies of a stroke on his ninth birthday and his parents commit suicide.

Victor, a drama situated in "a certain real spatial area," concerned archetypal beings whose moral problems, inner drama and anguish were not individual but rather collective. In order to strike his audience—hard and ruthlessly—Artaud had to be brutally frank in his *mise en scène.* This did not imply any desire on his part to scandalize or wallow in mire.

> There is in this play a terrible will for truth, for cruel light carried out to the dirtiest depths of the human unconscious.

Artaud sought to present this "drama" as a reflection or magical counterpart of man's inner being: to follow images through to their logical conclusion. For this reason, perhaps, he considered the fleeting character, Ida Mortemart, to be the most important figure in the play. She represented man's dualism; man riddled by his two opposing aspects: his enslavement to the physical and material on the one hand, and his longing for spiritual freedom on the other. Those who considered this role "foul" and "shameful", Artaud wrote, failed to understand its significance, its powerful and bitter aspects, and were content to merely dwell on what they considered to be vulgar. For Artaud, morality lay elsewhere.

> Nothing which is human can be dirty, if the situation where the thing occurs is poignant. And this one, as you can see, is completely so.[25]

But there were those in the audience—as always—who did not even understand the *truth* of the drama, but gobbled up and thrilled to what they considered the "smutty" aspects. This type of individual could never understand Artaud nor his conceptions; they accepted everything at face value, unable to ponder, to look within—blind to the world of secrets and hidden meanings, constricted by their perverse sense of morality.

Perhaps the most engrossing and profoundest of Artaud's *mises en scène* was the one created for "A Dream Play." An affinity existed between him and the Swedish Strindberg; one based on a blend of mutual pessimism, violence, ruthless and tormenting sexual conflicts. Strindberg felt, in fact, that mankind was a damned species, which, ever since Adam's fall, had been condemned to self-torture and punishment for crimes committed in a past life. "A Dream Play," however, differs from his other works because in this drama, Strindberg expresses compassion for the man who wanders blindly and aimlessly on this friendless earth. Perhaps Artaud had also been marked by destiny.

In the prefatory note to *A Dream Play* (1902), Strindberg explains that in this work he has attempted "to reproduce the detached and disunited—although apparently logical—form of the dream." In Artaud's directing, he underscored the "surrealistic" aspect of the drama; playing up the fanciful, mysterious and comic innuendoes.

The scene opens on an awesome, almost frightening castle called "The Growing Castle", surrounded by hollyhocks, piles of straw and manure. On top of the castle's highest tower sits a chrysanthemum bud. The two main characters, the Daughter and the Glazier, step out on the stage. The former declares that she believes there is a prisoner inside the Castle and it is her obligation to liberate him. The background disappears and reveals a bare room. An officer is seated there, apparently waiting to be freed. Now, however, he is not certain he wants to be liberated because he knows that whatever joy he might experience in the world, it will be followed by twice as much sorrow. The Daughter maintains that it is his duty to seek freedom. In a series of scenes involving a Maid, a Mother, a Lawyer, a Poet, a Gatekeeper, a Bill-Poster, the Dean of Theology, and more, this theme is battled out and built up on various levels and from different points of view. At the conclusion of the play, the Daughter takes her leave of all the people she has met in the course of her wanderings: she realized, finally, that man has been placed on this earth to suffer. The Castle is now aflame and the Daughter walks into it. The flower bud which was placed on the top of the tower in the beginning of the play now bursts into a huge chrysanthemum.

Since Artaud wanted to bring out the mysterious and cosmic elements of this drama, he ignored all rational concepts of time and space. Scenes and people shift about as though carrying out the demands of an arcane and inexorable will. In Act I, for example, audiences are presented with a forest of gigantic hollyhocks, the gilded roof of a castle, a gatekeeper's lodge, a billboard, a lawyer's office, and more. The background in each scene is at once real and fantastic; creating a certain *malaise* and insecurity within the spectator. The characters, furthermore, are like fleeting shadows who make their presence visible on stage, but who never seem to become living beings, acting and reacting as men and women. They are indeed the representation of an inner Bosch- and Breughel-like world.

One can readily understand why Artaud would be drawn to such a play. For him, the seemingly disconnected dialogue and incidents take on their own logic and form—as in a dream. Indeed, in "A Dream Play," Artaud could see the expression of his own poignant drama enacted before him: God versus man, good versus evil, the rational versus the irrational, reality versus the dream. And, Artaud affirmed:

> Strindberg revolted, as had Jarry, as had Lautréamont, as had Breton, as I have. We are producing this play as vomit against society.[26]

The Alfred Jarry Theatre aborted. Artaud had sought, unsuccessfully, to break the conventions of contemporary theatre and to obey the dictates of an "inner necessity." He had tried to dislocate the reality to which audiences were accustomed in the hope that they might achieve a deeper and more forthright way of considering life. Stage life, for Artaud, was a "continuation" of real life—his own—and a search for meaning.

People mocked and scoffed at Artaud's failure. He even became the butt of satire and ridicule, looked upon as an "eccentric", a clown, a jester. Few understood the excruciating pain he was now suffering, the smarting and gnawing hurt which comes with defeat. It could have meant his end. Artaud, however, refused to turn back. He would toil on—persevere in another medium, if need be. Despite the fact that he was shorn of practically all material subsistence, except for the few centimes he eked out from the occasional art and dramatic criticisms he wrote; divested of a following, save for a scattered few who could be counted on the fingers of one hand; the confidence he had in his vision was, strangely enough, left intact, perhaps even bolstered by the Alfred Jarry Theatre experience.

Artaud's ideas no longer remained in the vague land of untried formulas; they had become in his mind viable entities and as such, worth struggling for. Artaud felt these emotions deeply and inexorably—they pulsated within him, giving him the fire and strength needed to push forward.

Even now Artaud knew that in the end he would win out. He saw into the distance and realized that his personal sickness—from which his brand of theatre had emerged—was not yet ripe to turn into a collective malady.

CHAPTER IV

THE LIFE OF USHER . . . .

ARTAUD WAS DETERMINED to make his mark—someway, somehow —on his contemporaries. If the theatre had closed its doors to him, then he would direct his talents toward the relatively young film industry.

Artaud's capabilities, he felt, lay in the direction of acting and scenario writing. And he was very much aware of exactly those things which he had to offer a movie director. In a letter to Abel Gance concerning his acting talent, Artaud's judgment appeared incisive, incredibly perspicacious, as it had been years earlier in his *Correspondance avec Jacques Rivière*.

Artaud knew he could not play all roles because his characterizations were stamped with his own torments and nervous tremors. He could, however, be a character actor. Indeed, he declared he had found his prototype in the person of Poe's character, Mr. Usher. The similarities between these two men were frighteningly exact: almost as though time had been abolished, and Poe had modeled his character on Artaud. Both men possessed cadaverous complexions, lean bodies, haunting and incandescent gazes. Intensely focused eyes made it possible for them to ignore man's outer coverings and peer directly *within*. Pale and thin lips became a vehicle for uttering strange oracular pronouncements. Inhumanly sensitive, both Artaud and Mr. Usher had experienced the agony of deep sorrow.

Such an affinity as Artaud felt existed between himself and Mr. Usher had, startlingly enough, salutary effects: it made him feel he was not alone in the world; and through association, it enhanced his appeal as an actor, since he could compare his suffering with that of the fascinating Mr. Usher. With relative confidence he could tell Abel Gance that the man who has not known torment cannot create it outside of himself—except intellectually.

My life is that of Mr. Usher and his sinister hovel. The soul of my nerves is disease ridden and I suffer from this. There is one *quality* of nervous suffering which the greatest actor in the world cannot *bring to life in the movies* if he has not himself experienced it. And I have experienced it. I think as Usher had.[1]

I

Artaud had very definite ideas on the art of the cinema in general. It should not, he felt, be considered a "hybrid" art. Just as the theatre had its own distinct language, so the movies should discover ways and means of expressing its individual form. In the theatre, for example, there is a living flesh and blood reality for the spectator, because of the *physical* presence of the stage sets and living actors. The essence of the film art is *Matter*. In order to gain a sense of reality from the filmed image, the spectator projects himself on to the screen. In this manner, the movies, even more so than the theatre, can be a medium which makes enormous use of psychology. Because of the automatic participation of the spectator it can evoke the elemental instincts in man before they have become refined, diversified, and masked. For Artaud, the film is a vehicle in which the "human soul" can be viewed and examined "from all angles" and made to be as concrete and as plastic as is the human body.

Indeed, the film's enormous power lies in its peculiar ability to affect man deeply and intimately not only because of the spectators' automatic visceral participation, but because of certain elemental techniques, which make it possible to create never-before-possible images and sensations. For example, varying speeds and rhythms, closeups, fade outs, repetition, emphasis, distance and direct shots, trick photography, flashbacks, warping and distorting of images—all these techniques give the motion picture creator an enormous capacity for creating illusion. To transform and materialize the hidden elements and the fantastic phenomena in the world and in man and project these on the screen should be the goal of this new art.

The movies have a three-fold effect on the viewer: that of the sense image itself; the image in relationship to other images; and the symbolism inherent in any image. Imaginative use of camera can reinforce this triple possibility of suggestion and succeed to such an extent in shocking or mesmerizing the spectator, as to weaken all or most resistance on the part of his rational mind. The introduction of extraordinary material and subjects can also be instrumental in bringing about an intertwining of the projected image and the spectator's psyche. Mental barriers can thus be breeched; an inner world can be dredged up, and the psyche exposed to a whole series of new impressions and re-impressions.[2]

In many respects, the movies act far more directly upon man's brain than does the theatre. In fact, if a film avails itself of the proper mixture of ingredients, each film could become a catalyst within the individual viewing it.

> The cinema is endowed, particularly, with the power of an innocuous and direct poison, a sub-cutaneous injection of morphine. That is why the object of the film cannot be inferior to the power of the film's action—and must be connected with the marvelous.[3]

So sharply and directly does the film sometimes impose itself upon the spectator, that nothing can separate *it* from the *audience*. In the theatre, on the contrary, there exist many cleaving agencies which break the fusion: the stage and audience separation, the curtain, the lights. . . .

The potential of the film industry, Artaud foresaw, was so enormous, as to be virtually unfathomable. He anticipated the development of color and three dimensional films, but felt these aspects to be mere accessories. The wealth and depth of a film existed in its basic power and in the image. Nor was he in favor of "talkies" *per se*. As he wrote: ". . . talkies are foolish, absurd."[4]

But when he became aware that silent movies were doomed to oblivion, he realized that he too would have to follow the trend in order "to direct it."[5] At this time, he suggested the creation of a large screen (vista-vision or perhaps cinemascope) from which sound would emanate from all directions.

Well aware of the financial problems that were besetting producers of the 1920's, he suggested that shorts might be made instead of lengthy movies. These shorts would appeal to a limited number of people to be sure, but they would be money makers since the production expenses would be minimal. For one short, only two or three sets and a limited number of actors would be necessary. This particular type of short would be especially well suited to comedy, Artaud felt. Some French equivalent to the Mack Sennett type of humor should be created in France, but of course typically French.

Artaud's uncle, Louis Nalpas, director of Nalpas Productions in Paris, was aware of his nephew's advanced ideas concerning the film industry and of his desire to be included in it in the capacity of actor and scenario writer. He, therefore, put him into contact with the movie greats of his time: Abel Gance, Carl Dreyer, René Clair, Claude Autant-Lara and more.

Abel Gance, who had begun his career as an actor, was in the early 1900's one of the most renowned directors in France. He had made several important technical innovations and experiments in film-making: among them, the invention of the *caligarisme* technique, designed to send chills up and down the spectators' spine; the introduction of a new film to the film industry; the expression of the contemporary world as manifested in the romance of the machine age, by featuring images representing iron, steel, machines, vapor, and smoke . . . Gance' epic picture was *Napoléon* (1926); a film projected on three screens, an early precursor of the present day cinerama. It was considered one of the most original films, technically speaking, of its kind. Some of the scenes, particularly the tempest that broke out as Bonaparte was fleeing from Corsica, were tremendously frightening and powerful because of the wide expanse of the images flashed before the audience.

Artaud played the unforgettable part of Marat in *Napoléon*. Gance had given him permission to create his own character, to endow it with whatever personality he wished, providing it did not alter the spirit of the ensemble. Artaud used his face, primarily, to express Marat's personality. Marat, as Artaud played him, became a strange force of nature, disinterested in everything that was not related to his one great political passion.[6] It was in this role, that Artaud first saw himself projected onto the screen—his double—and it was a surprising confrontation to say the least. Others who knew him at the time, were equally startled: he presented a stunning picture on the screen and his incredibly volatile performance held the onlookers clutching their seats. Jean Cocteau spoke of Artaud's portrayal in this film as "the work of an alchemist" and described the image he conjured forth as unforgettable, that "celestial face hanging on the side of the bath tub . . ."[7]

Artaud also acted in movies directed by Marcel L'Herbier, an intelligent and cultured man. L'Herbier's approach, it might be said, was impressionistic. A bold innovator in the use of close-ups, he frequently deformed the faces of his protagonists in order to underline certain character traits for satirical purposes. In 1924 he completed "The Inhuman One" (*L'Inhumaine*), a picture for which the well-known writer Pierre Mac Orlan composed the scenario, Darius Milhaud, the music, and Fernand Léger, the maquettes. Artaud played a small part in "Money" (*L'Argent*) (1929), a film taken from Zola's novel in which certain scenes were marked for their striking realism. One year later, he portrayed one of the characters in L'Herbier's "A Woman for a Night" (*La Femme d'une nuit*).

Artaud's experience in the film industry included working with Claude Autant-Lara, formerly L'Herbier's scenic designer. In "News Item" (*Fait Divers*) (1925), Artaud interpreted the role of a handsome youth, Monsieur 2. A slow motion strangulation took place in this film which, it is said, was quite daring for the time. In *Tarakanova* (1929) directed by Raymond Bernard, the son of the famous writer Tristan Bernard, Artaud portrayed a young gypsy. For Léon Poirier, a specialist in the documentary, Artaud became the young intellectual of "Verdun, Visions of History" (*Verdun, Visions d'histoire*). René Clair, director of the famed picture "Under the Roofs of Paris" (*Sous les toits de Paris*) (1930), "Liberty for Us" (*A nous la liberté*) (1931), and the first film maker to be admitted to the French Academy, gave Artaud the part of the Gambler in *Entr'acte* (1924).

Perhaps one of Artaud's most exciting roles was that of Brother Massieur, the young monk who defended Joan of Arc, in Carl Dreyer's film *Jeanne d'Arc* (1928). This time Artaud played a saintly creature, calm and collected, with a mysteriously spiritual face. Working with Dreyer was a fruitful experience for Artaud. Inventive, Dryer opened up new vistas for him, expelled daring creations and points of view. About Dreyer, Artaud wrote,

> . . . . it was not a question of an aesthetic, a point of view, but of a work, a man concerned with elucidating one of the most anguishing problems which exists: Dreyer is concerned with demonstrating that Jeanne d'Arc is a victim of a distortion . . . the distortion of a divine principle. . . .[8]

Carl Dreyer, a Danish director, was an artist who insisted on a slow and deliberate pace in his films. He used environment to emphasize character portrayal: to striking effect in *Jeanne d'Arc*. All unnecessary details were removed in order to center on the main image which was then played up before the viewer. In many scenes, the faces of the protagonists were flashed on a black or white background. Dreyer felt that he came closest to obtaining psychological truth through the use of close-ups and facial studies on stark backgrounds. His favorite themes usually dealt with martyrs, vampires, witches or holy mad-men. They revolved about the powers of evil, the suffering of the innovent and the inevitability of death. It was always the dark side of man that Dreyer analyzed, the mysterious and supernatural, and perhaps it was this aspect of the director that intrigued Artaud.

Though one cannot call the impact Artaud made upon the film industry sensational, he did, however, create two stunning portrayals which are remembered even today: Marat and the Monk in *Jeanne d'Arc*.

II

It was as a scenario writer that Artaud thought he could win, if not fame, at least fortune. His scenarios possessed strange, haunting, frightening qualities; they were similar to something Mr. Usher might have envisaged, with characters suffering from some mental abberation or extreme agony. Humor was black; macabre. Horror, a trend towards the sordid, the occult, the mysterious, and the magical were other distinguishing features.

"The Eighteen Seconds" (*Les Dix-Huit secondes*) is a hair-raising drama and deals with man's thoughts during eighteen seconds of his life. It is as dense and concentrated in its action as a classical drama. In addition to its pronounced psychological point of view, Artaud uses for the first time a new concept in motion pictures: time differentiation. He separates or differentiates inner or unconscious time which knows no boundaries, from rational or conscious time which is limited. "The interest," Artaud explains, "resides in the fact that the events take place in eighteen seconds really, but the description of these events takes one or two hours on the screen."

The story! It is night. A man dressed in black is standing on a street corner. He is holding a cane and a watch. This man is an actor who is just on the verge of winning fame in his chosen field and of conquering the heart of the woman he loves. Suddenly, however, he is struck by a bizarre kind of mental sickness. Though perfectly lucid, he is incapable of translating his *thoughts* or *ideas* into gestures or words. He feels as though he were on the outside watching a series of disparate and contradictory images pass before him. He cannot reach his thoughts to grasp them; therefore, he is unable to act, and cannot come to grips with life. The image of a woman now comes into focus: beautiful, enigmatic, hard. A background fitting the soul of this woman emerges, a set filled with flowers and lit with brilliant lights. The man becomes so desperate he is willing and even eager to exchange his existence with anybody elses—even the hunchbacked newspaper boy on the street, provided he reacquire his *Intelligence.*

Several different images flash on the screen. The hunchbacked newspaper boy at a window; a glass ball, lit *à la* Rembrandt, changes its color and texture and the boy emerges from it like a devil, a man walks along the road with a stick. This same man opens a book, *The Kabbala,* lying on a table; policemen enter his room, put him in a strait-jacket and remove him to an insane asylum. He tries to fight his way free, a revolution breaks out in the asylum, and the doors are opened. The man is free and he has everything now except a normal mind. He falls asleep and dreams he is an actor, which he really is. He sees himself as the hunchbacked newspaper boy, kneeling at the feet of his mistress, who is his mistress in real life. Another image! The King is in his lodge. The actor also plays the King who has discovered that the hunchback is a usurper, that his hump is false, that the hunchback looks like the King and that he has robbed the King of his mind. The King wants to stop the show. The woman screams. She no longer recognizes the King as her lover because he has no hump. Suddenly, the King and the Actor become one. The room trembles. The previous images fly by in review. Eighteen seconds have elapsed and once again the man standing under the lamp post comes into view. He contemplates his wretched destiny and with no visible emotion, takes out his revolver and commits suicide.

The actor in the first image, alone and fearful, unable to master his thoughts, is in many respects Artaud himself: the Artaud of the *Correspondance,* of "Art and Death", the Usher-Artaud. But there are two men in this drama; the actor who appears before the world in any form and in any role he chooses, either as a Hunchback or as a King, and that other aspect, the anxious, anguished man, the slave of his own malfunctioning. The protagonist can hide these aspects of himself behind the various masks he assumes as an actor. The two aspects of time, the external rational time during which period everything takes place in eighteen seconds; and the inner, irrational sense that gives one the impression that everything is happening over an interminable length of time. These two aspects of time serve still further to differentiate the polarities within the protagonist's personality. The magic ball in the beginning of the drama, with its eerie light, permitted transformation to take place and gave the protagonists the ability to travel into different hemispheres and realms in his Faustian quest for wholeness.

The protagonist tries to escape from his personal anguish through mysticism. Yet, when he begins exploring the occult, reading the *Kabbala* and trying to decipher the meaning of the magic words and numbers written therein, society considers him insane and imprisons him in an institution. But a revolution breaks out and once again the protagonist is set free. Release then, or change can occur only after an overt act of destruction takes place, as is implied by the revolution.

The protagonist has a second means of escape: in the roles he plays. He portrays both Hunchback and King—the weak and physically distorted, and the very powerful. But the powerful King suffers from a mental deficiency and accuses the Hunchback of impersonating him and of robbing him of his mind and of his identity. Here, it is plain that the protagonist would have chosen an obvious physical deformity rather than a hidden and insidious one. Even the woman he loves chooses something she can see (Hunchback) rather than a mysterious and frightening disease like insanity (King).

Twice the protagonist has sought to escape and twice he has been rejected. First, by society and placed in an institution; and secondly, by the woman he loves when she rejects the King. Unable to find solace in escape, incapable of discovering his own identity since he is forever shifting about from one personality to another, the protagonist, in a supreme act of self rejection, destroys himself.

To conceive of a picture dealing with both rational and irrational time was quite a departure from film convention, as was

Artaud's entire approach. Perhaps that is why only one of his scenarios was ever made into a film; certain others lay buried in the pages of the *Nouvelle Revue Française*. Such was the fate of the scenario, "The Thirty Two" (*Les 32*) (June 1930). Readers were exposed once again to the mysterious world of the unconscious in which strange images and objects merge with one another or are superimposed one upon another, creating a world in which time and space are one.

The story begins in a small University town in Europe. A young handsome teacher is asked by his favorite pupil to come to his home after dinner. He is received most warmly by the pupil's mother and sister and is told that the sister, abandoned by her fiancé, is pregnant. The girl asks the teacher for occult intervention and comes to see him in his flask-filled laboratory the next evening at midnight. Suddenly, the young man's face changes; he begins gasping, and faints. Months pass. The girl has been caring for him all this time. He is now convalescing. A series of images float by: the young man walks toward a mirror; seizes a sword; and watches a spectator move about, who resembles him in all ways. There are quick scenes in which monstrous aquatic apparitions arise from a glass bowl. The young man has become hideous looking, as though he were the victim of a horrible passion; the girl leaves, frightened. He goes down into his cellar. When he sees his housekeeper, a strong and sturdy woman, snooping about, he informs her that the cases around her are filled with petrol and that if she touches them she will die. War is declared. The house is sealed and the young teacher leaves. The town suffers, lacking light and fuel. The Mayor and the Commissioner, having been told that there are barrels of petrol in the teacher's house, enter it through the cellar and discover thirty-two female bodies in the thirty-two petrol cases. Meanwhile, a vampire has been captured in Turkey. The Mayor, the commissioner, and the girl visit the hospital where it is being kept. His face has turned brown, his lips have thickened—he is hardly recognizable. Yet he is identified as the young teacher. The girl is both shocked and relieved at this knowledge.

In this curious scenario which resembles both the *Dr. Jekyll and Mr. Hyde* story as well as the *Blue Beard* tale, Artaud again indulged his bent for the horrible, the grotesque, the occult, and the magical. The hero in this drama is a murderer who remains undiscovered until the end. His protection is his "mask", that is, his outer charm and his teaching profession which "covers" his fundamentally evil nature. Yet, he is not completely evil, as witnessed by his helpful attitude toward the girl. Within him, however, are destructive forces over which he has no control. These evil elements manifest themselves in vampire-form, symbolizing the ugly, sickly side of man. In this respect, the school teacher-vampire can be likened to Artaud whose mental dilemma is also beyond his control. He is different from the protagonist in this drama, however, in that Artaud does not destroy others, but rather himself, unwittingly, through his own mental sickness.

The thirty-two murders committed by this vampire are perhaps another expression of Artaud's ambivalent attitude toward women. The housekeeper, energetic and strong, has been threatened by him, but not murdered. The young girl has remained unharmed. Her life might be endangered, were she to tread into forbidden (sexual) areas. Warning of this possibility was given in those instances when the young man's face became hideously distorted. Such physical ugliness was a material manifestation of an inner state, and a sign to the girl—to flee—which she did.

"The Seashell and the Clergyman" (*La Coquille et le Clergyman*) (1927) was the only one of Artaud's screen plays to be turned into a film. It was directed by Germaine Dulac, a former journalist and feminist, and first presented at the *Studio des Ursulines* on February 9, 1928.

From the moment Mme. Dulac agreed to produce "The Seashell and the Clergyman", rancor smouldered within her as well as Artaud's heart. Artaud was incensed by Mme. Dulac's conception of his script. Though she had followed his indications, image by image, she failed, he felt, to capture his essential ideas, both artistically and psychologically. Artaud reproached her for having misunderstood the spirit of his work and for having filmed "The

Seashell and the Clergyman" as though it were a dream, for having sought some kind of logic, either in the material itself or in the sequences *per se*. The images, he felt, should have been interpreted "in the sense of their essential, intimate, meaning," by means of their symbolism.

"The Seashell and the Clergyman" does not relate an unusual story, but rather "develops a series of mental acts which are deduced one from another." As one thought emerges from another, so associations emerge. From such contact of gestures and objects, mental and psychic situations are developed and reinforced.[9] In a foreword to the scenario, Artaud writes:

> You will look in vain for a film which is based on purely visual situations whose action springs from stimuli addressed to the eye only . . . untrammeled by psychological or irrelevant complications or by a verbal story expressed in visual terms.
>
> The visual action should operate on the mind as an immediate intuition.
>
> In the scenario which follows I have tried to realize this conception of a purely visual cinema, where action bursts out of psychology. . . .
>
> The scenario is not the story of a dream . . . I shall not try to justify its incoherence by the simple device of labeling it a dream. The scenario seeks to portray the dark truth of the mind by a series of pictures, self-engendered . . . but governed by an inherent and ineluctable necessity of their own, which forces them into the light.[10]

Perhaps Artaud's dissatisfaction with Mme. Dulac's interpretation of "The Seashell and the Clergyman" was tinged with personal reasons; he had hoped to act in his film and help in the directing of it as well. Evidently Mme. Dulac was not keen on this kind of collaboration.

When Mme. Dulac's film version of "The Seashell and the Clergyman" was shown, Artaud was full of anger and resentment. It is reported that he and a friend of his went to the showing, and when the lights were out, spoke in harsh, loud voices during the course of the film.

> The first voice: What is Mme. Dulac?
> The second voice: She is a cow.[11]

The Director of the Ursulines movie theatre, Armand Tallier, disturbed by the disparaging remarks leveled at Mme. Dulac, had the house lights turned on. He asked Antonin Artaud and his friend (it is said that his friend was Robert Desnos) to apologize. They refused. Instead, they added more insulting remarks to their already well-stocked larder. Artaud and other friends of his, who by now had clearly manifested their presence in the theatre, were asked to leave. Before departing, they smashed some mirrors in the hall of the theatre and screeched a medley of unusual sounds, such as "Goulou . . . Goulou. . . ."[12]

A film, Artaud writes in his introduction to "The Seashell and the Clergyman", can be considered in two ways: as pure or absolute cinema, or as "hybrid" art which seeks to translate and recreate on screen psychological states which properly belong to the theatre or to the literary arts and which do not really come to life on the screen. Artaud still felt that although the cinema's true *identity* or *self* had not as yet been discovered, directors should enlarge upon certain facets of this art.

Two types of films can be made: abstract movies with abstract forms and an interplay of light and shadow, pointing up the drama of each situation; or psychological movies which follow a story line.

In an abstract movie, forms or images on the screen that follow a particular rhythmic effect or certain sound vibrations, can act incisively upon the nerves of the spectator. They can force him, unconsciously, to recall certain past states. These blocks of time which emerge from the past, in turn, effect the spectator's present emotional state, working upon him intellectually at this point.[13] The screen drama would emerge from the various confrontations of these objects and forms as perceived by the spectator. The impact then would be *visual*.

Psychological motion pictures, which have a plot, are based almost exclusively upon the written word rather than the purely visual impact. The emotions stem from the text and the images on the screen are in effect translations of the word. it is not, Artaud maintained, a question of discovering an equivalent in visual languages of the actual written word, but rather of perceiving the intention of the word or action, the idea *per se,* and of projecting an equivalent image or action on to the screen where its meaning can be grasped intuitively by the mind of the spectator.[14]

In "The Seashell and the Clergyman," Artaud searched to create a "visual film", where the psychological aspect, the word, would "be devoured by the acts." He did not imply by such a statement that he wanted to do away with psychology *per se,* but rather to give the psychological aspect a more active and concrete form. Artaud insisted that for his screen play, only those images be used that derived their meaning from the "inner necessity" of the spectator and the author, rather than any objective "plot" situation.

"The Seashell and the Clergyman" is a series of illogical and disparate images and sequences, which do not follow any unified story form. The first scene shows the clergyman-alchemist pouring liquids from one vial into another (using an oyster shell for this purpose). He then smashes the emptied vial. The door opens and a much decorated Officer, wearing an enormous sword, enters. He stands shadow-like, behind the Clergyman. Suddenly, he grabs the oyster shell and smashes it with his sword. The room trembles. The Officer exits, the Clergyman follows, walking on all fours. Change of scene: a street. A carriage passes with the Officer and a Beautiful Woman beside him. Now the pair are in a confessional. The Clergyman, pursuing them, lunges at the Officer who turns out to be a priest and who vanishes into space. The Clergyman throws himself upon the Woman and tears off her blouse as though he were about to lacerate her breasts, which become transformed into shells. A succession of scenes: a dark road along which the Clergyman and Woman are running; a shadow, which the Clergyman strangles; an immense glass bowl into which he puts the shadow's head; a ship, on the deck of which the Officer lies enchained. The Clergyman is seen running under high vaults and stalactites; a ship passing back and forth; lights penetrating a ship's cabin; women cleaning the cabin and smashing the glass bowl in which a head appears and disappears; a governess in black holding a Bible. A priest runs into a house; a young couple prepared to be married who turn out to be the Clergyman and the Beautiful Woman. The Clergyman, now headless, descends a stairway which seems to be coming from heaven. He unwraps a package he is carrying and pulls out a glass bowl which he smashes and from which he withdraws his head. He rests it on an oyster shell. He puts the oyster shell to his lips, the head melts and is transformed into a type of blackish liquid which he drinks.

The Medieval alchemist—whom the Clergyman represents—tried endlessly to unite and transmute opposing substances. C. G. Jung has suggested that the secrets of chemical transformation, that is the alteration of substance, have parallels in psychic processes, "the unconscious phenomenon of nature . . ." It would seem that Artaud had a similar point of view, namely to discover the secret transforming substance, the activating "spirit" in every individual which, when penetrated and used to a purpose, may make him whole again.

The Clergyman-alchemist in his workshop is searching for something definite. The fluid which he pours from one vial to another represents the life force, the primal energy he is constantly trying to mold into diverse forms. The Officer, the Clergyman's shadow, is the darker side of his psyche. The sword he brings is symbolic of the aggressive brutality of the male. The oyster shell, a natural container, represents the feminine, protecting force. The glass bowl and the vials stand for the containers enclosing the imprisoned soul or mind. The successive smashings and cleanings of the bowl imply dissatisfaction of the casings or enclosing quality of the vessels. Yet, without some kind of casings, can man exist? The Clergyman who follows the officer on all fours is reverting to his child-like or animal-like state where hideous nightmares have a severe impact on the not yet solidly formed psyche. The sequence in which the Clergyman seems to want to disfigure the breasts of the Beautiful Woman indicate quite clearly Artaud's ambivalent attitudes toward the sexual, toward women: attraction-rejection, love-hate. The Clergyman implies the religiously oriented attitude toward life; the soldier, the opposite materialistic, power point of view: spirit contending against base matter. There are mutual attractions and antagonisms and excesses on both sides. The overly spiritual attitude may consequently be as destructive as the overly physical. The church, the woman in black holding a Bible, all represent in some way or another a safe and protective institution which man needs and yet will seek to destroy. The ship that carries the dreamer through and over the seas of the unconscious is instrumental in helping him get his bearings toward safe harbor. The dark roads on which the Clergyman and Woman are running are those which lead nowhere in particular, symbolizing, therefore, a search for some kind of psychological attitude. The headless Clergyman descending the ladder, the living communication between God and man, indicates man's inclination toward inflation. But, inflation from one standpoint is inadequacy from another. His head being severed from his body reveals the split between the rational or spiritual and the physical; between the side of him which is in no way related to the body and his human instinctual self. The black fluid distilled through a spiritual process, which he absorbs, indicates that spirituality when pushed to extremes becomes as black and as hurtful as brute unchannelled instincts.

Artaud's fragmentary, bizarre and somewhat chaotic scenario is a reflection of his own disparate efforts to stabilize the conflicting forces within him. The characters in "The Seashell and the Clergyman" are never whole human beings. They are heads or ears: they express animal instincts, or the forces of nature in their various manifestations.

Artaud did not regard the cinema as an art separate from life's processes. Rather, he saw in it, a means of discovering "the primitive arrangements of things." The motion picture camera was transformed by him into a vehicle capable of creating a new reality— one which might have the power of affecting directly the most remote areas of the human mind.

The author of additional film scenarios such as "Two Nations on the Confines of Mongolia" (*Deux Nations sur les confins de la Mongolie*) and "The Butcher's Revolt" (*La Révolte du boucher*); adaptor of Sevenson's "The Master of Ballantrae" and An-Ski's "The Dibbouk", he also wrote "a sort of French version" of Matthew Gregory Lewis' Gothic novel "The Monk" which he hoped to turn into a movie.

Artaud had always been drawn almost hypnotically to the amorphous reality behind appearances and also to the bizarre aspects of life; sadism, eroticism, satanism, sorcery, enchantment, violence, death, and magic. A believer in sorcerers, fortune-tellers, dervishes, and chiromancy, the supernatural had become something quite natural for him, another manifestation of eternal life. He was, understandably so, totally beguiled by "The Monk", about which he wrote:

> *The Monk* is impregnated with magic, soaked up in the real world which is made romantic by the hallucinating and realistic poetry of the high spheres, the profound circles of the invisible.[15]

"The Monk", a Gothic tale, so popular at the end of the 18th century and the beginning of the 19th, emphasized horrible, violent, or occult happenings, setting them against Medieval backgrounds of eerie castles, gloom, and isolation. "The Monk" is the story of Ambrosio, abbot of the Capuchins at Madrid, who is known for his religious zeal and for his devotion. Matilda, a young noblewoman so adores him for his religiosity, his manner, and his personality that she enters the abbey disguised as a monk. She soon reveals her identity and her passion to Ambrosio. He succumbs to her repeatedly, is discovered and condemned to death by the Inquisition. At Matilda's suggestion (she is, we learn, a demon in disguise), Ambrosio bargains with Lucifer for his release from punishment. The Devil, heeding his pleas, thrusts him into a desert. There, Ambrosio asks forgiveness for his past crimes. Lucifer is so angered by Ambrosio's repentence, that he dashes him to pieces against the rocks.

In his French version of "The Monk" Artaud made extensive changes. He altered the atmosphere and the tempo of the original novel; extraneous details and digressions were cut; important episodes were elaborated; lengthy poems were deleted; and the principal protagonists, Ambrosio, Matilda, Antoine, and others, given extensive character development.[16]

Just as the metaphysical incantations and magic rituals can penetrate deeply into man's psyche, so "The Monk", Artaud felt, would succeed in mesmerizing the readers, forcing them to follow the protagonists into that *other* realm.[17] Artaud expected each series of events in the story as well as each personality to act as a catalyst on the reader's unconscious. Furthermore, the sequences were to resemble dreams in that they fulfilled the characters' destiny: each character was to be experienced by the reader, and, hopefully, the viewer, as powerless before the forces of fate, as is the dreamer before his dream.

Though Artaud had high hopes of seeing "The Monk" turned into a movie, he failed to find a producer. So he stacked one more disappointment into his already high pile. Though his French rendition of "The Monk" was published in 1931, the returns were not sufficient to keep Artaud solvent.[18] Despite the publication of a few reviews; a bit part in a motion picture with Autant-Lara, work was sporadic and he was destitute. In fact, Artaud was so poor now that he did not even have a room of his own. He slept in the theatre near a boiler to keep warm.

Artaud's house seemed to be falling in on him, as had Mr. Usher's. Failure met him at every crossroad. Whatever form his endeavors took, rejection ensued. Yet, destiny seems to function sometimes in strange ways. The crushing defeat he now experienced in the film industry which resulted in a cataclysmic inner slaughter, could, perhaps, be looked upon from another point of view; as the proper dose of a *destructive* force, so unbalancing nature's system, and propelling her protective counter-element into action—her *constructive* side.

Whenever a tremendously brutal element is unleashed in nature—as it is during the time of a *plague*—bringing with it nearly total disorder, man's internal energy, his psychic fire *bursts* forth unhampered. Such a release of energy breaks down all barriers; it is comparable to an "immense liquidation", to the opening of a "giant abcess". The profoundest emotions can now be experienced by man in all their grandeur: pain, anguish, hate, love. Masks are shattered, façades are shorn. An extreme communicability arises between disparate facets of the individual's personality which activates his sensibilities, his powers, his strength and his *heroism,* driving him on to seek immortality in the work of art. True art derives from an original experience. As a result, it is endowed with a universal aspect that gives it long life.

Artaud had reached this stage. The flood gates had been torn asunder; the original experience was being transformed into a great work: destruction into construction. Artaud was now going to step into the most fruitful phase of his entire existence: as had, perhaps, symbolically speaking, Mr. Usher, when his house split first, then sank into the tarn.

CHAPTER V

NO MORE MASTERPIECES . . .

I

ONE NEVER KNOWS the tremendous repercussions a simple event may trigger off in one's life; the role it can play in the formulating of one's future activities. Artaud experienced such an occurrence in 1931 when he witnessed a production of the Balinese Theatre at the Colonial Exhibition in Paris. His heretofore vaguely defined theatrical ideas suddenly coalesced—as if in a dream.

Artaud had always been fascinated by Oriental theatre even during those early days when, as an apprentice actor in Charles Dullin's company, he spent long hours discussing the relative merits of Occidental and Oriental Theatre. At that time Artaud had been impressed by the fact that Oriental theatre was not psychologically oriented; that a production was looked upon as a sacred ceremony, where spectators could undergo a metaphysical experience; that there was no dividing line between comedy and tragedy; that the text of a play was merely a "poetic framework" from which the rest of the production emanated; that drama, tension, conflict, climax, suspense, analysis of character was not present, or else emerged as a result of certain standardized situations; that *Sturm und Drang* did not exist as the Westerner conceived of it.[1]

What had so impressed Artaud with the Balinese Theatrical performance he saw in 1931 was the importance accorded to gesture and facial expressions and the relatively unimportant role delegated to the spoken word. In a letter to Louis Jouvet dated August 2, 1931, Artaud expressed some of his views concerning the plastic element in dramatic art, so expertly used in Balinese Theatre. He described the impact of the visible action on stage and its effect upon man's unconscious; the emergence of the latter not only by means of the spoken *word,* but also by means of *gestures,* which should be looked upon as a kind of *hieroglyphic* or *symbol.* Gestures would thus act as transforming agents; communicating the mysterious and hitherto unrevealed contents of the author's, director's, and actor's unconscious and conscious intentions, making them visible on stage in the form of an elevated arm, a lowered finger, etc. Gestures, lighting and sound effects, considered from this point of view are laden with a certain magical force, empowering them to transform the amorphous into the concrete.

> . . . . I have always conceived of the scenic world as something impervious to everything which does not strictly belong to it, to the quasi-uselessness of speech which is no longer a vehicle for thought, but rather a suture, to the vanity of our sentimental or psychological preoccupations: in matters of the theatre, the necessity for the theatre to try to represent on stage certain strange aspects of the structure of the unconscious, all of this in depth and with perspective, with hieroglyphic-like gestures, which must be constructed in an absolutely new and disinterested mental frame of mind: all of this is fulfilled, satisfied, represented, and goes far beyond this, by the surprising realizations of Balinese Theatre . . .[2]

The fact that words are not the essential features in Oriental theatre appealed strongly to Artaud; he who had always had such difficulties formulating ideas by means of them and who described his struggles in this domain so pathetically in his "Correspondence with Jacques Rivière". Now Artaud was absolutely convinced that words are just incapable of expressing certain attitudes and feelings, and that these can be revealed only through gestures or sounds, symbolically felt.

> All true feeling is in reality untranslatable. To express it is to betray it. But to translate it is *to dissimulate it.*[3]

Therefore, objects, music, chanting, costumes, gestures, *and* words, used together are much more effective in bringing about powerful reactions in the spectator than are words used either alone or as primal factors in the spectacle. These aforementioned dramatic devices are transformed by each spectator who interprets them symbolically, into the image he feels the action demands. They take on, therefore, both a personal and impersonal meaning. A ball of red cloth, for example, displayed in a certain way on stage, implies the cutting off of an actor's head. Imitative harmonies, such as the hissing of serpents or the buzzing of insects, Artaud wrote in his article "On Balinese Theatre", lend a metaphysical and awesome quality to a production.

> It happens that this mannerism, this excessively hieratic style, with its rolling alphabet, its shrieks of splitting stones, noises of branches, noises of the cutting and rolling of wood, compose a sort of animated material murmur in the air, in space, a visual as well as audible whispering. And after an instant the magic identification is made: *We know it is we who were speaking.*[4]

The impact, consequently, of such a group of elements on the viewer is tremendous.

Artaud went still further in formulating his views. All the operative elements in Oriental theatre (music, costumes, objects, words, gestures, etc.), he reasoned, leave no space unutilized. A *concrete* sculptural quality is, therefore, created on stage which fills up the void about the actor.[5] Not only does such theatrical architecture add to the visual enjoyment of the spectacle, as Artaud saw it, but it captures the theatre's essential qualities: its metaphysical and spiritual aspects.

> There is an absolute in these constructed perspectives, a real physical absolute which only Orientals are capable of envisioning—it is in the loftiness and thoughtful boldness of their goals that these conceptions differ from our European conceptions of theater, even more than in the strange perfection of their performances.[6]

By means of a *harmonious* use of stage elements (gestures, voice, words, etc.) a Balinese theatrical spectacle succeeds in injecting a feeling of metaphysical terror into the heart of the spectator. When a spectator (a blasphemer) sees a strange and horrifying wooden form appear before him on stage, he feels he is viewing a manifestation from beyond, when he is actually seeing the image of his own blasphemy (in projection). When Dragons or other inhuman manifestations come on stage, Artaud wrote in his essay "Metaphysics and the *mise en scène"*, dread has been aroused within the audience by something concrete, not by language which is in itself an abstraction. The theatre, in this way, has become, symbolically speaking, the manifestation of something "inhuman" or "divine".[7]

Artaud sought to create an Occidental drama that would take on these solemn and frightening aspects present in Oriental theatre: where the "inner eye" would become operative. He looked upon everything on stage as symbolic, as a sign behind which lies a mysterious, fabulous, and dangerous reality. Reality, for the Westerner resides in "appearances", "show," "façade"; for the Oriental and for Artaud, true reality resides in the world "within" which resembles the Westerner's dream world.[8] It was the Oriental's reality, corresponding to the Westerner's unconscious world, that Artaud wished to represent on stage.

In addition to reflecting man's inner world, the theatre, because of its metaphysical and religious nature, must be a manifestation of cosmic reality. Consequently, author, actor, director, spectator, objects, color, sound, gesture, movements, rhythms, and word in the theatre arena, must be looked upon as differentiations or parts of the *cosmic whole*. Space, therefore, is seen as something alive, full—active—as part of the cosmic flow and not distinct from it.

Furthermore, since the theatre, Artaud felt, should be looked upon as a religious ritual and the *prima materia* of religions are myths: he advocated a theatre based on myths.

> The theatre must make itself the equal of life—not an individual life, that individual aspect of life in which CHARACTERS triumph, but the sort of liberated life which sweeps away human individuality and in which man is only a reflection. The true purpose of the theatre is to create Myths, to express life in its immense, universal aspects, and

from that life to extract images in which we find pleasure in discovering ourselves.[9]

A myth, it must be recalled, is a dramatic relating of those experiences or a description of those qualities which are deepest within man. Myths are the outcome of original experiences; not always personal, but rather impersonal or transcendental. In ancient times, for example, people believed that flowers, rocks, water, ice—all of nature's forces—were inhabited by Gods. Primitive man did not just watch the sun rise and set and accept it as such. He assimilated this external experience which then became an inner one. For instance, he likened the story of the sun's daily journey through the skies to a hero's fate. He did likewise with everything in nature: rain, thunder, harvest, drought. The fascinating and terrifying images man's unconscious produced, as a result of the experiences, took the form of dreams and premonitions and fantasies; they became symbolic expressions of an inner drama which he could only cope with by projecting into nature or the environment. These projected dramas or *Myths*, transcended the individual conscious mind in that they occurred everywhere, in all of mankind. Every culture has its Creation Myth, a God Myth, etc. and these myths, whose origins are in many cases prehistoric, are recorded sooner or later.

To the extent that the theatre of antiquity enacted man's dreams and fantasies (myths), it made possible the release of psychic energy in the spectator. For dreams, fantasies, and other products emanating from the unconscious are essentially composed of psychic energy. The theatre of antiquity, then, was giving form and reality to an element in man that is formless, tremendously powerful and to a large extent autonomous. It was a function, on the face of it, of tremendous importance: one to which Artaud wished the theatre to return.

But to merely reproduce the Myths of the ancients on a modern stage would be absolutely pointless to Artaud's way of thinking. It would not move audiences. New myths, therefore, must come into being and quickly, because Western man today, as a whole, feels cut off from nature and from himself. His rational, scientific development has given him a clearer understanding of his relationship to nature, but as a result, he no longer participates in the same mysteries as had the ancients. A cliff is a cliff—plain and simple—it is no longer a source of mystery, magic, fright, and excitement as it had been for the man of antiquity. Primitive man became familiar with his own inner drama, through analogy, in the processes of nature. Modern man has to find his way alone, unaided by alliance with either God, Nature, or even himself. But just as modern society cannot return to a more primitive level of existence, so 20th century authors must not worship the great writers of antiquity. Modern masses should not be blamed for their inability to appreciate a play like *Oedipus Rex*, Artaud indicates in his essay "No More Masterpieces" (*En finir avec les chefs-d'oeuvres*). If Sophocles' play no longer appeals to large audiences, it is not because people are devoid of torments (murders, wars, etc.) or that they no longer have a feeling for the "sublime". Modern man does not respond to the Myths as expressed by Sophocles, Aeschylus, Euripides and Shakespeare, because they are no longer part of his living religion. They are not *original* experiences. They are history, fine literature, the products of genius; but they do not reach into the heart of man and so are no longer valid.[10] The Judaeo-Christian Myths, for example, are no longer a real source of inspiration for the artist as they had once been in the Middle Ages and the Renaissance.

In Artaud's vital article "Metaphysics and the *mise en scène*," he discusses just this point: the decline in meaningfulness of certain Myths with reference to painting. Artaud had come upon a canvas of "Lot's Daughters" by Lucas Van den Leyden, a Flemish primitive who was known for his satiric, historical, and allegorical paintings, and who must have been deeply involved in the Bible. When Artaud saw the painting "Lot's Daughters" his senses (eyes and ears) were immediately touched. It was as if the painting had become animated and that both form and color beckoned to Artaud to follow them into their world. The mountains, the black tower, the boiling fire, the father's increasing sensuality as he

gazes upon his daughters—all these elements seemed to rise up
before Artaud and take on a life of their own. They had become
independent of their creator—the painter—just as the Myth
lives detached from its originator. Each part of the canvas seemed
to grow as he looked at it, in correspondence with his mood and
the depth of his projection. So profound was its impact upon
Artaud that he was immediately confronted again with the
eternal questions of Becoming, Fatality, Chaos, Equilibrium,
the Marvelous.

Modern painters, when trying to depict a Biblical scene usually
turn out a dry, lifeless, and uninteresting work simply because
they no longer believe in the Myths of their ancestors. They are
incapable, therefore, of finding a living response within their own
being and, so, within others. It is the task of the writer to discover
modern man's real sentiments about life, to dredge up from man
all of his buried forces, the *fire* which lives within him. With this
material the writer must create or express new myths. Today, man
must search out his own contemporary myth, declared Artaud,
force down the mask and reveal his inner sun, though it may be
coated with black.

Artaud called the theatre he wished to see come into being,
The Theatre of Cruelty. He wrote of his theories in two Manifestoes entitled "The Theatre of Cruelty", an essay "The Theatre
and Cruelty", and several letters on cruelty, though Artaud's ideas
on this subject are scattered in all of his essays written from 1931
to 1935.

The Theatre of Cruelty was to be a theatre which aimed to
activate man's "magnetic" nervous system to such an extent as to
enable him to project his feelings and sensations beyond the
usual limits imposed by time and space. This kind of theatre
would make it possible for audiences to have a powerful metaphysical experience while watching the spectacle on stage. After
undergoing such an emotional upheaval, the spectator would feel
cleansed and purified, ready for rebirth and renewed life.

What is cruelty? As used by Artaud, it does not mean "blood" or "carnage", though these might occur during a performance. The word "cruelty" must be considered from a philosophical point of view: to create, to breathe, to cry—any *act* is cruelty.

> I employ the word 'cruelty' in the sense of an appetite for life, a cosmic rigor, an implacable necessity, in the gnostic sense of a living whirlwind that devours the darkness, in the sense of that pain apart from whose ineluctable necessity life could not continue; good is desired, it is the consequence of an act; evil is permanent.[11]

Everything that is not dormant in life is cruel. When Brahma, for example, left his state of rest, he suffered. When a child is born, it knows pain. Death, transformation, fire, love, appetite are all *cruelties*.

> It is cruelty that cements matter together, cruelty that molds the features of the created world. Good is always upon the outer face, but the face within is evil. Evil which will eventually be reduced, but at the supreme instant when everything that was form will be on the point of returning to chaos.[12]

The moment unity no longer exists, pain must follow. Any change in a state requires motion, and conflict and cruelty begin: a change from dark to light, matter to spirit, inertia to movement.[13] When God created the world he did away with the original state of unity. When He cast Adam and Eve from paradise he further increased the division between man and himself and man and the cosmos. Before the Creation, and before Adam and Eve were cast forth into the world of antagonisms, life did not exist as we now perceive it—paradise is in actuality a state of union with the cosmos.

The "Great Fable of Creation", that is the change from unconscious unity to conscious individuality and multiplicity, is forever being enacted on different levels and is, Artaud felt, man's most traumatic experience. The drama *per se*, looked upon symbolically, is one of *Creation*. It is the enactment and re-enactment of the pain experienced by man as he is torn away from his stage of original unity, from "Mother Earth" or from "undifferentiated reality." Man is then forced into a state of multiplicity where he must act and react—therefore, live cruelly.

As the spectator sees and hears the story of Creation enacted before him, he is filled with nostalgia for the primordial condition he once knew—and which he had nearly forgotten. To reach this deepest of levels, a march inward, to discover unity with the cosmos, must be made. Such motion is shocking and painful; it is a voyage fraught with cruelty every step of the way.

> Everything that acts is a cruelty. It is upon this idea of extreme action, pushed beyond all limits, that theatre must be rebuilt.
>
> Imbued with the idea that the public thinks first of all with its senses and that to address oneself first to its understanding as the ordinary psychological theatre does is absurd. The Theatre of Cruelty proposes to resort to a mass spectacle; to seek in the agitation of tremendous masses, convulsed and hurled against each other, a little of that poetry of festivals and crowds when, all too rarely nowadays, the people pour out into the streets.[15]

The theatre then is to take each and every spectator on a journey inward: similar perhaps to Artaud's own voyage as described in "The Umbilicus of Limbo". It is an active force (a cruel one), which must work on the spectator always.

> In the same way that our dreams have an effect upon us and reality has an effect upon our dreams, so we believe that the images of thought can be identified with a dream which will be efficacious to the degree that it can be projected with the necessary violence. And the public will believe in the theatre's dreams on condition that it take them for true dreams and not for a servile copy of reality; on condition that they allow the public to liberate within itself the magical liberties of dreams which it can only recognize when they are imprinted with terror and cruelty.[16]

The theatre of cruelty for Artaud is a total experience. It is at once material and spiritual, real and imaginary. To establish the theatre of cruelty, theatrical techniques must be precise and as organized as the circulation of blood in the arteries. And, in order for the theatre to become a total theatrical experience, it must furnish real subjects which emanate from man's dreams: crime, eroticism, desire for utopia, cannibalism, etc. If the theatre, in such a case, turns out to be inhuman then it is a reflection of man's spasmodic and antagonistic inner life, the result of having been ejected into the world and forced to live *cruelty*.

A *dramatic technique* was necessary to give form to Artaud's theatrical concepts which were—and there is no doubt of this— unique. And such is the case despite a flood of theatrical inno- vators such as Adolphe Appia, for example, who felt that the answer to scenic art lay in Wagner's music-dramas and the emo- tions they engendered, the *Ausdruckskraft* which triggered off the force necessary to create the right theatrical structures and acting interpretations: Gordon Craig who essayed to conjure forth an inner reality by advocating a theatre based upon poetry, beauty, suggestion and imagination; Stanislavski who demanded that the actor identify with or live his role; Granville-Barker who ad- vocated a theatre based on exciting poetry and deeds, and so many more. No one but Artaud would have dreamed of asking the spectator to come to the theatre to live cruelty.

How would Artaud go about realizing the minor miracle of putting his ideas into concrete form? Of what would his tech- niques consist? Artaud reveals his system in a series of disparate lectures, manifestoes, letters, and essays written from 1931 to 1935 and published, for the most part, in the *Nouvelle Revue Fran- çaise:* "Metaphysics and the *mise en scène*" (1931), "On Balinese Theatre" (1931), "The Alchemical Theatre" (1932), "The Theatre of Cruelty" (First Manifesto) (1932), "The Theatre and Cruelty" (1932), "The Theatre and the Plague" (1933), "No more Master- pieces" (1933), "Letters on Cruelty", "Letters on Language", "The Theatre of Cruelty" (Second Manifesto) (1933), "Oriental and Occidental Theatre" (1935), "Two Notes" (1932, 1935).

In these works, familiar today to many devotees of the theatre, Artaud voiced his most profound ideas, *all* of which had emerged —not from any intellectual concepts—but rather from his own personal agony, like drops of blood staining the earth's surface.

Artaud's ideas throughout these works are never expressed in a cartesian manner, but seem to topple forth, helter-skelter—each as a result of some association or sensation which acts as a releasing agent for a torrential blast of new formulations. Such insights as are expressed by Artaud throughout these pages are revealed frequently by means of strikingly colored images: nightmarish and ghoulish figures scampering across its pages; cutting and brittle enunciations, onomatopoeias; cacophonous and deafening phrases. The reader, spellbound, tingling all over, his sensations aroused to the breaking point, as he makes his way through this labyrinth, this tremendously stirring and hyper-magnetised field of action, can actually feel Artaud's flashes of intuition, his heaving sighs of sorrow, his bursts of joy and hatreds, as he yields to revelation upon revelation. Artaud's super and sustained emotionalism, his psychic fire which he unleashes with stinging intensity, propels the reader on one of the most traumatic voyages ever taken; it also leaves him gasping for breath, bewildered, numb, trying to penetrate, to *see* into Artaud's exquisitely and intricately chiseled world of mosaic thought-patterns.

The specific elements of a Theatre of Cruelty spectacle will be taken up one by one: the role of the director; the actor and the breathing technique; gestures; words, sound effects; lighting; the stage and the theatre; objects; masks; accessories; decor; the play itself.

The *director*, according to Artaud, is like a magician, a master of "sacred ceremonies", a "Demiurge". He is a high priest, a God, a type of "unique creator" who brings about fusion of all the disparate theatrical elements (music, lighting, etc.), thereby creating unity from disunity. The director, therefore, animates the spectacle and the action—all the world which comes to life, even *matter*, and weaves it into a dramatic pattern which acts directly upon the spectator.[17]

A director should not and cannot commit a complete *mise en scène* to writing because it is something alive and mobile that grows as the play takes shape. "A *mise en scène* comes into being *before* the stage . . ."[18] A gesture, a movement, an intonation,

Artaud wrote, a sign, an expression, an attitude, cannot be contained in words, anymore than one can describe a *pain*. To try to set down a *mise en scène* by means of words alone is to limit its function and impact considerably. It must be thought out, felt and perceived by the director who is, after all, the central creator of any theatrical production.

If a director's function in part is to infuse life into the spectacle, the *actor* must do likewise when creating his role. An actor must materialize the sensations and feelings he seeks to bring out in his portrayal and can effect such result through *proper breathing*. Passion of every type has "organic bases", Artaud wrote. It is something physical and the rays emitted by a sensation from the body are likewise material. Every mental motion, every feeling has its corresponding breath, Artaud stated. It is the actor, through training, who must discover the right breath for the proper sentiment.

> The gifted actor finds by instinct how to tap and radiate certain powers; but he would be astonished indeed if it were revealed to him that these powers, which have their material trajectory by and *in the organs,* actually exist, for he has never realized they could actually exist.[19]

Indeed, the actor is like a boxer, Artaud reasoned. He must know and use his emotional world as the boxer knows his muscular organism. Only when the actor has become familiar with every aspect of his body, when he knows from where each emotion originates can he express every thought and sensation materially.[20]

> The belief in a fluid materiality of the soul is indispensable to the actor's craft. To know that a passion is material, that it is subject to the plastic fluctuations of the material, makes accessible an empire of passions that extends our sovereignty.[21]

Such a material concept makes it possible through "mathematical analogies" to penetrate a whole new realm: time and space in which the actor succeeds not only in linking himself with the character he is portraying, but of associating him with the forces of the cosmos.

To understand the secret of the passional time—a kind of musical *tempo* which regulates their harmonic beat—is an aspect of theatre long undreamed of by our modern psychological theatre.[22]

Artaud's metaphysical attitude in connection with breathing as a source of creation dates far back into history: to *Creation* which took place when God breathed "a living breath" into Adam.

> Effort sympathetically accompanies breathing and, according to the quality of the effort to be produced, a preparatory emission of breath will make this effort easy and spontaneous. I insist on the word spontaneous, for breath rekindles life, sets it afire in its own substance.
>
> What voluntary breathing provokes is a spontaneous reappearance of life. Like a voice, in infinite colors on the edges of which warriors lie sleeping.[23]

The *Kabbala,* Artaud wrote, divides human breath into six principal and arcane parts. The Orientals believe in the all-pervading Breath, the Buddha-Essence of the Buddha-Mind, the One, and that all life emerges from it and dissolves back into it.

The actor through breathing can also create a *being* (his double), that is, the character he wants to personify or an image or a mood. He can learn to commune with the forces of nature as well as with his own disparate parts by localizing the points where his muscles are affected by the emotion he seeks to portray: anger, sobs, guilt, etc.

> Another radiating point: the location of anger, attack, biting is the center of the solar plexus. It is there that the head supports itself in order to cast its venom, morally speaking.[25]

To know the secret of breathing is to be able to provoke life, to divine the *color* of the soul which is also made of matter and not pure abstraction: "The soul can be physiologically reduced to a skein of vibrations."[26] Artaud affirmed that one can go still further and stated that through breathing one could reach a more profound reality and return to one's origins. If an actor, he explained, does not possess a certain feeling necessary for his part, he can "sink into himself" by means of breathing and there discover and connect with the feeling he seeks to express.[27] The theatre looked upon in this manner becomes "the perfect and the most complete symbol of universal manifestation." The actor carried within him part of the cosmos and can return into it through his own organism, through his lungs.[28]

> In order to reforge the chain, the chain of a rhythm in which the spectator used to see his own reality in the spectacle, the spectator must be allowed to identify himself with the spectacle, breath by breath and beat by beat.[29]

Furthermore, the actor must know how to "touch" certain parts of the spectator's body in order to send him into a "magic trance." He can succeed in this because emotion has organic origins. When breathing properly the actor casts forth certain rays which strike the spectator in the proper place, provoking him to laugh or cry, as the case may be.

> To know in advance what points of the body to touch is the key to throwing the spectator into magical trances. And it is this invaluable kind of science that poetry in the theatre has been without for a long time.
> To know the points of localization in the body is thus to reforge the magical chain.[30]

Unlike the Western actor who looks *out*, who is "uplifted toward God" or to his role, and who "succumbs to exaltation" when he experiences religious fervor, Artaud's actor, like the Oriental looks *within* to find God, Self—or his Double.[31]

In addition to Artaud's breathing technique, he suggested that the actor—and the theatre in general—should be looked upon as an alchemical factor or process. Both alchemy and the theatre, Artaud explained in "The Alchemical Theatre" consist of the virtual and the material: both are reflections and externalizations of unconscious and primordial dramas within man. Both actor and alchemist create their realities by means of symbols and through illusion. The actor, for example, takes an amorphous and inanimate entity (his role) and tries to transform it into a life-like creation. In so doing, he reveals mysterious and powerful elements within man's psyche through projection. These unknown forces or this "psychic energy" is a force which lives within man—and the cosmos, and which is vital to the actor's art.[32]

Gesture is also of extreme importance in creating a momentous theatrical spectacle. It reveals the inner man. "Gesture is its material and its wits, and, if you will, its alpha and omega."[33] Gestures, however, must not be confused with pantomime, Artaud declared, a deformation of the mute elements of Italian comedy. Gestures are symbolic evocations of nature's aspects. They are signs of both inner and outer activities which can be made on stage and which act upon the spectator's imagination.

Though gestures and attitudes on the part of the actor are of supreme importance in Artaud's theatre, words should not be "suppressed" in creating a *stage language*. They should be given the importance they have in dreams, Artaud stated. The word is but one of many theatrical vehicles; to be combined with lighting, gestures, music, sound, facial expressions, etc. Western theatre, as Artaud had already indicated, relied too heavily upon the spoken and written word as a vehicle for expression. The word, as a result, had become an ossified and frozen means of conveying feeling, magic, and mystery in the theatre. Artaud was intent upon restoring to the theatre that which had been dethroned by Racine and his contemporaries in the XVIIth century when they gave primacy to the word and the psychological play.

Artaud relegated the *word* to its proper place as one of the ways of expressing and acting upon man's inner world. If words are to be effective, they must be manipulated like solid objects, Artaud explicated. They must act and react upon each other and upon the spectator.

> To make metaphysics out of a spoken language is to make the language express what it does not ordinarily express; to make use of it in a new, exceptional, and unaccustomed fashion; to reveal its possibilities for producing physical shock; to divide and distribute it actively in space; to deal with intonations in an absolutely concrete manner, restoring their power to shatter as well as really to manifest something; to turn against language and its basely utilitarian, one

could say alimentary, sources, against its trapped-beast origins; and finally, to consider language as the form of *Incantation*.[34]

The word is a concrete reality for Artaud and it must be uttered with the vehemence of the emotion that gave birth to it. Words are not merely a means of communication. He sought to restore to them their primitive functions and qualities, their incantatory nature, supernatural aura, mesmerizing and magical faculties— all lost to modern man. To recreate the role of the word necessitated first its destruction. Established words, meanings and sounds would have to be shattered before new content could emerge. Words then become as hieroglyphics, a visual translation for certain mysterious elements within man and the universe.

Sound effects played a very strong role in Artaud's conceptions. He made notations for background noises to be used in his dramatic productions. In fact, they were marked in such detail that they resembled a musical score. But even these notations indicating the concrete sounds he sought to reproduce in the course of a play could not possibly convey the sought-for impression, since no verbal description of a sound or vocal intonation or nuance is really possible. Musical instruments if needed during a theatrical performance should also be used as objects, symbolically, as do the Orientals, that is, as part of the decor. If modern instruments cannot produce the sounds the director considers necessary to his production, then ancient instruments should be used or new ones invented "based on special blendings of new metal alloys which can add new pitches to an octave, produce unbearable shooting sounds and noises".

Lights should be protagonists in the drama—actors. The interplay of lights on the stage can be a dramatic instrumentality designed to create an atmosphere capable of moving the spectator to anxiety, terror, eroticism, or love. Lighting is a force which can play on the mind of the spectator because of its vibratory possibilities. It can, Artaud declared, be cast down onto the stage in waves, in sheets, or in fiery arrows.

Costumes can be exquisite works of art as they are in the Oriental theatre; they can also capture the magic and mystery of the unknown. Modern dress, Artaud felt, should be avoided since it does not stir the imagination.

There should be no separation between the *stage and the theatre*. The theatre should be enclosed within four walls and be modified according to the architecture of certain sacred places: churches or temples, such as those in Tibet. There would be no ornamentation and the walls would be painted with lime to absorb the light. Audiences would sit in the middle of the stage on mobile chairs which will permit them to follow the play which unfolds around them. There will be galleries in the theatre, allowing the action to take place on all levels and dimensions; in height and in depth. This diffused action in space will grip and assault the spectator—as though a world were forcing itself in upon him: symbolically speaking, the outside world acting upon and stimulating man's inner world.[35]

The sense of the fragmentary and isolated nature of life as experienced in a series of diverse visual moments was, in part, what Artaud and the Surrealists sought to express in their paintings, movies, poetry, and the theatre. Artaud did not believe in the necessity for a visual center in a theatrical production. In the theatre, the audience must not see a performance as a concentrated whole, but rather as a succession of fragments or moments isolated in space. The rational mind must not synthesize or order the images it sees into consecutive patterns. Life itself is in a state of flux. It is the impact of these isolated fragments upon the spectator that is important.[36]

Objects—Masks—Accessories were to be used in the Theatre of Cruelty to help create a concrete theatrical language. These accessories and masks may appear on stage in the same size and shape as they do in the sleeper's dream world. They can, therefore, be huge or tiny, grotesque or beautiful, etc.

There was to be no *decor*, Artaud wrote. It must be noted that in old Chinese theatre there was no attempt at realistic scenery. The stage was decorated; that is, it indicated where the action was

situated (a palace, a lake, etc.) but it did not represent it. Proper-
ties were used symbolically: a wooden table and two chairs might
imply a banquet hall. Artaud felt that his actors, whom he called
"animated hieroglyphics", could, by the rhythmic use of their
voices and gestures express everything that was necessary.

A *play* must be topical, Artaud wrote, modern in its specifics,
and correspond to man's present problems and preoccupations.
Its general themes, however, should be universal and myth-like,
revealing the totality of man: social upheavals, conflicts of peoples,
races, natural forces.

Artaud's theatre in general then was designed to reflect cosmic
reality; inflict cruelty; that is, to be one of "extreme action, pushed
beyond all limits . . ." , enshroud and bombard each and every
spectator from all parts of the theatre with sensations of all kinds;
transform, alchemically, the amorphous into the plastic, thereby
creating a concrete poetry in space; force an actor's breathing to
affect and even regulate a spectator's psyche, to the extent of being
capable of strangling or choking him; look upon gestures as
symbols, clothing arcane elements, permitting them, therefore, to
stride the stage in myth-like grandeur.

Artaud compared his theatre to a plague; a disorder of the most
horrendous type which brings with it both social and psychological disturbances. Such a disease, symbolically speaking, unleashes
a "spontaneous" or "psychic fire"; during which time man is no
longer in control over his energies or his emotions which seem to
cascade forth. This release of energy which forces out passions of
all types (for example, incest and sexual abnormalities), provoking
horror and vertigo in the hearts of audiences, leads up to a collective expulsion or regurgitation, followed by a purification of
man through his own forces of evil. These tremendous "flames" or
"luminescent suns", as Artaud called them, which man discharges
either during the course of a theatrical performance or in moments of great stress (as during a plague) are also the same ones
which he later transforms in his fantasy into symbols and then
into the work of art.

A theatrical production then should give rise, as does a plague, to extremes of emotion. Spiritual forces would be trapped in this manner through shock, cataclysms perceived through projection on stage; a "superior analogy"[37] would arise from the severe trauma experienced. The dormant waves or forces present in the cosmos and in the human being, and the very secrets and mysteries of poetry would then reveal themselves to those able to *see* and *feel*.

Artaud outlined what was to have been a four act play, but was never completed: "The Conquest of Mexico" (*La Conquête du Mexique*). In a letter to Jean Paulhan (January 22, 1933), he declared that the outline and *mise en scène* for this work was the best example, so far, of what he intended for a Theatre of Cruelty production.[38]

Artaud opted for this subject: the conquest of Mexico by Fernando Cortez because of the universality of the questions it treated: man's drive to colonize, his need to brutalize his fellow man, his insistence on his right to convert the native from the old natural religion he professed to Christianity. In this work, "events, not men" as individuals are dramatized.

> Men will come in their turn with their psychology and their passions, but they will be taken as the emanation of certain forces and understood in the light of the events and historical fatality in which they have played their role.[39]

Since Artaud wanted to bring forth a theatre of symbols and myths, he chose super-human antagonists, conflicting civilizations and epochs to move above the scenic area and collide with great force. Though men would be acting out of their own personal passions and anxieties, they would be seen as individuals only in so far as they were part of an integrated whole, considered "in the light of events and historical fatality in which they have played their role".[40]

Montezuma,[41] the "astrologer king", was seen by Artaud as having two aspects: divine and human. His divine or collective side was that part of him that was attuned to the forces and laws of destiny, that accepted the cosmic dictates passively, knowing in advance that he was bound unalterably to the stars and that they determined his *way*. Dances and pantomines were to be enacted on stage to objectify and reinforce Montezuma's symbolic identification with the myths and astrology. Montezuma's human side, however, caused him to doubt himself, as well as the edicts of destiny, to be able to fight the conquering Cortez.

Act I opens on a tableau of Mexico, a country tense with dread, sensing an oncoming slaughter—the arrival of Cortez. Artaud describes fully the scenic effects: caves, forests, ruins; the lighting effects; the gestures; the attitudes of the actors; the sound effects consisting of melodies, groans, crashing waves and incantations. The intent was to create an organic atmosphere which was at once dynamic and frightening.

Act II unfolds on Mexico as seen by Cortez. The atmosphere of the second Act, as opposed to that of the first, is silent, immobile, stagnant.

> Silence concerning all his secret struggles; apparent stagnation and everywhere magic, magic of a motionless, unheard-of spectacle, with cities like ramparts of light, palaces on canals of stagnant water, a heavy melody.[42]

Act III, the revolt both actual and in Montezuma's mind, begins. Montezuma has become dual now: impersonal and personal; divine and human.

> Montezuma cuts the living space, rips it open like the sex of a woman in order to cause the invisible to spring forth.
> The stage is stuffed unevenly with heads, throats; cracked, oddly broken melodies, and responses to these melodies, appear like stumps. Montezuma himself seems split in two, divided; with some parts of himself in half-light, others dazzling; with many hands coming out of his dress, with expressions painted on his body like a multiple portrait of consciousness, but from within the consciousness of Montezuma all the questions pass forth into the crowd.
> The Zodiac, which formerly roared with all its beasts in the head of Montezuma, turns into a group of human passions made incarnate by the learned heads of the official spokesman, brilliant at disputation

—a group of secret plays during which the crowd, despite the circumstances, does not forget to sneer.[43]

The rebellion breaks out and fighting ensues.

Act IV dramatizes Montezuma's abdication. With his withdrawal from power, strangely enough, comes Cortez' loss of assurance. By means of multiple mirrors, the treasure, now placed on stage, and which has become Cortez' possession, seems to have become mere illusion. Lights and sounds grow and decrease; strange, distorted human figures fill the stage. Trouble is brewing. Not just one Cortez, but several now appear on the stage; a sign that the leader, as such, no longer exists, but only fragments of him. The vanquished are rebelling. After the bloodshed a religious atmosphere prevails. Heads are bent in prayer in preparation for Montezuma's funeral.

In "The Conquest of Mexico", the character Montezuma resembles Artaud in several respects. His passive acceptance of destiny as a profound and collective force can be likened to Artaud's feeling that he too was *destined* to lead a certain type of life, that his future had been dictated before he was ever born and that he was an instrument of a collective power. Artaud, like Montezuma, was a man with a secret knowledge, as symbolized by the treasure. There was also the human fighting aspect within Artaud which made him unwilling to let himself be devoured by society, his enemy, as symbolized by Cortez in the play. Unlike Montezuma, Artaud clutched at life as hard as he could, fighting desperately to prevent himself from dying of starvation which had been Montezuma's fate.

II

Though Artaud was the author of some of the most extraordinary articles, letters, and manifestoes on the theatre, he was not acclaimed by the general public nor even by his friends in the theatrical world. His ideas—as he was himself—were considered far too bizarre, too quixotic. To ask people to come to the theatre to undergo anguish? torture? to be healed? Such directors as

Louis Jouvet, Charles Dullin and Georges Pitoëff were far too busy trying to put their theatres on solid footing, making ends meet, to take the chance of working with somebody so strange, so unreliable—so "unreachable"—as Artaud. There seemed to be no common denominator between Artaud and the directors of his day. Artaud, the visionary, the man who wanted to direct part of the *Zohar* on a theatrical stage, was years ahead of his epoch; he lived in a world peopled with his visions and fantasies: one of *actuality,* where time and space do not exist. He was far removed from the work-a-day world and devoid of any practical sense whatsoever. Rarely, if ever, did he know where his next meal was coming from. He was growing thinner and thinner; gaunt; his eyes, by contrast, seemed to grow in size, and like the hollow caverns, inspired mystery, awe, and fright in those with whom Artaud came in contact. Dejection set in; increased, until it reached the saturation point, when for no apparent reason, Artaud suddenly became imbued with "fire". An immense conflagration blazed within him; new ideas poured forth, giving him the strength and courage, to ask Louis Jouvet for permission to read Georg Büchner's drama *Wozzeck* to him, to listen to his ideas for a *mise en scène* for this mystical drama. He begged Jouvet in letter after letter to make use of his talents in a restricted manner.[44] If Jouvet looked hard enough, he pleaded, there would be *something* for him to do. He took the bull by the horns in one missive and informed Jouvet he was sending him two *mises en scène:* one for Strindberg's "The Ghost Sonata" (1930), and the other, his own composition, a "talking-pantomime"; "The Philosopher's Stone" (*La Pierre philosophale*) (1931).

"The Philosopher's Stone" is a personal story as were all of Artaud's fictional writings; indicating his enormous struggle and preoccupation with his health. It is a strikingly original work; dealing with unconscious desires and obsessions; laden with symbolism of the most basic kind, strangely enough, akin to that of Wagner's *Nibelungen Ring.* An analysis of the "Philosopher's Stone," in that it sheds new light on Artaud's inner development, will be undertaken here.

Symbolically speaking, the philosopher's stone as well as the magic ring, gold and precious stones, have always been symbols of a treasure for which man is searching. The gold of the Nibelungs, for example, is a more 'civilized' form of this idea—the treasure which one attains with difficulty is, in psychological terms, *identity*.[45]

"The Philosopher's Stone" would then be, to a certain extent, Artaud's symbolic journey or quest for the treasure—his identity. The discovery of the treasure is not only a difficult, hazardous and terribly painful task; but frequently impossible. By means of imagery, gesture and attitudes (ideas so basic to Artaud's theatrical concepts), the protagonists of this drama are unconsciously cutting away layers of outer coverings, trying to penetrate into those dark yet fertile regions which surround the *Self*. For Artaud, judging from his previous scenarios (*The Seashell and the Clergyman*, *The Thirty-two*, etc.), such a quest begins in a scientific manner, usually in a laboratory of some sort, as it had with the alchemists of old. In "The Philosopher's Stone," the curtains part on an operating room.

Dr. Pale, a physician, has been carrying out certain experiments, hoping to discover the philosopher's stone. He is married to the beautiful Isabelle who is not only bored with her situation, but is sexually dissatisfied. She sighs and moans, making obvious her feelings. Harlequin, who loves Isabelle, offers himself to Dr. Pale for his sadistic experiments, just to be near the one he loves. Dr. Pale begins his work. First he cuts off Harlequin's arms, then his legs . . . Left alone after the operation with Isabelle, Harlequin and his beloved execute a series of erotic gestures. A child is born from their union which comes forth from under Isabelle's dress. It looks like Dr. Pale. More experiments occur. Dr. Pale keeps hacking away at Harlequin's limbs which must obviously come together again in some mysterious way after each operation. Harlequin returns, this time with his double: one aspect being handsome, the other ugly and deformed. Dr. Pale again begins cutting away at the handsome Harlequin. Exhausted from his arduous labors, he falls asleep. Another child is born. And as the doctor awakens, Isabelle and Harlequin, using their stomachs as spring boards bounce up into space "in a gesture imitating that of love."

The violence of Dr. Pale's experiments, the hacking off of Harlequin's limbs, indicate his extreme desire to destroy the healthy, the handsome, the love element in the world—all of which Harlequin symbolizes. Dr. Pale who can derive sexual pleasure only from sado-masochistic actions, cannot satisfy Isabelle. There seems to be no common denominator between husband and wife. His young wife finds an outlet in Harlequin and indulges abundantly in the sexual act, each time producing a child. Yet, strangely enough, these children keep looking like Dr. Pale. Why? The fruit of the erotic orgies is not normal since Isabelle is giving birth to sadism: too much sexuality (with Harlequin) implies an imbalance, as does too much intellectuality (Dr. Pale). Harlequin, in the last analysis, is Dr. Pale's double, his counterpart, each aspect loving Isabelle in its own way. In this triangular drama the woman gains spirituality, as does Harlequin (springing into space), through the sexuality. But the spirituality both Harlequin and Isabelle will know after bouncing up into space implies a total negation of the physical world.

One must take note of the importance of the *dismemberment* theme in this play: each time Dr. Pale cuts off Harlequin's limbs. Mythologically speaking, it is through the *cleansing, burning,* or *dismemberment process,* that transformation and rebirth can occur. It is just this transformation that Dr. Pale is seeking through his various experiments. He unconsciously wants to become a whole human being instead of just an extreme fragment. When in the Egyptian religion the evil Set caused Osiris to be dismembered, Osiris was reborn through the good work of Isis. Dr. Pale (Evil) is cutting away at Harlequin (the normal and handsome male), trying to kill that aspect of himself (the double) and by so doing, will, hopefully bring about a rebirth within his personality. In Dr. Pale's case, no matter how hard he hacked away, Harlequin could never be fully destroyed. The split within Dr. Pale is so great that no relationship can possibly exist between his polarities (his physical aspect and his cerebral or spiritual side). Only through Harlequin and Isabelle, that is, the aspect of himself that they represent, can Dr. Pale be reborn. But his rebirth is merely the rebirth of another single aspect of himself, since Harlequin and Isabelle symbolize only the sexual. After their sexual orgy they reject it and spring into space, negating all matter, as it were. No middle way has been found, no identity, no philosopher's stone—but rather more opposites which further divide the split within the personality.

"The Philosopher's Stone" indicated in many respects Artaud's feelings of dismemberment: his desire for wholeness, the constant torment caused by the unreconciled polarities within his own personality—the sexual and spiritual, the healthy and the sick, the ugly and the beautiful. Artaud's trinity (Dr. Pale, Isabelle, Harlequin) were projections of facets of his own being, aspects which unfortunately never came into balance with each other.

But when Artaud brought "The Philosopher's Stone" to the gifted but traditional director, Louis Jouvet, he felt such a work unsuited for his purposes, and answered Artaud negatively on all his other suggestions for dramatizations. Dullin and Pitoëff also steered clear of Artaud's monstrous and frightening half-humans which stamped his works. Yet, pathetically enough, Artaud's Breughel-like creatures were thirty years ahead of their time; their descendents via Beckett, Ionesco, Genet, dominate the present day "theatre of the Absurd."

Driven to express himself, still laboring under the illusion that people would finally listen to his ideas, Artaud composed another stage work "There is no more Firmament" (*Il n'y a plus de firmament*) (1931 or 2).[46]

In this frightening drama the world is presented as in a state of upheaval. Strange natural happenings have occurred. Scientists who in society are so lionized, on stage, are depicted in all degrees of stupidity and mediocrity. Yet, they are the ones, if they so wish, who can explode the world. Artaud's fear that the world, through man's efforts, or even through mysterious forces, would be destroyed was very real.

To make vivid Artaud's premonition of disaster he used sirens, violently percussive sounds and rhythms, echo-like noises, drum-rolls, chants, and litanies. His *mise en scène* called for darkness, explosions, music giving the impression of a cataclysm, chords that seem to fall in a medley or harsh claps. A series of colors are flashed on the stage, red, silver, green, white, yellow, but not one pure color among them, all nuanced; lighting effects give the impression of coldness or choppiness like the Morse Code. Crowds shuffle on to the stage in rhythmic groups, shadows appear and disappear; disconnected conversations, screams, voices expressing violence are heard; agonized and distorted faces emerge from nowhere; heads grow in size and take on excruciating expressions, as though experiencing the stigmata; bodies, with enormous heads and fists, advance, advance. . . .

Artaud added a new kind of character to his roster in this drama; namely, an impersonal-function type, The Great Sniffer (*Le Grand Flaireur*). This being walks on stage, larger than life, since he stands on stilts, and symbolizes man being led by his nose, as his name indicates. He is a man out of relation with himself; one who follows an over-developed or one-sided point of view; and who leads his flock of friends or followers into a distorted way of seeing things. His followers are made up of men with enormous arms and fists, unbalanced themselves, who follow him blindly. When the Great Sniffer utters his innocuous sentences, he draws them out, ending each phrase in an echo-like fashion and with "unbearable yelpings . . ."[47] The masses are attracted to the Great Sniffer's platitudes, which they interpret as words of revolt. After each tirade, banners, masts, torches and the sounds of plane motors fill the air, a concrete expression of the effect of the Great Sniffer's speech on the masses. The Great Sniffer then is the kind of person who leads groups, arouses people, captivates them into believing in his monstrous and distorted ideas: similar, in fact, to the "Great Figures" in Genet's "The Balcony."

In "The Philosopher's Stone," Harlequin and Isabelle bounced up into space and supposedly found their salvation in the higher spheres, though they had to give up their earthly existences to do so. In "There is no more Firmament," no answers are given, no escape is offered. Man is left to his own devices. He is alone. He must remain on earth and work out his own problems, anguishes and torments. And so it was with Artaud. No matter how original and vital were the techniques used in "There is no more Firmament," the script was rejected by one director after another.

Always hopeful, unwilling to take no for an answer, beseeching, Artaud approached Jouvet yet again with another idea. In a letter dated April 29, 1931, he sent him his *mise en scène* for "The Trafalgar Coup" (*Le Coup de Trafalgar*), a new play by Vitrac. Perhaps Jouvet would be willing to produce this play and let Artaud create the *mise en scène*? He admitted pathetically to Jouvet, that he was fully aware of the reputation he now had as an unreliable and quixotic person. But he wrote:

> You are certainly very much aware of the fact that this instability, these irregularities for which one reproaches me, stem only from the irregularity and instability of a life which has not found its goal. I am far less insane than one believes me to be: I would not be at all, the day I would be given important responsibilities and find myself able to make use of all of my energies in an interesting manner.[48]

Artaud did not want Jouvet to judge him on what he now called his quasi-"improvised" *Théâtre Alfred Jarry* productions. Circumstances had just been unfavorable at that time, he felt. Things had changed now. He was really ready to prove his mettle. He had something new and vital to share with Paris—his development of the plastic side of the dramatic act, the importance accorded to the senses, the symbolism of the gestures—all these elements which were in direct line with ancient theatrical traditions, he would use in an ultra-modern fashion. But Jouvet was sold neither on Vitrac's new play nor on Artaud's direction of it. So, once again, Artaud had to face up to disappointment, to vanished dreams—even worse—to a production of "The Trafalgar Coup" at the *Théâtre de l'Atelier* by Marcel Herrand and Jean Marchat on June 8, 1934, without Artaud.

From a practical point of view Artaud's endeavors had proved fruitless. Yet he worked: fought on as though some mysterious and guiding force gave him the necessary energy to keep going. A glimmer of hope loomed in the distance: Jouvet asked Artaud to read "The Cheaters" (*Les Tricheurs*) (1931), by Stève Passeur which he thought of producing at the time. But this glimmer faded into darkness when Jouvet had a change of mind and let the production idea drop. Charles Dullin gave the play on January 21, 1932—again, without Artaud. The theatre, Artaud had learned throughout the years, is one of those professions filled with staggering disappointments and when Jouvet asked Artaud, absolutely unexpectedly, to work on the sound effects for Alfred Savoir's "The Village Pastry Cook" (*La Patissière de Village*), Artaud finally smiled with satisfaction.

Artaud's task was not a simple one because he found himself thwarted at every step by Olivier Messiaen, the organist, who was supposed to implement Artaud's ideas on the organ, but who wanted to impose his own instead. Artaud was searching for certain

. . . . imitative sounds, simple and denuded, transposed in tone at times, but not musical ones, and within the other half, made up of composed sounds, it would be sufficient to reduce the composed sounds to the elements which compose them, and which we have searched to *isolate* in order to produce the entire register of sonorities corresponding to this play.[49]

The organ, Artaud contended, could absolutely not imitate certain real *sounds* which audiences could understand and to which they could respond. To use an organ to create unreal sound effects was to be hypocritical and this was not Artaud's way.[50]

After painful weeks of discussions and arguments, and emnity stemming from basic differences in personality and conceptions between Jouvet, Messiaen, and Artaud, "The Village Pastry Cook" opened on March 8, 1932 at the *Théâtre Pigalle*. It was not a success. Artaud, however, was not surprised by this outcome. Nor was he overly shocked when Dullin apparently agreed to let him direct Büchner's *Wozzeck* at the Atelier theatre and then either put off the project or changed his mind about it. The idea of establishing a "Theatre of Cruelty" program which was being considered by the *Nouvelle Revue Française,* which would act as its sponsor, also fell through.

Perhaps Artaud felt himself doomed at this point like Tantalus. In fact, an affinity with this mythological figure of the past might have inspired Artaud to adapt Seneca's play *Atreus and Thyestes,* which he entitled "Tantalus' Torment" (*Le Supplice de Tantale*). But nothing came of this project. Each time Artaud offered his talents, the doors of Paris' flourishing theatres were shut in his face and the stone of defeat swung menacingly above his head. It must have seemed to him that Tantalus' drama was his own—a Myth of the Damned.[51]

III

Artaud finally came to the conclusion that his physical suffering and mental outlook really made his being a "loner" inevitable. He could simply not operate hampered by anyone else's point of view. Henceforth, he would have to be his own master or not work in the theatre at all.

Artaud would walk alone. He was determined to realize his vision. He wrote "The Cenci," a dramatized Myth, which opened at the Folies-Wagram theatre in Paris on May 6, 1935.

A reading of Artaud's "The Cenci,"[52] without seeing the play enacted, is like viewing a frame with a faded picture. The written play is merely the framework around which the complete theatrical production was built. Because Artaud endowed his work with its own language and life, impossible to reveal on the written page, "The Cenci" became a living entity only on the stage.

Artaud based his version of "The Cenci" on Shelley's five-act tragedy (1819) by the same name and on Stendhal's translation (1837) of a XVIth century account of an historical event. The facts are uncomplicated. Beatrice Cenci was the daughter of Francesco Cenci (1549-1598), a sordid, cruel, sexually perverted Roman nobleman. His first wife had died after bearing him seven children. He then married the wealthy and beautiful Lucretia

Petroni. Later, he plotted the death of his sons and raped his daughter, Beatrice. Together with her step-mother and remaining brothers, Beatrice successfully plotted the murder of her father. He was killed by hired assassins; a nail was hammered in one eye, and another in his throat. The plot was revealed and the conspirators were brought to trial. Pope Clement VII refused the sought-for pardon, and on September 11, 1599, Beatrice, less than sixteen years old, and her mother and brother, Giacomo, were beheaded.

The Cenci story belongs to the ranks of the great Myths, Artaud felt, for it tells "truths" about man and God and its theme is impersonal. Though Artaud did not consider "The Cenci" pure "theatre of cruelty" he did hope that this play would involve his audiences to the point of shattering and bruising their complacency and by so doing prepare them for rebirth.

> I want the theatrical performance to take on the aspect of a devouring hearth where action, situation, characters, images will reach a degree of implacable incandescence: I also want the audience when viewing my spectacle to be plunged in a bath of fire, agitated by the action and encircled by both the spectacular and dynamic movement of the work. I would know such joy if I succeeded in making the spectator participate in the tragedy of the Cencis, with his soul and his nerves.[53]

"The Cenci", as conceived by Artaud, is a metaphysical dramatic creation. To make the impact of this powerful story of incest, adultery and murder more forceful, Artaud made use of his special theatrical language: the incantatory power of the word, concretized spatial movements, rhythmic effects, symbols, gestures, etcetera.

> . . . I have imposed nature's motions upon my tragedy, that type of gravitation which moves plants, and which one finds fixed in the soil's volcanic outpourings. The Cenci's entire *mise en scène* is based upon this movement of gravitation.[54]

Artaud asked the painter Balthus Klossowski de Rola to create the decors and costumes for this production. He was attracted to Balthus' paintings because they revealed a certain violence and had, at the same time, a tenderness and hypnotic intensity about them; the objects and people depicted frequently seemed like the materialization of dreams and fantasies, giving them the impression of being detached from the "outer world" event. The use of light in Balthus' canvases, his ability to evoke complete stillness and yet create the illusion of motion, the mask-like creatures which emerged full grown from his unconscious world all made him a fitting executor for Artaud's mythical drama.

Act I of *The Cenci* opens on a spiral gallery which has been so constructed as to give the illusion of limitless depth and height. Subtle rhythmic effects are brought into play by the image of these unending circular spirals. A feeling of giddiness envelopes both the actors and spectators as each is swept along in constant and continual rotation. This circular motion forces the audience to loose all perspective and balance, ushering it, gently at first, into a bizarrely exciting world. The spectator then becomes aware of the fact that mystical forces or powers are at work, that "gravitation" is operating, and that objects and people are forever being refashioned and transformed in this drama of tragedy and gore.

As the play opens, Francesco Cenci has just been informed by Cardinal Camillo of his willingness to pardon him for his latest murder, if he gives one third of his possessions to the Church. Cenci is angered by this request because it will deplete his wealth. Matter (symbolically, man's physical side) is an intrinsic part of Cenci's being and he could not thrive without it. Furthermore, Count Cenci feels belittled by the pettiness of the Pope's request; actually an exchange of matter for spirit.[55] The bargain suggested by the head of the Church makes Cenci all too aware of his subservience to the laws of the land, and the Pope's domination over them.

Cenci declares, however, that *in his own world* he is master of himself and his crimes.

> Behind the armed walls of my castle of Petrella, I feel myself capable of braving the Papacy's thunderbolts.[56]

The "castle" referred to in the above quotation, is, symbolically speaking, Count Cenci's outer-covering, his mask or persona.

This castle serves to shelter the undifferentiated world of his unconscious, protecting it from society, his enemy. In his "castle", Count Cenci is invincible. He lives according to his own transcendental law, not the Pope's *human* regulations. He feels no remorse, no repentance, no sorrow for the murders he has committed, he seeks to forge ahead in his designs: to grow blacker and blacker until his "blackness" glows and radiates, paradoxically enough, in the night. . . . "for me there is neither future nor past, therefore, no possible repentance. . . ."

Count Cenci is a Don Juan figure, type or Myth, according to Stendhal. He came into being as a result of Christian asceticism. It was the Christian ascetics who chose to kill the flesh in favor of the spirit; permit the spiritual or Godly half of man, the all Good, and the all Light, to become supreme. Man's other aspect, his physical, Evil, Dark, Satanic or Luciferian[57] half was to be crushed. Such a split in the human psyche, as had been established by Christianity, served not only to divide man against himself, but to create two Gods out of One.[58] Don Juan symbolized the repressed physical, instinctual, and therefore "evil" side of man; unrepenting, he and his likeness, Francesco Cenci, gloried over each crime. Neither of these men has a counterpart in antiquity where Fate or Destiny cause the heroes to experience guilt and repentance (Orestes, Oedipus, etc.).

Francesco Cenci and Don Juan are beings who consider themselves *above* and *beyond* Good and Evil, because God, the creator, made them what they are and, therefore, God alone is responsible for their acts. Since God has infused these heroes with His breath, and in so doing lives within them. They are then in part God and as such, like him, under no moral, that is, man-made law. They are, therefore, no longer responsible to society for their actions. They create their own governing agencies, incomprehensible, perhaps, to the limited mind of the average "rational" individual.

It could be stated that Cenci is, in actuality, very much bound by man's concepts and needs. He is *still* Man because he experiences the polarities in the world and within himself between Good and Evil. In an attempt to reduce the tension between the polarities, Cenci musters all means at his disposal and tries to march down the path of Evil, thereby penetrating, hopefully, into the *Absolute,* into *God,* into the *One,* where the tension of opposites does not exist.

Cenci's dogged attempt to incarnate Evil indicates his extreme preoccupation with Good or God's other aspect. If Count Cenci were not so obsessed with Good, he would not be so driven to his Evil deeds. Count Cenci aspires to achieve a condition of absolute Evil, by negating the condition of man, that is, by becoming inhuman. He strives as the saints did, but in the opposite direction; rejecting the Light or Spiritual aspects of Man and choosing to dwell in the physical half, and in so doing, tries to rise above and beyond man's lot.

Count Cenci dreams of identifying himself with *Destiny;* of carving out his own *Fate.* By leading events, by killing, by committing abnormal sexual crimes, by hating those around him, his children in particular, he will create his own law and dictate his Fate. "I obey my law which does not give me vertigo. . . . I seek and commit acts of evil through intention and principle."[59]

Artaud uses monologues as a means of informing audiences of the character's innermost thoughts; also as a means of breaking audience-actor empathy. Count Cenci, for example, prays at this juncture for the death of his sons, then begins to philosophize about the theatre and every day reality. In life, he declares, one speaks less and acts more; in the theatre, the opposite is true. By breaking the usual spectator-actor rapport, Artaud shatters one illusion in order to achieve an even greater sense of identification between actor and spectator a moment later.

Cenci continues to seek *absolute Evil.* He decides that the best way to reach his goal and feel joy at the same time, is to kill his own flesh and blood. "Evil after all," he says, "is not experienced without some kind of joy." To make the feelings of evil more pervasive, Artaud calls upon his intricate breathing technique described in "An Affective Athleticism". By means of breathing, Count Cenci seems to have been infused with certain mysterious and powerful elements; he seems to have grown in stature, to possess something inhuman or divine. The entire scene (Act I, i) is designed to inspire a feeling of metaphysical anguish. A spell has been cast upon the audience and, to shock the spectators back to the play's reality, Count Cenci strikes a gong with his sword. He causes, by this motion, a whole series of rippling sounds, thus adding to the supernatural aura of the spectacle.

Count Cenci organizes a tremendous feast, an orgy actually, to celebrate his pardon by the Pope. He invites both nobles and men of the cloth. In the Banquet scene (Act I, iii), which Artaud modeled after Veronese's painting "The Marriage Feast at Cana" (1573), a supernatural effect is created by the combination of stage sets and sound effects. Since sound and motion were *one* for Artaud, both the actors' motions and the sounds created by Roger Desormière, were designed to act upon the nerves of both protagonists and spectators. During the banquet scene, for example, the actors' steps were reproduced and amplified via recordings to heighten the violence of the action. The recorded steps sounded far more "real" and "significant" than the actors' actual walking sounds. The rushed steps and the trampling sounds of the guests at the banquet were represented by means of an amplified metronome oscillating at several speeds and played back at various intensities; producing an "obsessive" feeling, adding to the general *malaise* of the entire production.

As the festivities are about to begin in this banquet scene, heavy purple drapes are wind-swept into the giant hall from the outside. A "cosmic breath" seems to penetrate the room, a manifestation from the world beyond, the intangible forcing itself upon the visible and concrete reality. To underline this mystical note, the bells of Roman churches sound in muted tones, a fitting accompaniment to the intrusion of external cosmic forces, as symbolized by the wind-blown drapes. To achieve the proper volume of pounding church bells, Artaud pre-recorded the sound of the great bell of the Cathedral of Amiens. The recording was played during this scene and was diffused by four loud speakers situated in the four corners of the building, putting the spectator in the "center of a network of sonorous vibrations."[60] The resounding of these bells during the performance reached such a crescendo that it became deafening; actually painful to the ear.

As the Banquet scene progresses, and the noises drop onto the audience like sheets or waves, the voices of the guests begin to rise and also take on the timbre of resounding bells. A cacophony results from the vocal and bell sounds. Finally, all noises fade into the atmosphere.

Count Cenci now announces that his Myth has come to an end. With the passage of time he has become a *Legend.*

> I have descended today to tell you that the Cenci Myth has come to an end, and that I am ready to realize my legend.[61]

Like King Arthur, Charlemagne, Roland, so Count Cenci has become a legendary figure, a being disfigured by tradition, as exploit upon exploit become linked to his name. Count Cenci has renounced his personal existence and has, in his mind at least, become a collective figure. He tells his guests, with glee, of the death of his sons. To dramatize the "blackness" of his paternal character, Artaud showers the stage with flashes of light. The guests, stunned by Count Cenci's bestiality ask for "torches" to light their way out of the Palace, the labyrinth-like place, that domain of unchanneled instinctuality.[62]

The guests can hardly believe that Cenci could have killed his sons. "He's clowning," they maintain. No, Count Cenci was not "clowning." They then look at each other and wonder how many of them are guiltless. Not one guest claims absolute purity. To live in the world of men is to be forced into action, to be removed from that state of absolute unity where all forces exist together in harmony. Since earthly existence, by its very nature, cancels out the world of absolutes, no man is absolutely free of vice anymore than he is of goodness.

Cenci, the Black-Hero, has lived intensely and fervently, with one goal in mind—to attain a state of absolute Evil. He raises his cup of wine to his mouth and drinks to his sons' death.

> The priest drinks his God at mass. Who then can prevent me from believing that I am drinking my sons' blood.[63]

Cannibalism exists in everyone. Good Christians drink the blood of their God. And with the same religious spirit, Cenci imbibes, either symbolically or actually, the blood of his own children. Where is the difference? he asks. His children are within him now, part of him, as is God. To commune with God, for some, brings spiritual joy. Communion with his sons brings Count Cenci an equal amount of happiness. Count Cenci's desire for communion is motivated by his wish to return to the *One*, to the Universal or Eternal, to the Mother, to merge with the Infinite.

To underscore the dramatic effect of this banquet scene, Artaud created an intricate spatial and concrete rhythmic effect. As the guests first begin experiencing extreme fright at the Count's blasphemies, they rush toward the door. Silence follows. The guests then remain motionless, as if frozen in their places, congealed in space. After Count Cenci forbids them to leave, they seem to flow or glide back into the banquet hall in wave-like disorder. They stumble helter-skelter; their arms are outstretched, raised toward the heavens, as though they were battling an army of ghosts. They give the impression of struggling against some intangible, external, non-material force: the collective and uncontrollable instinctual element. These frightened guests now look like apparitions from a Goya or Breughel-like world of hallucinations. They have taken on a non-material vaporous aura. Their bodies seem to have vanished; what remains is reminiscent of a conglomeration of struggling forces or instincts. The guests are actually trying to destroy parts of themselves, their human condition, the unforseen and unknown elements within man which cause him to act in certain sinister ways.

As the guests battle out their fears, Beatrice begins to run around the stage, creating an invisible circle, repeating the ominous movement of the spiral staircase of the first scene. Artaud believed that such rhythms as the spectator experiences visually affect him physically, creating an hypnotic feeling. The guests, waving their arms about them frantically, as they fight off the unknown, create the impression of rushing about in somewhat straight lines. Such an image of the circle (eternal) and the line (ephemeral), symbolizes both aspects of existence: the cosmos and man's passage through it.

Beatrice stops before her father, the incarnation of Fate. He raises his hands to strike her. To increase the feeling of terror and danger which confronts Beatrice during this interlude, the guests, as a group, inhale and then "exhale a great cry." Making use of the system enunciated in "An Affective Athleticism", Artaud ushers in the cosmic forces once again, by the inclusion of rhythmic breathing, accelerating and slackening of pace and intensity with relation to the action. The guests then rush out in disarray as Beatrice, facing the crowd, continues her circular movements. The line then, formed by the guests, has been removed from the image; only the external aspect of the Cenci now remains.

Beatrice stays alone with her father. The torches are extinguished. The hollow and "cavernous" sound of the bell plus the eerie lighting creates a crypt-like ambiance. Silence settles like a blanket smothering all motion, visible and invisible. Only the deadly sound of the "viol" which may vibrate lightly and sharply in this interplay of universal magnetic forces, can be heard.

In this charged atmosphere, Cenci pulls out his last trick: *sorcery*. He will make magic and, like Mephisto, he will "charm" his daughter into acquiescence. He invokes the powers of the Night and Evil, and Beatrice, mad with fright, lunges for the door. But, Destiny, or Magic, has already begun its work. Cenci has joined the world of the occult, of hypnotic invisible waves which come to swallow all those who resist their grasp.

The Mythical Count Cenci again converses with his "muted castle", the keeper of his secrets. He apostrophizes descending night, his companion, his other self, the symbol of his immeasurable crimes—even those he has only imagined. The acts which live within Cenci (incest, murder, sacrilege, adultery) are no longer his alone. They belong to humanity.

And Beatrice has become aware of her father's powers. She should despise him. Yet, in some strange way, she is drawn to Evil, tantalized by its beguiling force. A fitting stage accompaniment to Beatrice's conflict was established by Artaud in the form of bird images. Birds are heard screaming and screeching at this point. It is uncertain, however, whether they are the kindly winged creatures which have, throughout the centuries, symbolized the soul and the spiritual aspect of man, or the birds of prey which swoop down from above, seeking to destroy their victims. So Beatrice, as symbolized by the birds, is possessed by these two forces within her: her desire and longing for the good and the spiritual, and her attraction for evil. "I should hate but cannot," she states.

Beatrice (Act III, i) narrates a dream she has had many times since childhood, as impersonal as is Cenci's *act*. In the dream, Beatrice sees herself in the nude. Beside her there is a beast, breathing furiously, as is possible only in a dream. Beatrice wants to flee, to hide her nudity. But she also hungers and thirsts. A door opens and she discovers other *things* panting and moving about. Suddenly, and from all directions, a whole population of hideous and famished beings emerge. In vain, she tries to flee, to pursue the light she sees beyond. She runs and each time she feels she can no longer keep going, she awakens.

Such a dream, another version of the "Beauty and the Beast" myth, indicates Beatrice's real conflict, her bondage to the physical or evil aspect of life. Beatrice is caught in the midst of hungry and panting beasts, an expression of her father's lust and her own. If the world of light (spiritual) is to be reached, the starving beast must be left behind. But the world of light is inaccessible to mortals who live in a differentiated world. The real question here would be to satisfy the beast in man and not kill it. This requires the maintaining of balance and harmony between spirit and flesh, which seems to be an impossibility for Beatrice, at this point. The ascetics who tried to kill the beast in man by starving it, made it all the more ravenous—hungry animals are far more insistent than fed ones. The fact that Beatrice keeps running indicates her desire to escape her Destiny, the hungry side of herself, as represented by the animals in her dream and her Father in actuality.

Artaud had Count Cenci murdered by two mutes who expressed

by means of gestures what the voice was incapable of evoking. The fears of the assassins at the magnitude of their crime and their revulsion at the thought of committing it, was far more effectively portrayed by means of their silence, their stylized attitudes, their rhythmic breathing and the macabre lighting, than if the portrayal of these emotions had depended merely on the articulated word.

The assassins (Act III, ii) walk with measured steps, grimacing now and then as they plot and plan. This slowing down of pace increases, strangely enough, the speed of their activity and aggravates the suspense. A storm now rages. The wind howls. Beatrice, her brother Bernardo, and Lucretia, her stepmother, appear and join the priest Orsino, her other brother, Giacomo, and Count Cenci, who walks at the end of the line. They look like statues or shadows, performing the celebrated *Danse Macabre,* so popular in the Middle Ages. The wind blows more fiercely now than ever. The audience hears strange voices pronouncing the name CEN-CI four times in prolonged, sharp tones, rising or falling in pitch, resembling the tonal waves of birds in flight. To increase the obsessive effect of the voices, Artaud had Roger Desormière use the *Ondes Martinot.* As a result, frightening and inhuman sounds emanated from the recorded voices of the actors shouting out or whispering the name CENCI-CI . . . ."crossing each other, first remote in time, then huddling together in gusts, thereby reaching an impressive crescendo brutally cut."[64]

Only the assassins' silhouettes are visible (Act IV, i). Then two gun shots are heard. Night clutches everything, the lighting ceases and the audience learns that the murder plot has failed. God does not want Cenci to die or to repent—not yet. Cenci returns to the stage and wonders why he was created? Why is he supposed to repent? After all, he is neither responsible for his crimes nor for his destiny. God who created him is the guilty (responsible) party.

> Repentance is in God's hand. It is up to him to regret my act. Why did he make me the father of a being which invites my desire?[65]

Count Cenci does not repent. But he is forever preoccupied with God. That he is conscious of doing *Evil* indicates his awareness and obsession with its opposite. Had he really been amoral, had he reached the depths of degradation as he had so desired, he would have merged with the "black", thereby becoming oblivious to evil and its opposite, good. He would have been swimming in that unlimited domain of unity where good and evil cohabit in harmony.

Beatrice will not give up. She will have her father murdered. She manipulates the assassins' actions as though they were automatons. She even gives the impression of playing a game of chess, trying to figure out what pawn she must next move. She hands the assassins two daggers. They take them; their actions have become unreal—wooden.

Cenci, an Oedipus-like creature in certain ways, now staggers forth on stage. He covers his blinded right eye. Cenci who has carried out his own law, going beyond man's limited vision, has become a Martyr, a Christ figure, in reverse. And in an *imitatio Christi,* he too dies in a nail-hammering ceremony.

Fanfare and noise are now heard and they grow louder with every passing second (Act IV, ii). Blinding light floods the stage ushering in a super-human or sub-human aura; the light of Hell or of Heaven, indicating perhaps the passage of Count Cenci from one world to the other. Semi-circles are drawn on stage as the guards walk round and round. Lucretia, Beatrice's mother, like a somnambulist tries to penetrate the center of the circle. The occult effect of the circular motion underscores the mythical nature of the drama. The guards finally encircle Beatrice and Lucretia. Bernardo, the son, rushes into the circle. He is pulled out by Cardinal Camillo who has decided to free him for personal reasons. The others, however, will fill out their role in the circle of destiny, enmeshed in man's continuous and eternal conflicts. Man's warring instincts are concretized on stage by the constant breaking of the semi-circles, indicating the eternal friction between each half-aspect of man during his earthly existence.

The torture chamber (Act IV, iii), with its wheel which is forever turning, should resemble, Artaud wrote, a factory. Sinister sounds hoot forth every now and then, piercing the atmosphere in wave-like formation. Bernardo, whose hands are tied, walks around his sister Beatrice. She moves about on stage in cadence with the turning wheel,[66] to which she is tied by her hair. Bernardo looks at her admiringly because he believes she is above and beyond pain. No longer running from destiny, she has accepted her role in the earthly drama. But what he is still unaware of and what the audience now learns as she chants her poem, is that *Life*, as she has experienced it, has been a *dream;* and *death* which she will now know, is *reality*. Her soul she now returns to God, the creator, who will cure it of "life" or of the "fire" which it now experiences. Beatrice's conceptions resemble in certain respects the Hindu's belief in earthly reality as illusion. For only when the veil of matter or life has been lifted, will Beatrice know Reality, God, the Universal Breath.

As Cardinal Camillo, still a victim of his earthly and sensual law, tries to extract a confession from her, she informs the world that the Pope's cruelty and brutality is on a par with Count Cenci's. Though he is supposed to represent the forces of Good— he is Satanic. Beatrice is unafraid. Only those "deprived of liberty", her step-mother Lucretia interjects, know fright. Those who have experienced freedom live in a world rid of constricting barriers imposed by man's rational mind (society).

Beatrice's life-dream is now dimming. She has become detached.

In Artaud's "The Cenci", Beings and Events—the Myth—stalk about on stage. The human forms they take, their gesticulations, motions, words and sounds produce "a kind of synthetic whirlwind, in the midst of which the spectacle takes on the aspect of a veritable transmutation."[67] The creatures that people Artaud's stage are manifestations of vast forces at work within nature. They possess their own cry, their own rhythms, and move about in an inhuman atmosphere where Fate has worked out its finale, long before the drama has commenced. With almost mathematical precision, in spatial geometric patterns, and according to the subtle rhythms of gravitation, Destiny propels the "events" along.

For Artaud, this drama of cruelty was particularly significant. He was in actuality portraying his own conflicts on stage in an attempt to gain freedom from the worldly ties which forever pained him. Cenci's struggle was in many respects Artaud's struggle to see *beyond* the world of appearances into the realm of primordial unity where Good and Evil are either non-existent or co-exist. However, neither Cenci nor Artaud succeed in merging themselves into the world beyond. To have succeeded would have meant rejecting the human condition—an impossibility.

Artaud had great hopes for "The Cenci", but it ran for only seventeen days. It was, of course, a financial failure and the critics were nearly unanimous in their condemnation of the play. Lucien Dubech, critic for *Candide* wrote:

> The text, which, thank God, one hardly hears, is marked by ghastly sounds. Mr. Antonin Artaud is convinced that he is renewing dramatic art in this manner. Let us not hurt him.[68]

Francois Porché in *La Revue de Paris* felt that "The Cenci" was an "insult to dramatic art, to the acting profession, to everything that we venerate. . . ." Artaud answered:

> . . . . the French public is not ripe enough for a feast fit for Gods, the tragedy of the Cenci brings with it an unusual atmosphere; more than one spectator experienced it as something noxious.[69]

The failure of "The Cenci" came as a great blow to Artaud. It made him feel more solitary and more dejected than ever.[70]

Artaud's Theatre of Cruelty as an institution never came into being. The only Theatre of Cruelty play ever produced was "The Cenci", and Artaud had said that even this work was not genuine Theatre of Cruelty. When "The Cenci" failed, Artaud not only saw the end of the road coming, but he had reached it, despite the fact that he had been twice thrilled in recent years; when he saw the Marx brothers in "Animal Crackers" and in "Monkey Business." He considered their performance which he described in "Two Notes" extraordinary: the poetic, imaginative, artistic, humorous, magic quality was unique; their gestures unparalleled. Artaud's emotions were again aroused to an unusual pitch when he saw Jean Louis Barrault's "dramatic action" based on William Faulkner's novel "As I Lay Dying" (*Autour d'une mère*). Artaud knew Jean-Louis Barrault well. Indeed Barrault had "experienced" his influence, having read his works and spent long evenings with him talking about the metaphysical and poetic aspects of the theatre. It was Artaud who incited the young Barrault toward the creation of something unique in the annals of the theatre, his performance in "As I Lay Dying." Artaud had been so entranced and exhilarated by the simplicity of the story related (a mother has died and her coffin is being transported to town for burial), by Barrault's "marvelous horse-centaur" which circulated about the stage throughout the performance, that he wrote an article about it, included in "Two Notes." Artaud eulogized Barrault's spontaneity, his vigor, his stylized and mathematically precise gesticulations, the inaudible "concert of cries" which emanated from the stage and which succeeded in creating a sacred theatrical language, a mystical atmosphere which worked directly on the soul.

> His spectacle demonstrates the irresistible expressiveness of gesture; it victoriously proves the importance of gesture and of movement in space. He restores to theatrical perspective the importance it should never have lost. He fills the stage with emotion and life.[71]

But Artaud had to leave France. He was empty, drained, totally and completely. Were he to remain in his country, he would either disintegrate, or be consumed by his own vital energy. He was convinced of this now because he *knew* he could *see* into the future. He had implied as much in "Heliogabalus or the Crowned Anarchist" (*Héliogabale ou l'Anarchiste couronné*), a two hundred page documented, philosophical, and metaphysical study of the Roman Emperor (202-222), in which he draws certain parallels between numerical symbolism and Heliogabalus' life. Number symbolism fascinated Artaud increasingly as time went on. It may be said that, in certain ways, he geared his life according to astrological calculations and numerical symbolism, also around the image of fire. Indeed, the image of fire so preoccupied Artaud, that in February 1935, he signed a contract with Gallimard for the publication of "The Life and Death of Satan the Fire" (*La*

Vie et Mort de Satan le feu), for which he received an advance of one thousand francs. But only fragments of this work have been unearthed and we know no more about Artaud's intentions nor even whether the work was completed.[72]

In January 10, 1936, Artaud sailed from Antwerp to Havana and from there to Mexico. It was during this trip that the perfect title around which Artaud would group his series of essays, letters, and manifestoes he had written between 1931 and 1935, was "revealed" to him—"The Theatre and its Double." This work, published only in 1938, became in time one of the most extraordinary volumes ever written on the theatre.

With the discovery of the right title for his volume, armed with letters of introduction to the Under Secretary of State of Foreign Affairs and to the Minister of Fine Arts in Mexico, to journalists, artists and writers of note—Artaud was going to turn over a new phase of existence: encounter a breathtaking world: discover some primitive, magical layer of himself, and perhaps of mankind, through association with the ancient Tarahumaras tribe in Mexico.

Artaud *had* to find something tangible—amid this sea of floating enmity which was his world!

PART THREE

THE NEW REVELATIONS
(1936-1948)

.·.

I had not conquered by force of spirit this invincible organic hostility, where it was me that did not want to continue, in order to bring back from it a collection of motheaten imagery, from which this Age, thus far faithful to a whole system, would at the very most get a few new ideas for posters and models for its fashion designers. From now on it was necessary that whatever lay buried behind this ponderous trituration, which makes the dawn one with the dead of night, be dragged out in the open and put to use, that it serves precisely for my crucifixion.[1]

CHAPTER VI

THE LAND OF THE TARAHUMARAS

I

WHEN ARTAUD'S CARGO SHIP pulled out of Antwerp, such a withdrawal, looked upon symbolically, indicated a determination to sever ties with a past and an intense desire to discover the new. What Artaud was leaving behind was his withered world: that part of himself which had chalked up blocks of fabulous failures, frustrations, pain, anguish, at having been unable to found a theatre of cruelty or of even succeeding in communicating his ideas to others in theatrical circles. Something had gone wrong—dreadfully so. Exactly what? He was convinced that an answer to this question would be "revealed" to him—eventually.

Artaud's decision to journey forth in search of "enlightenment", was fraught with excitement; pleasant and perilous. What he had feared most of his life, what had plagued his very existence and which he had described so poignantly in his "Correspondence with Jacques Rivière," would now have to be dealt with urgently, blindly, totally, if the results of his quest were to be fruitful. The terrible gamble would have to be made—to first face, then leap into the *void*. What could result? Renewal and Illumination—or total Annihilation.

To sever oneself from the work-a-day world which is what an immersion into the void necessitates; to become part of the cosmic universal forces, to join the collective and in so doing renounce one's individuality, even temporarily, is what many would consider a definition of insanity. Such is the path Artaud had chosen to follow: to burn and destroy—and like the phœnix arise from the ashes renewed, with tremendous riches gathered from the infinite cosmic realm, granted to those who can *see* as it had been to the Angel of the Apocalypse. But *if* Artaud should never ever return from these depths, that *Other* existence, remote and all-powerful which heaves its sighs within every being, and is looked upon from our world with fear and trembling . . . Artaud would risk it. The choice actually was no longer his.

When Artaud's ship docked in Havana in January 1936, *something* strange and exciting seemed to tingle in the air. So intense were his emotions at this point that an incident which might have seemed innocuous to someone else took on great significance for Artaud. A negro sorcerer gave him a stiletto which had originally come from Toledo (Spain). It measured about twelve centimeters in length and had three hooks attached to it. Artaud did not consider his stiletto an ordinary weapon. He sensed a power hidden within it, something magical. The stiletto became his talisman, and, henceforth, it did not leave Artaud's possession.

II

Artaud arrived first in Vera Cruz, then Mexico; more confident because he had his stiletto in hand, certain the outcome of his adventure would be positive and fruitful.

Mexico shocked him. It reminded him of a city which had been blown up by an earthquake, and which had remained petrified at a certain level in its evolution. He was horrified to discover that the Indians living in and around Mexico City were considered "savages" by the inhabitants of that city, and that the most popular movement these days was to "civilize". . . . Preachers of all types had set out to convert the Indians; some bringing the Christian gospel, others, the "Gospel according to Karl Marx". These missionaries were regarded by the "uncultured" Indians as Montezuma had looked upon Cortez—as "infantile preachers".

Artaud became more and more antagonistic toward the so-called civilized man with his ready-made attitudes and phobias. Was he viewing a facsimile in Mexico of what he had rejected so bitterly in Europe? Would there be no difference between the European's outlook and the South American's? Artaud's anger grew as the days sped along and the similarities rose to mountainous proportions. Four centuries had elapsed, he mused, and still white error persisted—now more virulent than ever. His resentment of the patronizing and aggressive attitudes of the whites grew daily. And so his heart pounded with relief when he learned that though the whites had done their best to proselytize as many Indians as possible, causing the eradication of countless tribal units, there still remained certain ancient secrets as yet impenetrable to the white man: secrets of healing through plants, occult sciences.

Artaud was chafing at the bit—anxious to plunge into the unknown, the void and bring about his own healing. But there were pressing problems to which he would have to attend before he could venture forth. He was in desperate need of funds. He, therefore, contributed articles to the government-sponsored newspaper *Nacional Revolucionario;*[2] delivered a series of lectures at the University of Mexico on February 26, 27, and 29, 1936, entitled: "Surrealism and Revolution", "Man Against Destiny", and "The Theatre and the Gods".

These lectures can be looked upon as a review of Artaud's whole career; a summing up of what he had experienced during his life in Paris; spiritually and artistically.

Surrealism, which he had encountered in 1924, he considered, now that he could look upon it with the proper perspective, as a true moral revolt, "man's organic cry, the bucking of one's own inner being against all coercion". And these thoughts he expressed most vociferously in his first lecture "Surrealism and Revolution". Surrealism was a movement, he explicated, which sought to rebel against the Father, and all that he symbolized; all forms of material and spiritual oppression; that is, father, country, religion, family. And Artaud still considered himself a Surrealist, unhampered by the politically constricting influence Breton had imposed upon this movement by joining the Communist Party.

Artaud believed violently in artistic freedom, and cried out against pat answers and overly simple ideologies. Youth, he said, is starving for "human truth", as he himself had been, and not so long ago, when he had arrived in Paris in 1920—frail, but bubbling with enthusiasm and swelling with hope. At that time and even at this point, he was aware of the dangers besetting the 20th century city-dweller: constrictions of all sorts, but most important, the fact that man had been led astray from *real life* nature. Cut off from nature, he has forgotten how to "look at nature, feel life in its totality". As a result, he has become a fragmented and faceless being instead of the *whole* man he once was, centuries and incarnations back.

As a good Surrealist, Artaud still suggested the dethronement of Reason. Reason has run wild with power, he declared, in his second lecture "Man Against Destiny". It has led man to consider the fruits of his thoughts as the *only real truth*. Man has failed, however, to replenish his soul, to nourish his feelings in the source of all things—the physical universe. The thinking and feeling aspects of man have not kept pace with each other. The ancients were balanced personalities because they reached beyond their ideas and their dreams, right into nature itself. They felt the collective forces hidden within the images revealed to them in their dreams. They allowed themselves to experience *these forces* and forever struggled to remain in contact with them.

What Artaud sought for himself and what he intimated in these lectures was a return to the root of everything, to *chaos* in the mystical sense, to those living and breathing forces within the cosmic which lie behind the symbols and signs man views about him. The interesting shapes and forms (crosses of all types, swastikas, circles, triangles, points, numbers, etc.) which Artaud had encountered thus far in Mexico, had once been charged entities, with the ability to evoke meaningful experiences in the heart and soul of the viewer. At present, these same symbols, for the majority of people at least, are impotent, meaningless markings. The fire which such signs had once aroused within the human psyche must be rekindled by searching for "the bases of a magic culture which can still burst forth from the forces within Indian soil".[3]

This *fire*, interpreted as creative energy, should also manifest itself in the theatre, Artaud declared in his third lecture "The Theatre and the Gods". Such intensity and power would be proof of its living quality and reveal the hidden "secrets of culture". Europeans, Artaud stated wryly, have a tendency to consider *culture* as existing in the written text alone. If that were so, if no written records remained of a country's history, it would follow then that no culture ever existed, an absurdity on the face of it. For Artaud, culture implies a discovery of the secrets of life, the possibility of setting up certain rapports with the cosmos. Culture includes the *whole of man* in all of his aspects, as he moves about in space, aware of every phase of his nature that works in harmony with all the others.

> I call organic culture, a culture based on the mind in relationship to the organs, and the mind bathing in all the organs, and responding to each of them at the same time.[4]

Culture as a spatial concept is related to Artaud's theatrical ideas. The stage area is looked upon as a spatial entity in a state of continuous flux where things move about freely from one form to another and "find their own faces, and under the faces, the sound of life".[5] The theatre becomes a macrocosm for the actor (and all those connected with the theatrical venture) who is not removed from nature, which lives within his limbs and spirit, in harmony with the world's breath and the universal rhythm of the cosmos. From such immersion the actor can build what Eric Bentley termed a "Dionysian theatre" of "energy and visionary power".[6] A real theatre of cruelty, when natural forces impress themselves upon the actor and spectator alike, bombarding them ceaselessly, can now come into being.

Artaud was more eager than ever to return to nature and the divine spectacle; to flee civilization—even Mexican—which had severed him from the physical universe, left him fragmented, stranded, isolated on a rapidly sinking and shrinking segment of land. He sought to discover true culture—in the ancient, mysterious, and magical world of the Sun-worshipping Tarahumaras Indian tribe. The next lap of Artaud's trip became a certainty now that the artists and intellectuals in Mexico, so impressed by his lectures and articles, had signed a petition asking the President of the Republic to make it possible, financially speaking, for him to transform his dream into reality. The necessary funds were made available to Artaud who then embarked on a series of fantastic experiences and adventures.

So much of Artaud's life is geared to the supernatural, the *déjà vu,* the mystical and the magical, that it becomes incumbent upon me to relate a strange and prophetic dream Artaud had the night before he landed at Vera Cruz. He dreamt about a woman to whom he had been attracted when he was eighteen years old. She was now a widow and was offering herself to him. At the very moment when he was about to consummate his act, her husband came forth from the shadows. Even before the husband had stepped onto the scene, a child literally barred Artaud's passage to the woman.[7]

If the sexual act is looked upon as the union of opposites, this dream indicates that the opposing and apparently irreconcilable forces within Artaud (spirit and matter) were still poles apart. Artaud was forcibly reminded again, therefore, of the split within him and his unconscious desire to make himself *whole.* Perhaps by working backward in time, he felt, reverting back into man's earliest layers of existence, to the primitive Sun cultures: the peyotl-imbibing Tarahumaras, he might so deeply tap the spiritual source of life as to attain unity with the cosmic forces; and thereby achieve harmony within his own being.

III

Artaud was ready to begin his perilous journey into an "anterior" world—a remote land of mythical origin.

It was in August 1936, that Artaud set out for the high mountains, the home of the Tarahumaras Indians. Though their villages were located only forty-eight hours north of Mexico City, Artaud felt, upon seeing them, as though he were *re-entering* a past existence. This race of approximately 40,000 pure red Indians lived in the same state of development as had man before the flood. At all odds, the Tarahumaras Indians should have perished or degenerated centuries ago. Yet, they had not. They had resisted disease, war, famine, and so-called civilizing and proselytizing elements.

When Artaud left "civilization" to join the Tarahumaras in their mountain retreats, he was armed with his "holy" instrument, his little stiletto from Toledo which possessed as much power for Artaud as a cross blessed by the Pope for the Catholic. As Artaud made his way up the mountains on horseback and on foot, he had a premonition that all would be well with him, that after immersing himself in the ancient religious rituals practised by the peyotl-imbibing Tarahumaras he would "wash" away the fears and anxieties that had tormented him all his life, and which clung to him with the strength of a ravenous lion attacking his prey. Artaud felt that he would at last succeed in re-entering the *real* world—through the primitive. "I had suffered enough, I thought, to deserve a little reality."[8]

He was strong, stimulated by some strange and supernatural power. So much so, in fact, that he decided to give up the heroin habit. He was convinced that the primitive force which now lived within him possessed curative powers. As he ascended the mountains, he threw his last dose of heroin into the torrent. His torture began. He suffered physically, he wrote, as he never had before. After four days without drugs, the withdrawal pain and anguish of the addict usually subside somewhat. Not so for Artaud. "I was seeing red, literally," he wrote, "it seemed to me that the road was burning. . . ." The pain had increased in virulence after the sixth day. His body, in fact, had so altered because of his excruciating torture, that he looked like a mass of flesh and bone, like "an enormous, inflamed gum. . . ."[9]

Perhaps the acuteness of his physical torment made his reactions to what he saw that much more potent. He felt himself

bewitched by the Indians whom he saw about him. He marveled
at their sheer strength. Living close to nature, they had discovered
its secrets and could climb up and down from their high mountain villages, through torrential waters and thick underbrush, and
over jagged and steep cliffs, slippery as wet slate. Artaud added,
"I cannot help thinking that they have conserved the force of
gravitation, natural to the first men."

A world alive with magic, with haunting rhythms, images and
artifacts seemed to be closing in on him. He was dazzled by the
extremes of color. He could understand why it was said that the
pre-Renaissance Italian painters had discovered their breathtaking blues not in Italy, but in Mexico. The intensity and
excitement of the colors seemed to grow more pronounced
as Artaud penetrated further into the heart of the Tarahumaras' land.

The region's topography, the shapes and forms he saw about
him in this strange country astounded him. There were certain
natural land and rock formations which seemed to have been
pressed directly out of the earth. In some areas, these forms took
the shapes of men's tortured bodies: elsewhere, of gods' heads
peering from behind rock clusters; of drowned men half eaten by
stone; a statue of Death holding a child in its hand; a man lying
on a stone, his arms open and his hands nailed as they pointed to
the four cardinal points, a man "quartered in space".

Whether it was the mountain or myself which was haunted, I cannot
say, but I saw similar optical miracles during this periplus across the
mountains, and they confronted me at least once every day.

Maybe I was born with a body as tortured and counterfeited as
that of the immense mountain; but it was a body whose obsessions
might be useful: and it occurred to me in the mountain that it might
be just useful to have an *obsession for counting* . . .

I saw in the mountain a naked man leaning out of a huge window.
His head was nothing but an enormous hole, a sort of circular cavity,
where successively and according to the hour, the sun or moon appeared. He had his right arm outstretched like a bar, and the left
was also like a bar but drowned in shadow and folded inward.[10]

Still more signs appeared in Artaud's path, indicating the Tarahumaras' active geometric conception of the world: triangles, clover designs, the Egyptian *crux ansata,* numbers (3, 4, 7, 8) frequently repeated, etc. These shapes that Artaud saw about him were natural phenomena, that is, adorning not only the mountainside, but embodied in the designs painted on the clothes worn by the natives, in the decorations used inside and outside their houses, in their rites and dances.

At every crossroad one sees trees *deliberately* burnt into the shape of crosses, or of beings, and often these beings are doubles, and confront each other, as if to express the essential *duality* of things; and I saw this duality reduced to its prime element in a sign . . . enclosed in a ring, which struck me as having been branded on a tall pine tree with red-hot iron; other trees bore spears, trefoils, acanthus leaves surrounded with crosses; here and there, in sunken places, corridors choked with rocks, rows of Egyptian ankhs deployed in files; and the doors of Tarahumaras' houses displayed the Maya world-symbol; two facing triangles whose points are joined by a bar; and this bar is the Tree of Life passing through the center of Reality.[11]

The symbol of the cross which resembles the human body and which Artaud found repeated in all shapes and forms in Mexico and particularly among the Tarahumaras Indians, is an age-old symbol used by the ancient Egyptians, the Orientals, the Central and South Americans, etc. The Aztecs, for example, in order to win the friendship of the goddess Cinteotl, used to nail a young boy or girl to the cross every spring, after which they shot him or her with an arrow; Osiris was pictured on several occasions as a crucified god, mourned by both Isis and Nephthys; in primitive Christian art, Christ stood before the cross with open arms and was not featured nailed to it. The cross, wrote C. G. Jung in "Symbols of Transformation", symbolizes the tree of life or the tree of knowledge, which are both extensions of the Mother symbol, an emblem of fertility and fruitfulness. When a hero or God, therefore, is nailed to the cross, such an act, interpreted symbolically, implies a union between the hero-God and his Mother, or the conquering of death by a renewal of life.

That Artaud became so aware of these many archetypal images about him was an indication of the intensity and richness of his own inner world. It is interesting to note in this connection that other artists, namely Sergei Eisenstein, have experienced similar "revelations" which transcend any rational explanation. Marie Seton, in her excellent biography of this film maker, describes the changes which came over him during his Mexican trip in 1931. He had gone there to direct *Que Viva Mexico*. When he began work on this film, the mystic qualities he sought to bring forth in his film made him all the more sensitive to the ever-present supernatural powers at work about him. When he realized that the motif of the triangle kept cropping up ever more frequently in the composition of his picture, he was convinced that the use of this "primal form" had been dictated to him by a "supernatural consciousness" and was not "his work" alone. In fact, this certainty was so keenly felt that he constructed "a whole theory of composition" upon it which he never published, however, for fear, perhaps, of being ridiculed by the "rationalist".[12]

Artaud believed in similar supernatural forces and spirits and pursued his journey backward into time with ever growing fervor. Tantalized by what he had already witnessed; strengthened by what he knew would be revealed to him, he ventured forth on what he predicted would be something fantastic. Behind the living symbolism he saw about him in the form of strange signs and forms, an arcane science lay hidden, of which the Tarahumaras were masters; a science far older than the mysteries hidden in the legend of the Holy Grail or the Rosecrucian sect; one which might date back to the very beginnings of man. Just as the *Kabbala* is a work, Artaud wrote, wherein the "music" of Numbers "reduces the material chaos to its origins, and explains by a kind of grandiose mathematics how Nature orders and directs the birth of forms, which she brings forth out of chaos",[13] so everything about him seemed to obey and be ordered by hermetic numerical forces, the secrets of which these peyotl-imbibing Indians had known for centuries.

The Tarahumaras Indians, Artaud learned, believed themselves to be the descendants of a race of Fire-bearing men who had served three Masters or three Kings. It was said that these Masters were on their way toward the Polar star, and had stopped amid the Tarahumaras tribe way back in time. A similar legend is related by Saint Matthew[14] when he declared that the three Magi, guided by celestial indications, had come from Persia and were going to Jerusalem. Modern thinkers consider the Magi to be not kings nor priests, but rather men of science, students of celestial astronomy who had come from Arabia, attracted to the West by the discovery of a new star. The Tarahumaras' belief in the existence of three Masters or three Kings was strikingly similar to the belief of the other great Solar traditions in Egypt, Assyria, Chaldea, Persia, South and Central America, etc.

For the worshipper of the heavenly fire, as was the Tarahumaras Indian, the visible Father or God is the Sun. The adoration of the Sun's strength (or God's strength) means in actuality a worshipping of the great regenerative force of Nature and (or) the energy of the archetype: as witnessed, wrote C. G. Jung, in "Symbols of Transformation", by the nimbus around Christ's head, the halos around the Saints, the star over the head of the twelve apostles, etc. Indeed, the Sun cult has been expressed symbolically throughout the centuries in one form or another, by means of the Egyptian cross (*crux ansata*), the swastika, the double cross, the great circle with a point in the middle, two triangles opposite each other, three points, four triangles in the four cardinal points, the twelve signs of the zodiac, the sun wheel, etc.[15]

It was no wonder then that Artaud was drawn to the cult of energy and regeneration that was the Tarahumaras' Sun-worshipping religion. With them, he experienced a certain feeling of serenity and of quiet. On the mountain tops where they dwelt, so high as to seem to reach right up to heaven, he listened and was stirred by their Creation Myth; understood for the first time why they considered themselves to be part of the first and original race.

They are made of the same Fabric as is Nature, and as all the authentic manifestations of nature, they are born of an original mixture.[16]

The Tarahumaras believed they were dropped from heaven to earth; that Nature which caused them to fall upon the earth also directed them to think like "man"; that they evolved into their present state as did other parts of nature. Indeed, the Tarahumaras Indians, Artaud declared, are preoccupied with their origins, as were Piero della Francesca, Fra Angelico, Piero di Cosimo and Mantegna with theirs. These Renaissance artists who painted so many nativity scenes did not do so because of their religious fervor—Artaud was now convinced of this—though they were devout, but rather to satisfy their longing to discover the secrets and origins of life itself.

In this land of the Tarahumaras Indians, Artaud experienced a totally new and haunting sensation. When viewing these primitive folk in their native habitats he was certain he had *already* seen them somewhere some place before; but was quick to add that he was *not* experiencing the *déjà vu,* usually a vague kind of feeling. Artaud's visions, on the contrary, were precisely situated; in fact, they were like historical reminiscences. He pursued them. What was being revealed to him now was something so unbelievable as to make it shocking. Artaud not only saw the Tarahumaras as they were today, but their ancestors the ancient Fire-Bringers, come forward to him, make certain markings throughout the land, an 'H' in particular. Had this been an isolated happening, the impact of its magnitude would not have been so startling. What made it incredible is that Plato had mentioned this same sign in connection with the people of Atlantis and their cities which were constructed around a central figure—in the shape of an 'H'. Artaud was not one to believe in 'absolute' imagination, that is, that something arises from nothing. A mental image is "the detached member of an active image which has lived some place. . . ."[17] There was a link, of this he was certain, between the very ancient and the present, the remotest and densest regions in the world and the most sophisticated.

There was no doubt that what Artaud was experiencing, psychologically speaking, was a sudden and direct contact with archetypal contents revealed to him in the form of images. These archetypal contents which belong to the collective unconscious are part of man's legacy to man: that aspect of him which he leaves to posterity. Artaud was on his way to total communion with the void in the form of these images. Danger, therefore, confronted him; a hyper-fascination with an archetypal image implies an over-preoccupation with what is common to all men: a rejection of the personal element within man and a reverting to, or submersion within the psyche or the unconscious. For a certain kind of individual, such a "sinking into self" or immersion into the *void*, is a source of healing and power since it has a beneficial effect upon the psychological well being of the individual: it gives him a feeling of being part of a whole or belonging.[18] In Artaud's case, however, his withdrawal into himself, the past, and the collective could, on the other hand, provide a destructive escape mechanism for his unconscious deepseated fear of living in the work-a-day world. But then, perhaps the effect would be salutary since Artaud had said that he had not gone to Mexico because he had been unable to find his proper niche in French society, but rather to "hunt out the living basis of a culture, the notion of which seems to be disintegrating here;" also *to find himself.*[19]

It was little wonder then that Artaud was fascinated by a people whose culture was rooted in the *soil* and in *fire:* soil (symbolizing stability, mother nature, as the source of nourishment) and fire (creative energy, a mystical fire) "which participated at once in the spirit of fire and in the soul of light. . . ."[20] Indeed, culture, as we have already seen, meant fire to Artaud, that is, the burning of energy. And the whole of Mexican cosmogony, in fact, resided in the four mythical images first alluded to by Heraclitus: fire, heaven, earth, water.

No network of man-made dogmas marred the intensely close relationship between the Tarahumaras and the transcendental force they worshipped, Artaud concluded, and so fanaticism was non-existent. They adored an all-encompassing force, the "Essential," the "Principle," that is, the origins from which Nature formed itself: storms, wind, silence, sun. Though conquerors tried strenuously to destroy Mexican religions in general and the power of the native Gods in particular (the trinity of gods Tezct-lipoca, Buitchiboloch, Quetzalcoatl), they failed because the natural divinities persisted and continued to furnish a way of life for the natives.

The Tarahumaras Indians, Artaud affirmed, render homage to a universal principle which is at once Male and Female. The hermaphroditic principle which symbolizes a union of opposites, is represented in the headbands worn by the natives, at times red and at other moments white, indicating that within their race, the Male and the Female exist not only simultaneously, but complement one another.

Artaud was perhaps so fascinated by the symbol of the hermaphrodite because it indicates a primitive state of mind which is present at the very dawn of life, when differentiation is barely visible or understood. With increasing development, irreconcilable opposites come into focus: friction, energy and as such creativity. One must recall that the symbol of the hermaphrodite played an important role in both Greek and Gnostic culture; in the natural philosophy of the Middle Ages, in Catholic mysticism with Christ's androgini. It signifies a longing to go backwards and at the same time, a desire for the attainment of a future goal: to subdue conflicts, to heal.[21]

Artaud's fascination for the androgyne as a transcendental force is perfectly understandable. This bi-sexual primordial being became for Artaud a symbol of the unity of personality, of wholeness, indicating a union also between conscious and unconscious worlds. The heart of the Tarahumaras' cosmogony lies in the symbol of the hermaphrodite as it is manifested in the hallucinatory and self-fertilizing peyotl plant. The peyotl plant is cylindrical in shape and measures from fifteen to twenty centimeters in length; it is covered over with silk hairs and bears a solitary pink flower. It is considered sacred by the Tarahumaras Indian and necessitates a long harvest period accompanied by all types of pilgrimages and celebrations. The peyotl plant opens the way to *Ciguri.*

The Ciguri rite of the Tarahumaras Indians is one of creation and regeneration. It permits the Indian to gain knowledge of the existing *void* and of the infinite: of the *infinite:* of the reality which emerges from these two entities and of its eventual shaping into a body. The Indians never pronounced the name *Ciguri*, nor did they like to hear it. It filled them with fear; not as the Westerner conceives of this emotion, but rather as one filled with a "sense of the sacred".

The peyotl plant for the Tarahumaras Indians, affirmed Artaud, opens the way to *Ciguri*. Ciguri is a man-God who inhabits the peyotl plant. Whoever takes the right amount of peyotl cannot lose his rational self in fruitless hallucinations because God is within him and is working with him. The believer, Artaud explained, gains sight into the Infinite or into Tutuguri, the Sun. But since Ciguri is also the God of self control and balance, to take too much peyotl would be to offend Him. In such an event, any beneficial action Ciguri might take upon the individual would be annihilated and would be replaced in the believer's body by the Evil spirit.

To swallow the white powder derived from the "divine" peyotl plant meant for the Tarahumaras Indian, Artaud explained, to partake in the flesh and the blood of their God Ciguri. By so doing, each person shared in the attributes, the powers and the beneficial effects of this God. The custom of seeing God incarnate and in substance was by no means peculiar to the Tarahumaras Indian. One need only pick up the "New Golden Bough" and there one is confronted with a list of similar customs: for example, twice a year the Mexican God Huitzilopochtli, made of dough, was broken and eaten with great ceremony by His worshippers; the Brahmans considered rice-cakes given up in sacrifice, as a substitute for human beings, the rice-cakes were converted into the real bodies of men by priests. Whether the God was human, plant, or corn made little difference: the plant or corn became his body; when he was a vine-god, the juice of the grape was considered as his blood. And so, by eating the bread (flesh) and drinking the wine (blood), the worshipper partook of the real body and blood of his god. Therefore, the drinking of the wine in the rites of a vine-god, Dionysus for instance, was not an act of drunken debauchery any more than was and is the eating of the host and the drinking of the wine in a Christian service. On the contrary, it is believed to be a solemn sacrament.[22] When the Tarahumaras Indian experienced the sacrament or God within him, his entire countenance changed, Artaud noted.

The Tarahumaras Indian does not fear death. He believes in metempsychosis and looks upon his body as something transient and so attaches little importance to it. In fact, he considers it, in part, as Evil. But not completely so, since the body also has its good points because Ciguri created it, and finds refuge from the elements within it. When the body withers, however, Ciguri is set free to roam about and make His way into another.

Only through the white powder made from the hermaphroditic peyotl plant can the believer gain some kind of understanding of Ciguri. No one, however, has the right to touch this white powder until he has gone through an initiation ceremony which consists, in part, of being struck by the glaive (spear) of a certain old Indian chief. Only in this way can he learn to perceive *Tutuguri* (the Sun), which means, mystically speaking, traveling from the *multiple* (man's earthly state) to the *one* (the mysterious reassimilation into the *All* or into the *Sun* or *Tutuguri*). Such a dissolution of the individual's psyche is usually followed by a re-forming —a kind of rebirth.

Once the initiate, Artaud wrote, is under the influence of peyotl he is aware of his own dual nature. Unlike the Occidental, the Tarahumaras Indian distinguishes that element or being within him which is *personal* from that part of him which is *impersonal*, which belongs to the *Other* or the *Master of Everything*.[23] It is by means of peyotl that the believer's personal consciousness assumes the role of separating and distributing agent. As one of the natives told Artaud:

There is, he said, in all men an ancient reflection of God, in which we can still contemplate the image of this infinite force, which had one day thrust us into a soul and this soul into a body; and it is in the image of this Force that peyotl had led us, because Ciguri is recalling us to him.[24]

Artaud underwent the initiation ceremony and was struck by the Indian chief's glaive. He felt no pain as a tiny drop of blood emerged from beneath his skin. Artaud was then given a few grains of peyotl which he immediately swallowed. Suddenly, he felt himself filled ". . . with a light I had never possessed . . ." as though he were present, he stated, at the very birth of mystery. He could by means of peyotl . . .

> . . . plunge forth into the arcane original myths, enter through them into the Mystery of Mysteries, see the face of the extreme operations by which MAN FATHER, NEITHER MAN NOR WOMAN has created all.[25]

Artaud saw the Sun Priest begin drawing a series of symbols in the air, as though he were drawing forth forms from space. Certain forces hidden within the shadows of the universal design began to emerge. Artaud experienced an utterly extraordinary sensation; as though he were being turned upside down and inside out, living on the other side of things . . .

> One no longer feels the body one has just left, which gave you assurance because of its boundaries, on the other hand, one finds oneself much happier as part of the limitless, rather than just belonging to oneself; because one understands that what was oneself has emanated from the head of this limitlessness, this Infinite, and that one is going to see it. One feels as though one were part of a gaseous wave, from which an incessant crackling emerges from all parts.[26]

Aldous Huxley described his experiences with mescaline in a similar vein in his essay "Culture and the Individual." When he entered this realm where "culture-conditioned habits", relationships, and associations have vanished, he felt himself gliding into another phase of existence; from this vantage point he could no longer understand the one he had just left.

> . . . . the world will now reveal itself as not only unimaginably beautiful, but also fathomlessly mysterious—as a multitudinous abyss of

possibility forever actualizing itself into unprecedented forms. New insights into a new transfigured world of giveness, new combinations of thought and fantasy—the stream of novelty pours the world in a torrent, whose every drop is charged with meaning.[27]

For Artaud, peyotl became that precious element needed to cross from one world to another. Though peyotl was taken on several occasions during the year by the Tarahumaras, Artaud was told, the plant, during those times, was only used as a modifying agent. The great peyotl festival took place but once a year and was accompanied, Artaud affirmed, by special dances. It was only after having imbibed the peyotl powder that the initiate could begin to understand his God: his soul and nerves had been touched by His power as manifested in the peyotl.

IV

What Artaud was about to witness was so incredible as to be beyond belief: something he had known intuitively all these years: insights which had risen forth from those most primitive layers within himself: revelations he had presented in his brilliant series of essays ("The Theatre and its Double")—what Paris' theatrical world had rejected *en masse* via blocks of unpleasant epithets. On a mountain top, removed from civilization, Artaud was going to watch and partake of a religious ritual: a true *theatre of cruelty* spectacle.

The sky was ablaze, as though mirroring the intensity of what was about to transpire. Artaud watched the Priest-Sorcerers come down the mountain side with all the accessories necessary for a religious (dramatic) ritual: baskets, crosses, "mirrors gleaming like patches of sky".[28] A vision possessed his eyes: worlds far distant seemed to cling together as the past shot forth, invading his present. "The Nativity" of Hieronymus Bosch bounded about in his mind.

The kings, with their mirror-crowns on their heads and their rectangular purple robes on their backs—to my right in the picture—like the Magi of Hieronymus Bosch.[29]

The ceremony began. The faces of the initiates, who had already taken communion by eating their peyotl god, took on an almost inhuman expression: a strange glow and illumination. The stage was set: the "ring" had been drawn. Around it glowed the forbidden area where evil breathed its destructive force. Here, no mortal was allowed to tread, so horrendous would be the consequences. Within the "ring" (stage) "a history of the world is danced" from dawn to daybreak, around a fire, the reflection of the eternal Sun. The Priest-Sorcerers thumped the ground with a stick, traced magic numbers (usually an 8) in a series of intricate geometrical designs (triangles, circles, etc.) in order to "restore lost rapports".[30] After this, they spat not saliva from their mouths, but the "breath" of life, the symbol of creation. They walked upon the stage together with the dancers armed with six hundred small bells of horn and silver, glaring, sparkling, lending dramatic excitement to this decor of magic and myth. The lighting effects dazzled; the sounds emanating from this array of beings and things devastated. Each dancer whirled. They seemed to lacerate space with their "coyote" calls, shooting through the land like bristling arrows. Their gestures became more violent, as though they wanted to taunt destiny, tempt danger; and they drew closer and closer to that forbidden area in which Evil was held captive.

> He plunges into it headlong and with a sort of hideous courage, in a rhythm which transcends the Dance but seems graphic of Disease. And we imagine we see him emerging and vanishing by turns, with a movement suggestive of I know not what obscure tantalizations.[31]

The dancers, Male and Female symbolizing the Principle, gestured now in a menacing and warring manner; then fled from one another only to bump against each other once again.

> It's because the principles were not in the body, did not succeed in touching the body, but remained, obstinately enough, like two immaterial ideas, suspended outside of the Being, always in opposi-

tion to Him, and which made, on the other hand, of *their own bodies*, a body where the idea of matter is volatised by CIGURI.[32]

Artaud watched the CIGURI RITE dance which is essentially one of Creation, as spectator-participant, parishioner-officiant. Transfixed, as sensations from all quarters of the universe seemed to pour in on him, forcefully at first, then with bated impact; he was invaded by a sense of the Sacred, of Danger, of the Inhuman. Slowly, virtually unconsciously, he slipped into the elements of the alchemical drama he had described so vividly in his essay "Alchemical Theatre" (1932). Reaching into the heart of the Myth—the Mystery—he became part of the Essential transforming process in nature.

Object and subject at once, Artaud both partook and looked at what transpired before him: the whirling and twirling of the dancers and Priest-Sorcerers; listened to the strange guttural emanations pounding away at his ear drums; dazzled by the brilliant play of light and shadows cast by the reflecting elements of the sun, the fire and the mirrors in the "ring". Signs, Symbols, Gestures cut through the atmosphere swept on to him; his senses became activated to the breaking point, it seemed, when an acute feeling of elevation possessed him. All converged in this upsurging of vibrant waves.

The performance continued as actors veered about, pursuing their mimodrama; tinkling their bells; casting voluntary shadows on the stage floor as they persevered in their endless gyrations, silhouetted against a blistering sun. Another series of Symbols now etched themselves on stage, as though they had emerged bodily from "The Book of the Dead": crosses, mirrors, holes, beams, all manifestations of the two Principles (Male and Female) which lie buried in Matter. The Priest-Sorcerers feeling compelled to obtain some tangible proof of the efficacy of their ritual filed past the flames; bowing, curtseying, marching, crossing themselves.

So there was this rolling vault, this material intricacy of screams, tones, footsteps, litany. But above all, transcending all, this impression, which recurred, that behind all that, and more than all of it, and beyond it, still something else was hidden: namely, *the principle.*[33]

Still entranced, the Priest-Sorcerers stepped off the stage, indulged in "uncouth purgation" as the dancers heaving, swirling, screaming, shrieked out their anguished joy.

The water ritual, the second and final act of this spectacle, followed. It consisted in the uttering of strange pronouncements while water was being sprinkled on the participant. The Priest-Sorcerers then taking out their graters, the most sacred of all religious accoutrements used to exorcise the elements, rattled it first on the initiate's head, then struck him with it. The real world now became visible to the baptised, the one no ordinary man can *see,* but rather the one which Ciguri reveals to him.

Artaud lay on the ground now, he wrote, "so that the ritual would descend upon me, so that fire, litany, screams, dance and the night itself like a living human vault might wheel as a living being over me."[34] Slowly, he was losing consciousness of his body; his individual self had withdrawn into the Infinite. Merging with actuality, Artaud was assimilated to the breath of creation howling through the trees.

The *Theatre of Cruelty* spectacle Artaud had witnessed was no longer just a series of abstract notions he had committed to paper, but rather, a glaring, vital and living force. It had been felt so intensely by him as to cause a "giant emptying out" and "replenishing" of emotions: an action and inter-action similar to that encountered during times of plague and which Artaud had already explicated so accurately in "The Theatre and the Plague" (1933). This tremendous energy which had derived from an original experience, activated Artaud's sensibilities, his powers, his strength and his *heroism.*—Years later, another poet-mystic, Jean Genet, whose acute sensibilities also dug deep into the forces of nature, objectified his reactions to a religious ritual in "The Screens" and "The Blacks": true theatre of cruelty plays which were enacted not on a mountain top this time, but on the stages of the great cities of the world.

Artaud had a glimpse of the *void* when he underwent the peyotl rite. Renewed now, he was certain that the universal forces with which he had come into contact during his Mexican venture, inhabited him now and in some *magic* way protected him against all *Evil*.

It was November 1936. Artaud, in good spirits now, was homeward bound.

CHAPTER VII

THE SEPARATION

WHEN ARTAUD RETURNED to Paris in November, he was swelling with hope. So pleased was he in fact, that he revealed a desire to attempt some conformity to society's norms. He wanted to get married. Before his departure for Mexico, in 1935, he had met a young Belgian girl, Cecile Schramme. Upon his return, in 1937, he became engaged to her.

Artaud's letters to Cecile, which run from January through April 1937, are replete with extraordinary tenderness, love, and devotion. Expressing his preoccupations and hopes for their future together in certain missives; he virtually explodes with joy in his letter dated February 19th: "I love you because you have revealed human joy to me."[1] Yet, he was not one to be falsely deluded. On January 31, he wrote and spoke plainly and honestly; informing Cecile of what he foresaw to be his destiny: something so "abnormal", so "astounding", that only a "miracle" could help him. But he could not, he concluded, live in the hope of a miracle. When his moods grew too dismal, he placed his trust in universal protective forces which he believed would certainly come to his aid: "Think of the Powers which keep me, which keep *you*."[2]

Since Artaud wanted everything to be just right before getting married, he decided once again to rid himself of the drug habit. For this he needed money and the Ministry of National Education was now prepared to give him six hundred francs toward this end; friends also contributed to realize his urgent request. But cures in general are always difficult, and this period spent in the clinic was no exception. On March 3, he wrote to Cecile expressing his profound and deepening affection for her; but also, the difficult road which lay ahead for both of them. A month later, when he realized his cure had not been effective, he took a second one; suffered even harsher tortures this time.

Despite these provisional setbacks, Artaud had cause to be pleased. Jean Paulhan, editor of the *Nouvelle Revue Française*, expressed a desire to publish some sections of articles Artaud had written for *El Nacional* in Mexico. Paulhan's request encouraged Artaud to pursue his writings; indeed, it triggered off a period of extreme creativity. He had plans: to recount what he had seen in Mexico, but not in travelogue form. Rather, it would be "a meditation on unsuspected aspects of the mind and of existence," nourished by the sensations, ideas, souvenirs which were gushing forth from him now with geyser force.[3]

In the spring, Artaud was invited to Brussels to deliver a lecture on his Mexican trip. The Schramme's asked him to stay at their home. The lecture, scheduled for May 18, was announced in the Brussels newspapers. But as far as can be ascertained, no newspapers carried any report of it. From what can be gathered, it seems that Artaud began to talk to and on the point, but slowly veered from his subject and began to lash out at his audience, throwing a wild array of invectives at it and the gathering ended in disorder. Marcel Lecomte, a spectator, declared that Artaud became more and more violent as time elapsed, and toward the end of his lecture, screamed out with eyes half-closed and wearing an expression of convulsed agony: "And by revealing all this to you, I have perhaps killed myself!" Another account of the occurrence ran as follows: Artaud told his audience, "Since I have lost my notes, I shall talk to you about the effects of masturbation among the Jesuit fathers."[4]

Whatever the facts may be, there is little doubt that Cecile's father, a member in good standing of Brussels' bourgeois society, was shocked by Artaud's behavior. Cecile's engagement was broken. Artaud's venture toward matrimony had been short-lived. Such an outcome, however, was to be expected. Artaud's quixotic temperament, his distaste for the sexual, and his nearly constant head pains, were hardly conducive to a bourgeois life.

After his break with Cecile, Artaud seemed to lapse into a state of confused sorrow. To his old friend Dr. Allendy, he confessed, "I no longer know what is normal or supranormal. I only know what is: that's all."[5] To Manuel Cano de Castro, who had taught him to read Tarots, he wrote of the vision he had had: a certain woman would give him the will and strength to "destroy" his own "destruction"; she would "deliver" him from the "poisons" which now threaten him.[6] To André Breton, he expressed his violent indignation for the world in general, and further declared that the only reason he accepted life at all, was that he was convinced the world would perish before he would.[7] In another letter to Anne Manson, a young journalist, he described the burning sensation of which he felt himself to be a victim; the drugs he had used to extinguish the tortures of a separated and dissociated personality.

> I do not know what I am, but I *do know that for twenty-two years, I have not stopped burning* and I have already said that I have been turned into a pyre.[8]

The burning sensations of which Artaud had already given an account in his letters, essays, and poems, he was convinced, the whole world would soon know. Indeed, in "The New Revelations of Being", a slim brochure which he had written, he had prophesied, by means of an ingenious numerical symbolism, that the world would be destroyed by fire. Such annihilation would occur, he suggested, five months after June 3, 1937.

There will be, Artaud affirmed in "The New Revelations of Being," an immense upheaval, during which time Heraclitus' four elements (earth, water, fire, air) will be transformed into four warring forces and total, willful destruction will follow.

> It means that burning is a magic act, and that we must consent to burning, burning in advance and immediately, not a thing, but *every thing that represents things for us,* in order not to expose ourselves to being burnt up whole.[9]

After total annihilation by Fire, a re-evaluation, a revision of all values will occur. For example, the present imbalance between the Male and Female principles in the universe will be rectified. "The absolute Male of Nature," Artaud wrote, "is already stirring in the heavens and longs to regain his former grandeur and stature." With the strengthening of the Male principle, will come the resurgence of the Spirit which it symbolizes. The Spirit will then gain ascendency within, causing a de-emphasis or even an eradication of an over-developed sexuality as symbolized by the Female principle. Evil also will be diminished, since "Evil comes from the darkness of Women". Artaud predicted that the cataclysm will terminate a world cycle dominated by women; man will then reign supreme and as a result, the masses (female symbol) will once again be controlled by the spirit. This destruction by fire will annihilate every conception held by man, each instinct of which he is a victim, all disease that corrodes his body, images embedded in his brain and psyche. Fire or burning, symbolically speaking, leads to the destruction of one form of life and to the birth of another. It is an initiation from one state to the next. As for Artaud, what would become of him? Not death, but separation. "I am not dead," he wrote prophetically, "But I am separated."[10]

Artaud came to the conclusion that the world would be destroyed on November 3, 1937 because of a special cane with three hooks and thirteen knots. The ninth knot bore the symbol of "thunder" and this number, according to numerical symbolism, signifies destruction by fire.

Artaud's friend René Thomas had given him this cane, which it had been said had once belonged to a Savoyard Sorcerer and also to Artaud himself in earlier incarnations. In fact, Artaud affirmed, this very cane was mentioned in Saint Patrick's prophecy. It had even been used by Christ in the desert when he struggled against the demons. A drop of this blood still remains on it; and while it has been rubbed off with water many times, it returns, nevertheless. This cane has magical powers. Artaud estimated that it had two hundred million fibers with special

signs representing "moral forces and prenatal symbolism. . . ."[11]
The cane seemed to take possession of Artaud as the months
passed. He carried it everywhere and showed it to André Breton
and other friends during the months of May,. June, and August
1937. He had had the cane tipped and it struck sparks against the
pavement as he walked with it. In fact, the cane with all of its
associated symbolism became so important for Artaud that he felt
compelled to leave for the land of its origin, of Saint Patrick—
Ireland. There he would seek to discover traces of the ancient
tree worshippers, the Druids, who might have fashioned this
magic weapon.[12]

> I am in search of the last authentic descendant of the Druids, those
> who possess the secrets of druidic philosophy, who know that men
> descend from the God of Death "Dispater" and that humanity must
> disappear by water and fire.[13]

Little is known about Artaud's trip to Ireland which, he said,
Jesus Christ had ordered him to take.[14] The only available infor-
mation has been gleaned from the letters Artaud wrote his friends,
particularly André Breton, Anne Manson, and Jean Paulhan.
According to these letters, Artaud landed at Cobh on August 14,
1937. He was in Galway on the 17th; in Kilronan, Inishmore on
the 23rd. He returned to Galway on September 5th, where he
stayed at the Imperial Hotel. He left Galway for Dublin on
September 8th. "I am leaving Galway and going toward my
Destiny . . ."[15] In a letter to Anie Besnard and René Thomas
dated September 14th, Artaud confessed he had finally penetrated
"the mysteries of the World with Jesus Christ's cane" and that
Jesus Christ had spoken to him,[16] that He had revealed the future
to him. In another missive to André Breton dated also on September 14th, he expressed a sudden fear of losing his friend's friendship. He had been forced, he pursued, to give up many things
"during the course of an abominable existence. . . . even the idea
of Existence." Frequently, however, certain mishaps serve a
purpose. His search for "INEXISTENCE" had led him, he wrote,
to the discovery of God.[17] By the same token, Artaud frowned

with contempt on organized religion and suggested that Christ
would arise "to punish his Church" by bringing forth "an Enraged (force) who will *raze* ALL the Churches and will force the
Initiates to practice their rites underground".[18] It is no wonder
then that Artaud later wrote the following about the Irish and
their church.

> The Irish are stubborn Catholics, and the basis of Catholicism is to
> taste God the ego in the mass with all of its obscene tendencies, with
> the obscene phallic weight of a praying tongue, as though from the
> breath of its chest it lasciviously ejaculated its milk during an orgasm.[19]

Matters came to a head in this regard when one afternoon
Artaud went for asylum to a Jesuit convent. He did not know the
monks were in retreat at the time and when they did not respond
to his knock he began banging on the door and screaming out his
annoyance at their silence. The Jesuits, discomforted and confused, called the police. A street fight ensued and a policeman
nearly broke Artaud's back when he struck him with an iron bar.
Artaud was imprisoned for six days following this episode. The
facts surrounding this strange incident are dim.

As a result of his arrest, Artaud was forced to set sail for France
on September 29. As for the cane, it had been left under the
mattress where Artaud had hidden it at Saint-Jean-de-Dieu's
shelter in Dublin, the day before the street fight. Artaud was so
quickly and unceremoniously evicted from Ireland that he was
unable to recover his cane. He was comforted, however, by the
knowledge that he still had in his possession the magic stiletto
from Cuba.

On board the ship Washington which was taking him back to
France, there occurred an incident which was to have sad consequences for Artaud. At around three o'clock in the afternoon,
when Artaud was in his cabin, two men entered; the steward and
the chief mechanic. They had come to fix something and were,
therefore, carrying a monkey wrench. Whether Artaud misunderstood their intentions and thought he was going to be attacked or
not, is not known. He did, however, do something which was

interpreted by these men as an act of violence. Perhaps he pulled his magic stiletto? It is not known. In any event, he was immediately seized and put into a strait jacket. When the ship docked at Le Havre, Artaud was taken to a mental institution. Later, according to Artaud, he was "martyrized" by the French police at Le Havre. Artaud's longest agony was just beginning. The destruction of the world that he had so positively predicted as indeed happening—was the destruction of *his* world.

II

Artaud seemed to be the tool of forces beyond his control. And this state of affairs was to continue for the next nine years as he was sent from one mental institution to another.

For the first weeks of his confinement Artaud's situation was aggravated by the fact that neither Dr. Allendy, Jean Paulhan, Robert Desnos, André Breton, not even Artaud's mother had any idea of what had happened to him. His whereabouts were a mystery. In November, Jean Paulhan wrote a letter of inquiry to the French Consul in Dublin. They informed him of the incidents which had taken place in Dublin and of Artaud's departure on September 29th. According to Mme Mallausséna, Artaud's sister, the poet's mother then rushed to Le Havre, where the ship from England was supposed to have docked. There she tried to discover some clue as to her son's whereabouts, and, on consulting the authorities, was advised to go to Quatre-Marre Hospital in the outskirts of Rouen. She found her son, but he did not recognize her. He had fallen into a *world* completely his own: impenetrable to the outsider.[20]

Shortly afterwards, Artaud was sent to Sotteville-les-Rouen; from there to Saint-Anne, where he remained for three years. He was totally apathetic and was declared autistic and incurable.[21]

Conditions in mental institutions were particularly dreadful because World War II was in progress. Food and heat were very short and discipline was extremely rigorous. Artaud's head was shaven and he was required to wear the uniform of the insane.

Yet, it was at this time, strangely enough, that he began to recover slowly. For the first time since his internment over two
years before, Artaud began writing letters. He asked for his
mother. He asked his friends to do their utmost to try to have him
released. On April 7, 1939, he wrote to Jacqueline Breton: "I am
a fanatic, but I am not crazy." On November 9, 1940, he sent a
letter to Roger Blin begging him to do his utmost to have him
released from Ville-Évrard. To Charles Dullin, he confessed that
he had been struggling desperately for a year and a half now,
against an *evil*, that nothing had relieved his agony, that Satan
had barred the path of rescue. From Pierre Souvtchinsky, on
August 10, 1941, he begged for heroin, cigarettes, and bread.[22]

In 1943 Robert Desnos succeeded in arranging for Artaud's
transfer to the institution of Rodez. Due to the severe restrictions
on food, Artaud had become so emaciated he looked like an
ambulatory skeleton. At Rodez, however, he was placed under the
care of Dr. Gaston Ferdière, a poet in his own right and a man
interested in Surrealism and in Artaud. He not only tried to build
his patient up physically, but talked with him at great length,
trying to discover some way to cure the terrible force which so
gnawed at his psyche.[23]

It has been reported that at this period in Artaud's life he
suffered from coprophilia and glossolalia, frequently losing track
of the ideas he was pursuing during a conversation. This kind of
lapse indicated the interference of an unconscious dynamism, resulting in the total eclipse of an idea at that moment. Artaud was
so retrenched in his own world, so overcome by his "other preoccupations" that the rapport with the "normal" "outer" world
ceased. He would begin telescoping his syllables, indulge in
verbal gyrations, make strange noises, change his intonation and
the vocal range of which he was a master: speak first in a sonorous,
then monotonous, and finally in an insipid register; whereupon,
he would break out in mellow and full tones. At meal time,
Artaud frequently stopped eating, quite suddenly, and for a few
seconds or minutes would go through a whole series of rituals
such as spitting, getting down on his hands and knees and

psalmodising, drawing magic circles, indulge in auditive hallucinations, gustatory antics, belch in rhythmic patterns, etc.[24]

There were days when Artaud had difficulty speaking, even formulating words. He smiled without apparent reason, suffered from a variety of tics, his gestures were incomprehensible—he was unable to complete even the simplest act. At other times, hours were spent in articulating words forcefully, injecting each syllable with a kind of metallic ringing sound; treating words as something concrete, actual beings possessing potential magic forces. For the non-initiated, or those unable to understand Artaud, these syllable-words seemed to blossom forth helter-skelter; for Artaud, however, they created a tapestry of verbal images and rhythms. He believed that words were not only instruments enclosing potential meanings, but also harbingers of friendly and enemy forces, emanations of a superior will which hovered around mankind eternally. Artaud projected onto those who surrounded him the forces he felt existed in the words they uttered. There were periods, when he treated those who cared for him, came to see him, or even other patients at Rodez, in what could be called a quixotic manner—at one moment he expelled feelings of hatred, at others, adoration. One could never tell, however, what his reactions would be at any specific moment.

Artaud's delusions and fantasies sometimes played havoc with him. For example, he was absolutely convinced that André Breton had come to Le Havre the day he had arrived from England. Despite machinegun fire, Breton tried to rescue Artaud from the hands of his tormentors, the police; later, the doctors who were going to incarcerate him. Artaud was so certain of the reality of these events that he related them to Breton. The founder of Surrealism denied the entire incident, pointing to the fact that he had not been near Le Havre the day of Artaud's arrival. Yet, Artaud remained adamant in his belief.

Living in a world retrenched from society was nothing new for Artaud. His unconscious realm had always played an important part in all of his activities and might even serve to explain, in part at least, his poor theatrical acting. When Dullin and Pitoëff had asked him for natural portrayals in the 1920's, he brought forth the most complicated. His characterizations were a composite of mechanical gestures accompanied by extraordinary facial motility, far beyond the part's requirements. It must be recalled in this connection, that ever since childhood, Artaud had camplained of periods of uncontrollable stuttering, twitching of facial nerves followed by periods of relaxation. Unconsciously then, he projected into his roles. Furthermore, he had always been drawn to the same type of parts: unbalanced individuals, traitors, perverts, addicts of one sort or another; and these, he played extremely well. For example, he acted King Basilio in Calderon's "Life is a Dream"; a believer in sorcery, magic, and evil, with unusual dexterity. He endowed the Angel in Molnar's *Liliom* with a kind of somnambulistic quality which was extraordinary. An explanation for such portrayals can be extrapolated: Artaud associated almost totally with his roles; in fact, he became that person at that particular moment. Such an associative attitude becomes even more visible in certain screen parts. The anguish he portrayed, for example, as a soldier haunted by a pathological fear of bursting shells in "The Wooden Crosses" was incredibly real. Artaud's face was so contorted, the torture so deeply felt, that he could not just have been 'playing' the part; he must have actually felt it. Furthermore, Artaud believed that pain could never be just 'acted', it had to have been experienced to be real.

In the 1920's Artaud's disease was still circumscribed. Relating to reality was possible. By 1942, however, the situation had been altered. He could frequently hardly distinguish inner from outer reality. In fact, Robert Desnos, who had gone to see him, wrote to Dr. Gaston Ferdière on January 26, 1942:

> I found him in a state of complete delirium, speaking like Saint Jerome and no longer wanting to leave (for Rodez) because he was being moved from the magic forces which were working for him. . . .[25]

Artaud seemed to have slipped beyond any recall. Dr. Ferdière, therefore, felt it advisable to use electroshock treatments and insulin therapy. Artaud, strangely enough, was fully aware of what was happening and complained bitterly, even rebelled, against these shock treatments. He feared a permanent loss of memory. The suffering he was now forced to endure was not only severe, increasing as time went by, but, he declared, virtually inhuman.

Artaud dove into a state of total despair. Concomitant with the electroshock treatments came the loss, disappearance or removal of all his material possessions. He suddenly felt as though he had been shorn of every human vestige. His papers, manuscripts, brown crocodile wallet with his initials engraved on it, and his precious stiletto from Toledo with its red leather case had all vanished. There was something so terribly pathetic in his cry of despair, as though he were being humiliated—degraded—to his very depths.

Dr. Ferdière, certainly aware of Artaud's depression, tried to inject a note of positive therapy in his treatment. He encouraged him to write and it was at this period that "In the Land of the Tarahumaras" (*Au Pays des Tarahumaras*) was rewritten; the most important section of a two hundred page work, "Trip to Mexico" (*Voyage au Mexique*), which had been lost during the course of Artaud's peregrinations. Also forthcoming now were a series of letters to Henri Parisot, his publisher in Paris, which was destined for publication under the title: "Letters from Rodez" (*Lettres de Rodez*) and the "Supplement to the Letters from Rodez" (*Supplément aux Lettres de Rodez*).

III

In his writings from Rodez, Artaud expressed his most profound preoccupations, analyzed his frame of mind, and developed his metaphysical, mystical, and spiritual beliefs. In fact, he wrote:

> My confinement was thus a religious matter, an affair of initiation and spells, of black magic and also most importantly of white magic, however unpopular that may be.[26]

The study of religions and their mysteries had always fascinated Artaud. Now, however, it had taken hold of his every thought. In a letter to Jean-Louis Barrault dated April 15, 1943, he declared that he had become a devout believer in Catholicism; that God in the form of Jesus Christ, with the help of His Angels, had now come to his aid, to chase the demons from him.

> Antonin Artaud returned to the Church and to the Catholic and Christian faith of the Church of Jesus Christ in Dublin, on September 1937, and he confessed and took communion on a Sunday morning in a church in this town where he had come to return Saint Patrick's cane which he held in his hands in Paris in June, July and August 1937.[27]

Shortly after this experience, Artaud repudiated all of his writings except for his "Correspondence with Jacques Rivière", the "Theatre and its Double", and "The New Revelations of Being" because the others did not express his intense feelings for God.

Artaud's religiosity had now become so extreme, that he swallowed one hundred and fiftytwo hosts. Indeed, in a veritable *imitatio Christi,* he concluded that the sufferings which had been inflicted upon him had been decided upon by God who had chosen *his* body, as he had Christ's, in which to descend. Artaud claimed, in fact, that it was because of his preoccupation with Jesus Christ that he had gone to Mexico. The Tarahumaras Indians were, he suggested, really worshipping Jesus Christ in their Sun-adoring Tutuguri Rite.[28] In fact, each Indian Priest considered himself "a terrestrial emanation" of God's "Virtu" and "Force", identifying himself with "one of his Rays . . .". The Sun and Jesus-Christ are, according to Artaud, synonymous. Furthermore, the Tarahumaras, representatives of the highest form possible of the human conscience, were also the harbingers of Jesus Christ's doctrine.[29] This was made absolutely clear to Artaud after his myriad visions in Mexico: not only did he see almost every conceivable type of cross linked for the most part with the solar image, but also the flames of the Bleeding Heart— and distinctly.[30] He explained further, that Jesus Christ, the

"Healer", had given the Tarahumaras peyotl, a plant capable of opening "the doors of Eternity" to the soul.[31] Worshippers imbibing peyotl could, therefore, come into contact with the universe's elemental forces: the "pre-conscience" and so see themselves as they are and had been centuries before their present existence. This is just the experience Artaud had known in Mexico. Revealed to him also at this time were those evil forces existing in the cosmos. While he had believed in their existence for many years, Artaud had never seen them as *plainly* as now; before they had taken root and come into being. Past—Present—Future —the inner and the outer world—all were rolled into one Reality for Artaud.

Since God represented the Self for Artaud; to be removed from Him implied total dissociation with the psyche and the ensuing pain which comes with such a break. Furthermore, Artaud had indicated that the Sun and God were one and the same thing. To project on to such an image revealed the intensity of Artaud's inner dynamism. Solar force, a symbol of psychic energy, belongs to the archetype or the unconscious, a collective force which cannot be controlled by the individual's personal will. Artaud then was at its mercy. He could not differentiate between his personal and his collective unconscious; they overlapped.

When he spoke of being inhabited by God or of experiencing the divine, he felt his personal power and stature increasing; with a corresponding lessening of what he considered human weaknesses and failings. Such an identification with Deity results in an inward thrust, a withdrawal indicating a solemn wish to reject the "lowly" state of man and to "raise" oneself to the godly heights. This overly introverted state brings forth further dangers: greater access to both the personal and impersonal unconscious, but a diminution in the ability to relate to the conscious world.[32]

The riches dwelling in Artaud's depths had now become transformed into living and active phenomena. Childhood memories arose with the vibrancy of an actual event; an impersonal historical past also surged forth in bizarre formations. For this reason, Artaud could talk or write about—and lucidly—his five spiritual daughters: the lost language; his own appearance at Golgotha where Jesus had been crucified; his incarnation as Jesus; his two relatives now at Rodez and whom he loved so very much, the young Catherine and her older sister Catherine; another soul, Cecile, the girl he was supposed to marry in 1937, which was trying to contact him at Rodez but was prevented from doing so by outside forces.

Indeed, as time passed, Artaud's unconscious became so active and powerful an instrument as to permit him to create a whole theological system of his own. He was convinced that the evil forces had extended their hideous tentacles onto society; clutched at individuals with their steel-like embrace; cast their spells whenever need be. When they insinuated themselves into the bodies of humans, they imposed their superior force or will upon the person in question; prevented him also from fulfilling his mission in life.

Artaud had been the victim of these forces since the beginning, he explained, but became aware of them only in 1915. They had succeeded in causing him to be born; in "impairing" his mind; in preventing him from fulfilling his destiny as both man and artist; in forcing him to say things he did not want to; in making it possible for him to be stabbed in 1915; in sending him to jail in Dublin in 1937; in seeing to his confinement in a mental institution ever since.

Artaud recounted the intricate machinations of these evil forces in his "Letters from Rodez". It had all happened, he wrote, at noon, 1915, while walking along a street in Marseilles, he was suddenly stabbed in the back by a pimp. The assassin told him, however, that it was not *he* who had perpetrated the crime. In fact, he had done his best to avoid committing this act; but he had been strangely possessed by a force which had clutched at his very soul. Artaud was convinced that his assailant was speaking the truth. It was an Angel—of this there could be no doubt—who had committed this crime and not the man who stood before him.

It is interesting to note in this connection that it was in 1914, just a year before the ostensible stabbing had occurred, that

Artaud had suffered his first depression; had been taken to a doctor who had given a negative diagnosis. The stabbing Artaud described was, if interpreted symbolically, a perfect imagistic description of the emotional pain he must have endured as a youth during his first mental breakdown. The trauma had evidently been so profound as to cause him a lasting impression; so acute indeed that he could recall the symptoms—like a knife stab—and their effects, nearly thirty years after the sensation had been experienced.

The Angel which Artaud believed had struck him in Marseilles when he was a youth, had reappeared, he felt, once again in Dublin in 1937. Furthermore, it was this *same* Angel (or Evil Force), which had prevented him from ever really accomplishing the things of which he was capable—of fulfilling his destiny. Now he was determined to do his utmost to rid himself of this strange power which had infiltrated his very fibers. He had gone to Mexico to try to discover the secret source of this magic force so that he could gain control of it or eject it from his system once and for all.

Such a belief in good and evil forces was not new for Artaud. He had mentioned their existence in his "Correspondence with Jacques Rivière". Even at that time, he had confessed being a prey to outside forces over which he had no control; which had deterred him from transforming the sensation-emotion into the concrete word. He had always sought to discover the root of these powers which he knew to reside in the occult. He studied, therefore, the *Kabbala,* the "Tibetan Book of the Dead", the "Egyptian Book of the Dead", etc.—with the purpose of trying to find a possible cure for himself.

That man's will is at the mercy of cosmic force is one of the basic tenets of all religions. Such a power may reside in the image of the godhead or another equally alluring. For example, many Saints and Mystics believe themselves to be inhabited by Divinity. Once they have become possessed, they are convinced that they are carrying out the will of some superior force; but certainly not their own. Some deeply religious people have experienced the *stigmata* they maintain, in one form or another; others have had visions of heavenly beings speaking to them, coming toward them, embracing them, etc. The list of such visitations is long. The dividing line which can be drawn between those fervently religious beings who live enshrouded in their contemplations, experiencing abnormal or extra-ordinary fantasies and visitations; and the insane, who dwell in their unconscious world, is indeed a tenuous one.

In this connection, it is interesting to note what Balzac had to say. Influenced by Lavater, Mesmer, Swedenborg, Saint Martin and the Illuminists, he felt that mysterious souls and forces hovered about the universe which was alive and forever permeated by a "vital fluid." Further, he believed that there were secret correspondences which united the visible and the invisible, and that metempsychosis and mental telepathy existed. In *Louis Lambert* (1832), Balzac created a character whose so-called insanity opened wide the door to a new world—for those who *understood*. Louis Lambert, whose senses had developed beyond the average, indeed, to such an acute point that he saw beyond the realm of reality, right into the future and could recall the past at will, was considered insane by the world. His wife, however, who "lived in his thought", understood the arcane language of the super-intelligence he personified, wondered why people wished the return of such an individual to the conventional and limited world of the 'normal'.[33]

Artaud in certain ways might be called a modern Louis Lambert. He saw beyond the natural frame of existence; lived in a world of extra-normal vision. His imagination, forever stimulated by the tiniest sensation, permitted him to grasp hidden meanings, penetrate into deeper stratas of existence, helped him gain *sight*.

As the days flew by at Rodez and his thoughts were devoted more and more to matters of religion, he became aware of the stultifying role organized religion had played in mankind's existence. The church in general, Artaud wrote, had "distilled everybody's perceptions," circumscribed both inner and outer worlds. Furthermore, Artaud was convinced that Catholicism was at the root of the bewitching forces which had been torturing him ever since 1915. Indeed, the entire church hierarchy was crippled, he now believed, with charm workers who initiate both black and white masses and other soul-begetting devices. The fresh and original experience which man had known centuries back and upon which Occidental religion had been based, had long since shriveled. The dogmas and rites which now secured the church's existence were series of machinations devoid of any profound meaning. The "loam" which is "the very body of the soul" can no longer be felt by an individual who follows the rules and regulations of established religions. Christ, Artaud maintained, had tried to hunt out the "loam", to relegate this regenerative force to his paradise; other religious sects put it to their own secret use. Today, those pretending religiosity, worship empty shells, façades, screens. Organized religion has become a deadening and leveling force in the world. In a letter from Rodez dated September 7, 1945, he wrote:

> . . . . I was stupid enough to say that I had been converted to Jesus Christ when Christ is the one thing I have always despised the most, and that this conversion has been the result of a horrible bewitchment which made me forget my own nature and made me swallow . . . a frightening number of hosts . . . at Rodez.[34]

In Artaud's "Supplement to the Letters of Rodez", he made his position on religion perfectly clear, stating on December 9, 1945 his total and complete renunciation of both baptism and of Christianity. He renounced Jesus Christ whom he called "the horrible little bewitcher from Judea." He renounced Christianity because it was a religion which concentrated on exteriors, on outward manifestations of "piety", and because its priests were hypocrites and "each priest a criminal".

Artaud's rejection of Christianity did not relieve him of his sense of being held in thrall by some great interior force. His agony continued, but was to a certain extent relieved by his love for poetry.

Poetry was Artaud's very life force. He needed it to survive. It was an instrument which could put him in touch with the infinite; one capable of creating a world of its own, of possessing a soul which could suffer and agonize. But poetry, Artaud explained, is a lost art today, comparable, perhaps, to the by-gone rites practised in the ancient mystery schools. If poetry is to be a living thing, it must be the product of a human experience: it must express suffering, agony, joy. Each word must be sweated out, squeezed out drop by drop, like blood, and like fecal matter emerge from the human body. When Artaud was asked to translate Lewis Carroll's "Jabberwocky", he worked on only a fragment of it because it "bored" him. Furthermore, it smacked of "affected infantilism." While "Jabberwocky" contained interesting words coined by the writer, this poem was not really nourished by the author's blood. It was a cerebral linguistic success. It had not been torn from him; it was devoid of a soul.

> Anything that is not a tetanus of the soul or does not come from a tetanos of the soul, such as poems by Baudelaire or Edgar Poe, is not real and cannot be considered poetry.[35]

Only authors who had known personal anguish could write lines sufficiently powerful to brand the reader. "Jabberwocky" is the work of a "castrated" male, an intellectual "profiteer" who fed on somebody else's pain.

> *Jabberwocky* is the work of a coward who did not want to suffer his work before writing it, and this is obvious.[36]

Even the fecal passages in "Jabberwocky" are those of "an English snob," Artaud explained. They are unreal because they were unfelt. His is undigested poetry from which no scent emanates. It is, therefore dead: that is devoid of the life processes constituted in the eating, digesting, and evacuating of all cosmic resources. "I like poems which stink . . ." Artaud wrote, because "they smell of life."[37]

To write poetry is to infuse it with the breath of life; to recite it, is likewise a creative process. Once a poem is injected with life it can move or project life into someone else's being or inflict pain, as the case might be. Under the right circumstances, the poem itself becomes, symbolically speaking, the breeder of life and so, develops its own sexuality. An entire universe can, therefore, come into being if a poem is interpreted properly; forces will arise, spirits invade, "internal magic" transmitted from one body to the next; sexual energy freed, and emotions, feelings, sensations, thoughts flow forth in an infinite array.[38]

Strangely enough, when Artaud recited poetry for Dr. Ferdière, a man well versed in literature art and music, he failed to understand Artaud's theories which were, in actuality, a projection onto poetry of his theatrical techniques. When Artaud put his breathing system, described in "An Affective Athleticism" to use, he injected his readings with an incantatory quality, scanned certain syllables, treated words as concrete objects, and in so doing brought forth a new language which was ejaculated forcibly or limpidly from Artaud's lips, with all the beauty or ugliness as he willed into the emanations.[39]

Artaud was preparing two books, he explained, "Surrealism and the End of the Christian Era" and "Measure for Measure", both to deal with the discovery of a new language. Indeed, Artaud was working on a whole new system of expression: neologisms, verbal gyrations, syllabic sounds, a glossary of verbal images—all in an attempt to inject life into poetry and to unearth hidden and secret meanings, making it possible for him to rediscover the original language, the one pre-dating the erection of the Tower of Babel. The word-sounds created by Artaud, expressing waves, feelings, sensations were comprehensible to him, but not to the psychiatrists at Rodez who labeled it glossolalia.

> orka ta kana izera
> kani zera tabitra[40]

or again,

> ratara ratara ratara
> atara tatara rana[41]

The above syllabic sound patterns were examples of a language Artaud claimed to have deciphered and written about a long while back. He had made public his discoveries in a book which disappeared in 1934. It was written, Artaud further explained, in a new language which all people could understand no matter what the nationality.

Whether Artaud talked about religion, poetry, the theatre—or most any topic at this period, he forever referred to the fecal, the sexual, and the anal. These aspects of life had always been important to Artaud, but now became increasingly so. His atavistic fixation on these matters might be compared with the obsessive interests of primitives and children in the visceral regions. In the Solomon Islands, in New Guinea, and in other regions where primitive man lives, everything that comes out of the body (semen, spittle, sweat, dung, breath, words, and flatus) was considered as part of a creation myth.[42]

Artaud's obsession with the sexual, however, differed from that of the primitives in an important respect. Primitive man looked upon sex as something natural, creative, mysterious, and marvelous. Not so Artaud. Consciously he rejected *everything* sexual. He made this perfectly clear in "The New Revelations of Being", when he predicted the destruction of the Female Principle (sexuality). Indeed, Artaud was so repelled by the mere idea of sexuality that he could not accept the fact that he was born out of his mother's uterus. It was too ignominious a concept.

> . . . . I Mr. Antonin Artaud, born on September 4, 1896, in Marseille, at 4 Rue du Jardin-des-Plantes, from a uterus in which I was in spite of myself and with which I had nothing to do even before, because this is no way of being born, to be copulated and masturbated for nine months in a gaping membrane which devours without teeth as the Upanishads say: and I know I was born in a different fashion, from my works and not from a mother, but the MOTHER wanted to take me and you see the results in my life.—I am nothing but pain.[43]

During his confinement it has been said that Artaud never mentioned the name of his father whom he had always detested and rarely spoke of his mother with whom he had lived, more or less off and on, in Paris since his father's death on September 24,

1924. Artaud's hostility toward his parents was so strong that he felt he was nobody's child; that he had come into being from his own anguish and spiritual torment.

As Artaud's schizophrenia became more and more circumscribed, the subjects which could be mentioned without ushering forth an abnormal frenzy of emotion became fewer and fewer. For example, it was said that when the subject of a beautiful woman or of a couple was broached, Artaud was thrown into a state of turmoil, of aggressivity, of virtual hysteria. Reactions such as these, however, had diminished to such an extent that Artaud seemed to be functioning well enough to be finding his incarceration really unendurable. He besieged his friends with pleas for his freedom.

By 1945 the war was over and Artaud was able to see visitors. Among the first to come to visit him were the painter Jean Dubuffet, Marthe Robert, his wife, Arthur Adamov, Colette and Henri Thomas. These friends were intent upon obtaining Artaud's release from Rodez. But such a release involved serious problems. It must be recalled that Artaud had been interned by force and according to French law, his release would have to be agreed upon by an administrative body. In France, the family usually asks for the patient's release, but in Artaud's case, this was not possible since his family did not approve. His mother, therefore, had never been informed of the steps that were being taken for Artaud's release. Actually, according to Mme. Paule Thévenin, Artaud was on very bad terms with both his mother and his sister. Dr. Ferdière, however, sympathetic to obtaining Artaud's release, asked his friends to comply with two requests.

The first request: that sufficient funds be collected before Artaud's release to assure his support for several years to come. A fund-raising committee was organized and headed by Jean Paulhan. On June 7, a gala benefit performance was given at the Théâtre Sarah Bernhardt at which famous actors and actresses read some of Artaud's works. At another benefit sponsored by the Galerie Pierre, certain paintings and manuscripts given by the artists and writers were auctioned. Over one million francs were thereby collected.

The second requirement: that Artaud be placed in a private rest home so that his diet and health regimen could be supervised. Mme. Paule Thévenin, the wife of a doctor, went to see Dr. Achille Delmas at Ivry, a man who had been the doctor of Roger Gilbert-Lecomte and of Lucia Joyce, and whom she described as having "innate tact and great generosity".[44] He agreed to take Artaud.

Now that both requirements had been met, Dr. Ferdière and the administrative committee agreed to Artaud's release from Rodez. It was Dr. Ferdière, in person, who accompanied Artaud to Paris. He wrote:

> I accompanied Artaud myself to Paris. The souvenir of this night on the train, still today tears my heart. Leaning with his elbows on the brass bar, we pursued a friendly conversation, not to say affectionate; I felt Artaud's deep attachment, his full confidence in me, and I also felt my anguish for his future.[45]

CHAPTER VIII

THE DEEPER VISION

ARTAUD ARRIVED IN PARIS ON MAY 26, 1946. He went directly to Ivry about twenty minutes away from the heart of the city. There, Dr. Achille Delmas received him. Dr. Delmas displayed great kindness and understanding in his handling of Artaud. In fact, he gave him the keys to the large front gate of the rest home and said: "Monsieur Artaud, you are in your own home, here are the keys."[1] It was no wonder then that Artaud's health improved.

During the first few weeks at Ivry Artaud lived in the new building. One day, however, as he walked through the park with its burgeoning flowers, he noticed a charming XVIIIth century pavilion set apart from the rest of the establishment. It was said that Gérard de Nerval had once lived in it. Artaud was so taken by the small building that after returning from a short stay in the South of France, he asked Dr. Delmas for permission to move into the two room pavilion. Though Dr. Delmas was not wholly in favor of such a move, he understood that Artaud *needed* this isolation; this separation from the other people at the rest home. He consented, therefore, to Artaud's request, though he was fully aware of the discomforts involved in such a change. There was no heat nor was there water in the pavilion. Artaud's meals, therefore, had to be brought to him daily; also, huge logs to warm his quarters on chill fall mornings or icy winter nights. Despite the kindness extended to him by his friends and Dr. Delmas, physically Artaud was a changed man. The years of deprivation had taken their toll in many ways. His health was poor due to the malnutrition during his years of internment, he had lost his teeth, and his hair had thinned. He looked like a shrunken old man whose haunted eyes stared out of a deeply furrowed, sallow face. Yet, by no means had he abdicated from life, retaining somehow his creative, combative force. In fact, he wrote more than ever now. He wrote anywhere and everywhere, in restaurants, subways, cafés, standing up, sitting down, in bed, in note books on scraps of paper. As he said to Mme. Paule Thévenin, "After nine years of silence, I have so much to say."[2]

Artaud's writings were not haphazard. He had certain projects in mind. He wanted to produce and direct Euripides' "The Bacchantes" because it was, in Artaud's opinion, a perfect theatre-of-cruelty play. But Parisians were still not ready for Artaud's theatre. Having *lived cruelty* under German occupation, they were not prepared to see it objectified on stage. Artaud's plan, therefore, never came to fruition.

Nevertheless, he was not neglected by his friends and admirers. The Club d'Essai asked him to read one of his texts for a radio program. He agreed to do this and chose: "The Patients and the Doctors" (*Les Malades et les médecins*) (1947). But he failed to satisfy his audiences. Indeed, his readings were compared to the declaming of Albert Lambert, Sarah Bernhardt's acting partner at the Comédie-Française, a man whom Artaud did not admire— not one bit; in fact, he considered him a mummer.

This small setback did not dampen Artaud's spirits. He was accustomed to far worse. Furthermore, he was still experiencing something exciting and relatively new for him—freedom—and he wanted to enjoy it to the hilt, as far as his personality would allow him. He looked toward the future. He was alive, active, capable of expressing himself. And this was the most important truth of them all right now. And so, when Henri Parisot who had just translated three poems by Coleridge, asked Artaud to preface them, he acquiesced in letter form. In Artaud's scathing letter (November 17, 1946), which he labeled "Coleridge the Traitor" (*Coleridge le traître*), he not only explicated his ideas concerning the XIXth century poet, but about poetry in general, and also the conflicts raging within him at this very time.

I

Artaud believed that poetry must be experienced, brutally if necessary. Like the theatre, it must under no account be mere entertainment. Tracing the word *poème* etymologically, he declared that *ema* in Greek means "blood" and *po-ema* probably means "the blood afterwards." Poetry, therefore, like the dramatic arts, must draw blood: "For what has been made of blood, we have made into a poem." A poet who chooses to avoid blood, who seeks to glide over reality and truth, is no poet.

Artaud took Coleridge as a case in point. A frightened, weak man, Coleridge eventually refused to give of himself completely in order to create poetry; and he *realized* his failure. For this reason, he could not enter into the category of the *poètes maudits* as did Baudelaire, Poe, Nerval and Villon "outcasts capable of *transpiring* at a given moment, of ejecting that little black mucous, that waxy fart of hideous pain at the end of the turnstile of blood . . ."[3]

Coleridge was complex, for he was double in the beginning: on the one hand, there was the strong and courageous man who did not seek to avoid the blood necessary to speak plainly and "completely"[4], on the other there emerged the will-less being who sought to skim over life's pain. The "Rime of the Ancient Mariner", a recounting of the poet's inner struggle, has a confessional and autobiographical element about it. The crime of the seaman who shot an albatross, a bird of good omen, and his subsequent supernatural punishment and penance which is related in the poem, is a symbolic representation of Coleridge's own crime and expiation. The mariner was, in certain respects, Coleridge himself who had killed his own sensitive and poetic facets, those which sought to experience the pain of life. In so doing, however, the poet had destroyed part of himself, his strong side and permitted the weak elements in his personality to flourish. This poem's fascination is further enhanced by the fact that a whole cosmic drama is present in full: crime, punishment, death, and transfiguration.[5]

Artaud begrudged Coleridge the fact that he had betrayed the real poet in him by seeking the easy path and in so doing lost all of his vital creative forces. Such was not the case of Isidore Ducasse, better known as the Count de Lautréamont.

In Artaud's "Letter on Lautréamont" (1946), he pointed out the steps the writer had taken to resist every kind of coercion stemming from self or from the "hypocritical citizen". Lautréamont had remained "bone-hard" in his struggle to retain his individual personality and never once cast aside the anguish of torment. He lived it fully. The conflict raging between the two aspects of his personality (the Lautréamont side which personified the collective forces of the unconscious and the Isidore Ducasse aspect, symbolizing the personal side) had a salutary effect upon the poet. Such action (cruelty) increased his inner dynamism. But this positive achievement was in a way only temporary because the weak and underdeveloped personal consciousness was unable to fully cope with the collective unconscious. The horrendous and monstrous images forever swept into consciousness ended by overwhelming and killing it. The individual Isidore Ducasse died so that the collective Count Lautréamont would be permitted to live on in his works.

> And this is not called an uprising of chattel against the master, but an orgy of the collective unconscious trespassing on individual consciousness.[5]

It was because such a struggle had taken place, Artaud explained, that one can differentiate between such poets as Poe, Nietzsche, Baudelaire, Nerval—arch individualists—and "the funnel of everybody's thoughts," Lamartine, Musset, Pascal, Chateaubriand.[6]

Artaud's assessments of both Coleridge and Lautréamont are particularly interesting in the light of his own emotional frame of mind. He considered Coleridge a traitor because he was unable to grapple with those painful forces emerging from the collective unconscious which brought forth the blood of creation: and Lautréamont, a hero, for fighting his battle and dying physically in so doing. Affection and admiration on Artaud's part always went to those who struggle and ache, for he could best relate his own torments to them. Such was not only true in the case of poets, but of artists as well.

II

Art had always played an important role in Artaud's life. Even during the early years: the two years spent in the sanatorium in Switzerland (1918-1920) in particular, where the doctor in charge had encouraged Artaud to draw and paint for therapeutic reasons. In the 1920's in Paris, Artaud had become acquainted with artists and art dealers: André Masson, Elie Lascaux, Joan Miro, D.-K. Kahnweiler—Cubists, Dadaists, and Surrealists. He was drawn to their new way of seeing things; the breaking up of form and surface; of color and space; the fragmented nature of the visions they presented, the metaphysical innuendoes which permeated their works. Perhaps the shattering elements, the tangled rhythms, the destructive and violent forces he saw in these artistic manifestations mirrored his own inner world.

An artist himself, Artaud appreciated originality and imagination in others. When asked to contribute reviews to art shows, he had always proven to be a stimulating and discerning critic. Like the great art critics of the past—Diderot, Gautier, Baudelaire— Artaud saw *into* the canvases before him: they became living entities, capable of awakening his senses; arousing and sucking them up in some way or another. Never did Artaud attempt to write a critique of a painting just because he was asked to do so. His judgments could not be cerebral, superficial or hackneyed. He had to experience a painting, be seared by it in order to pour forth his ideas. A painting spoke to Artaud, made him vibrate— with glee or with horror. It attracted or repelled him; it remained an objective entity or it drew him into a state of vertigo as he watched the lines etched on to the canvas move about in a maze of color. A painting was a theatre of cruelty spectacle—an active, compelling vital work—or else it was nothing.

Artaud had always felt a particular affinity for certain artists:

Cranach, Delacroix, Giotto, Cimabue, Breughel, Le Nain, Klee, Modigliani, Picasso—just as he had a propensity for playwrights: Euripides, Ford, Seneca. These painters had an "untranslatable" and eternal quality about them. There were others, however, who left him unmoved. Matisse, for example, was an "incomparable trickster", Albert Gleizes "boring"; Picabia, amusing because of his inventiveness; Gromaire, powerful, in fact his canvases made him "one of the most considerable temperaments of our epoch."[7] An artist's craftsmanship, his ability to draw or execute objects *per se,* his linear construction, was secondary for Artaud. It was the "expression", the artist's "ideal", his "vision", a "certain sum of humanity through colors and features," the "truth" of a painting which counted.[8]

Certain painters stirred Artaud more deeply to song than others. Vincent Van Gogh's canvases had always succeeded in creating a series of explosions within Artaud's own personality—now more than ever. Familiar with everything that related to Van Gogh, his correspondence with his brother Theo, the various biographies which had been written about the artist and his work, Artaud realized that the same unconscious content living within the painter's being—a chaotic and seething mass ready for the painful process of disintegration and rebirth—came into sudden contact with his own whirlwind personality; each responded to the other in some strange and mystical manner.

It was during the month of January (1947) when Artaud went to see the Van Gogh exhibit at the Orangerie Gallery in Paris that a sudden collision of emotions (Artaud's and Van Gogh's, as revealed on the canvases) gave birth to an extraordinary essay: "Van Gogh: the Man Suicided by Society" (*Van Gogh le suicide de la société*).

There are conflicting reports as to the genesis of Artaud's article. Pierre Loeb, an art dealer in Paris, to whose home Artaud went directly after seeing the Van Gogh exhibit, described the poet as being "overwhelmed, in a state of extreme exaltation." According to Mr. Loeb, who was aware of Artaud's fervent reactions to the canvases, the conversation was recounted as follows. "Why couldn't you write a book on Van Gogh?" queried Mr.

Loeb. Whereupon Artaud went up to the first floor of his host's home and began writing in what Mr. Loeb declared to be "his rapid, nervous writing . . ." The text was completed in two afternoons.[9]

Mme Paule Thévenin, whose devotion to Artaud after his release from Rodez was unstinting, described the genesis of "Van Gogh: the Man Suicided by Society," in a somewhat different manner. She reported that several days following the Van Gogh exhibit, Pierre Loeb sent Artaud a letter in which he enclosed several newspaper clippings concerning the art show. One of these articles, written by a psychiatrist referred to Van Gogh as being one of those "degenerates of the Magnan type." Incensed by what he considered to be a callous and superficial way of viewing genius, Artaud retorted by writing "Van Gogh: the Man Suicided by Society." According to Mme Thévenin, Artaud wrote this work which won him the Sainte-Beuve prize, in five or six days.[10]

In "Van Gogh: the Man Suicided by Society," Artaud brought new depths of vision to the field of art criticism. He looked upon the plastic arts as an externalization of self; painting, as a device by which man's mythical heritage could be renewed and made to live again, where unconscious archetypal images could be made to dance their dance of the hours, confronting, stifling, crippling, or unburdening the heart of the spectator. Painting for Artaud was a material manifestation of an immaterial myth, the stating of an intangible *reality*. To interpret such a mythical reality, Artaud declared, requires genius, and this is just what Van Gogh possessed.

Furthermore, painting was a manifestation of the occult, a hypnotic agent. Each object on a canvas, each color, each line and stroke was looked upon by Artaud as a "talisman", a force serving to draw the viewer's vision *inward*. This altered vision, plus the viewer's intuition, imagination, and feeling, created a new state of being, a fresh world with a just-born sense of self.

In "Van Gogh: the Man Suicided by Society," Artaud maintained that Van Gogh was endowed with powers beyond the average. He was a man of extraordinary vision, and therefore, his personality differed from that of others. Artists who see things in a different light cannot function according to the dictates of society and cannot be expected to follow the behavior patterns of the so-called *normal* human being.

> . . . . for Van Gogh was a creature of superior lucidity which enabled him, in any circumstances, to see further, infinitely and dangerously further than the immediate and apparent reality of facts.[11]

Since artists are simply not the same as the average human being, they are misunderstood, lonely, forced even to live in mental institutions, or some other form of social isolation, because this is the easiest way for society to cope with those they consider to be the "problem artist".

Artaud certainly, unconsciously or deliberately, identified with Van Gogh. Both men were victims of society's indifference to and incomprehension of their gifts. Both men found their deepest release in their creative work. They were equally the victims of doctors, in particular, psychiatrists. Indeed, Artaud went so far as to blame Van Gogh's suicide on his psychiatrist, Dr. Gachet. Artaud was convinced that Dr. Gachet really hated Van Gogh and the *genius* that lived within him. In fact, he wrote that psychiatrists as a whole are jealous of those possessing imagination, feeling, and intuition, to a profound degree—qualities belonging only to the genius. Instead of going along with Van Gogh in his creative fantasies, Dr. Gachet, who did not understand the *illuminated* artist, tried to rid him of all of his so-called peculiar ideas. Even Van Gogh's brother Theo, materially so helpful to him, considered the artist to be suffering from some kind of delirium. These, are the destructive attitudes of the highly rational human being who cannot possibly understand the hyper-sensitive artist who moves about in a much different world, responds to other stimuli, is far more profoundly affected by his surroundings than is the average individual. In fact, one can say that the true artist, such as Van Gogh, has reached a phase of existence which is unknown to most people, the stage of *direct creation*.

> . . . . in which disorderly thoughts surged back
> through the invading discharges of matter,
>   and where thinking is no longer exhausting,

and no longer exists
and where the only thing is *to gather bodies,* I mean

TO PILE UP BODIES[12]

The artist of genius is not a well-functioning, well-meaning, easily adaptable person who sees life in all of its routine—yet limiting aspects and is willing to cope with it. The genius artist has *enlarged vision.* His paintings are like bursts of *fire.* Possessing the force of an atomic bomb, they are endowed with the power of transforming conceptions: social, religious, and political institutions—even nature itself. Their optic is different. When Van Gogh painted his tides, his tempests, his suns, images charged with violence and love, they became occult powers suffused and infused with extreme energy and creative force. Though his colors (discordant reds, greens and yellows) on first sight created a sense of turbulence; in their totality, they reflected inner harmony and beauty. Under Van Gogh's every brush stroke, nature itself seemed to rear its "hostile flesh", to strike, to flay, whatever came into contact with it.

Artaud did not describe each painting he saw at the Van Gogh exhibit. Such a project would have been pointless and impossible because Van Gogh did not paint lines and forms, but rather "things of nature in full convulsions". He did, however, dwell lovingly on the succulent and living qualities of Van Gogh's color tones, as well as his "terrible sensitivity" which shot right through Artaud.

There are, however, certain paintings Artaud did single out: the "Crows over the wheat field", painted two days before the artist's death, for the sinister and enigmatic feeling which pervades the atmosphere; "Wheat field, at night," "The Aliscamps", "Vincent's Bedroom" and others, affected Artaud as though a raw nerve had been exposed. He knew from these canvases that *all* of Van Gogh had participated in their creation: his flesh, blood, and mind. They were projections of the artist's inner rhythms and vibrations in which both the man and the animal within him had been revealed; works in which color, texture and form combined to express the violence Artaud had so craved for and also to bring forth something of striking beauty. Artaud experienced a visceral empathy: complete contact between painter, canvas, and viewer.

Van Gogh's "Sun Flowers" also manifested tremendous action (cruelty), like exploding meteors, irradiating sparks, forceful and swirling lines, presenting brilliant flashes of lightning—and from within this energy, the artist's face seemed to appear to Artaud, that "bloody red face" burst forward and moved toward him. Van Gogh, the creator, was

> . . . evoking for us, in front of the fixed canvas, the enigma pure, the pure enigma of a tortured flower, of landscape slashed, pressed and plowed on all sides by his drunken brush.[13]

Artaud appraised paintings and drawings as he did everything else, from a metaphysical point of view. Form and color, harmonies and relationships were not a painting's only important features; the picture as a whole had to be in complete agreement with the rhythms of the universe as well as with man's inner movements and responses. A painting must be a part of a whole, yet it must strike at the very heart of the individual viewing it; penetrate deep within the viewer's unconscious, create a "mosaic of images," according to its own "irrational disorder. . . ." Van Gogh's paintings accomplished just this for Artaud. In these canvases, Artaud commented, nature itself was ready to rise in all of its beauty and horror in order to display its stormy light, its *sun* buried within its black folds. Within this *chaotic* mass, which Artaud so clearly discerned, unity and multiplicity co-existed; creation as man knows of it has not yet taken form and shape, each motion, feeling and idea was preparing itself for its new life, gathering strength all the while to rise up and act out its agony.

Van Gogh's canvases present viewers with life in the raw, divested of all extraneous elements, already breathing its breath into object and form; giving the impression of being able to *see through* things and beings, of *filling* and being part of a *void*. Artaud had been confronted with a similar void when viewing

André Masson's paintings in the 1920's. In them, he saw beyond the physical and colorful masses brushed on to the canvas—right into those dismal depths of columns, suns, mountains, surrounded with dead air, mirrors and black moons. From this other world, emerged mystery and magic, a whole new cosmic optic which he again felt when faced with Van Gogh's paintings.

> Why do Van Gogh's paintings give me the impression of being seen from the other side of the tomb, from a world where finally his suns will have been the only things that spun around and lit up joyously?
> For it is not the whole history of what was one day called the soul which lives and dies in his convulsive landscapes and flowers.[14]

Artaud also dwelled on the incredible faces painted onto Van Gogh's canvases. About a self-portrait by Van Gogh, he wrote:

> Van Gogh's gaze is hanging, screwed, glazed behind his naked eyelids, his thick wrinkleless eyebrows.
> It is a look that penetrates, pierces, in a face roughly-hewn like a well-squared tree.[15]

Facial features were also explored in a poem Artaud had written for the presentation of his own "Portraits and Drawings at the Galerie Pierre" (July 4-20, 1947). In this poem Artaud calls the human face "an empty power, a field of death" that has never yet fully revealed itself; a mystery to which the painter must give form. The artist must seize this amorphous entity from its depths; drag up its profound meaning from oblivion, free it and so save it from "perpetual death". Though man's face has existed for thousands of years, no artist, from Holbein to Ingres, to the present day, except for Van Gogh, has ever succeeded in making it talk. Van Gogh

> has extracted from a human
> head a portrait
> that is the
> rocket explosive of
> the beating of a burst
> heart.
> His own.[16]

Van Gogh forces the face to express the mysteries hidden within
and behind the material mask:

> by a void eye,
> and returned to the inner world,
> thoroughly drains all
> of the most specious
> secrets of the abstract world
> where the non-figurative painter
> can delight,—[17]

Art in any form, whether pictorial dramatic or musical, must
express man's inner reality by whatever material means at his
disposal. To be able to knead his feelings and instincts, to make
them take on a form comprehensible to others, to crystalize sentiments and thoughts, is the artist's only valid and eternal manner
of expression. Creation of any type had always meant for Artaud
a *search within:* now, as it had in 1925 when he wrote:

> In the course of this search buried in the limbo of my conscience,
> I thought I felt explosions, like the clashing of occult stones or the
> sudden petrification of fires. Fires which would be like insensitive
> truths miraculously vitalized.[18]

Artaud's contribution to the field of art criticism cannot be
unduly stressed. He made it live at a time when this art had
disintegrated to an unbelievable degree: it had become an aca-
demic exercise, not even that, a superficial and unintelligible
retort.

III

Artaud was *still* searching—and more desperately than ever
because strangely enough, he felt life's impact more fully now—to
exteriorize his emotions and thoughts, turning them into mobile
matter which could inflict the string of truth on his readers and
spectators, had become his goal. When on January 13, 1947, he
was asked to lecture at the Vieux-Colombier, Artaud was fully
prepared to expand his audience's optic by striking at their complacency first, by destroying the status quo of the conformist, by

introducing them to another world of unlimited vision, where cruelty (action) writhes like a bleeding serpent ready to pierce matter's destructive mask.

Artaud's lecture was entitled *Tête-à-Tête*. It drew an unexpected crowd. In fact, there was a frantic rush for tickets just before curtain time at 9 o'clock. No one had any idea that Artaud's performance would attract so many spectators and few, therefore, had bothered to reserve seats in advance. Six hundred people filled the tiny theatre, one hundred of whom had to stand. Among the spectators were André Gide, André Breton, Roger Blin, Jean Paulhan, Arthur Adamov, Albert Camus, Henri Pichette, producers, journalists, doctors. . . .

The air was expectant as Artaud walked on stage. Emaciated, his hair disheveled, he began reading some of his works.

Artaud le Momo, a poem, was part of the program. By *momo*, Artaud might have been referring to "Momos", the Greek God of raillery, sarcasm, and night. This latter aspect of "Momos" had perhaps endeared him to Artaud for it is during the dark hours, both real and symbolic, that imagination plunges into the very depths of both spirit and matter. The poem is replete with all facets of Momos' personality: from pleasant folly to the most bitter hatreds. In *Artaud le Momo*, the obsessive revulsion which Artaud felt for anything of a sexual nature is expressed with bristling passion. Lashing out at the very thought of being the product of a sexual union, he flaggelates God for having permitted the lascivious act of sexuality to exist; for having so deeply hurt him, and for having intentionally wounded the poet who is forever confronted with the repulsive story of sexual birth. Satire, irony, and immense bitterness are imbedded in those lines in which Artaud grapples with death, entombment, and mummification. Refrains such as the following are inserted, every now and then, to intensify the bitterness of his feelings and also to add to the religious flavor of the poem.

> O dedi
> O dada oyoura
> O dou zouvra
> A dada skizi. . . .

These possibly meaningless syllables which could sound, when read aloud, like an incantation or a religious prayer, were considered by Artaud as a means of invoking some cosmic force or being; also, possibly as a first step in conjuring forth that era which ante-dated the Tower of Babel Myth, as previously mentioned, when the language barrier was non-existent.

In the poem *Centre-Mère et Patron-Minet,* another poem Artaud read on that evening at the Vieux-Colombier, he again expresses his revulsion for the sexual birth, his extreme hatred for the copulating couple father and mother, for the evil two, whom he curses and condemns: "I condemn you because you know why . . . I condemn you . . ." In *La Culture indienne,* also included on the program, Artaud smothers himself in his obsession. In vivid, striking, sensual images, he pounds out in a circular construction his hatred for the "buggering" mother and father: the objects of his pitiful and fearful revolt.

Artaud's performance at the Vieux-Colombier was over. It was midnight. The audience was shocked. Friends and strangers were transfixed, as though welded to their seats; not knowing how to respond, except in stunned disbelief. An astounding, frightening, horrendous experience as described by Maurice Saillet, a journalist, in the following manner.

> . . . . when his impetuous hands fluttered like a pair of birds around his face; when his raucous voice, broken by sobs and stumbling tragically, began to declaim his splendid—but practically inaudible poems, it was as if we were drawn into the danger zone, sucked up by that black sun, consumed by that 'overall combustion' of a body that was itself a victim of the flames of the spirit.[19]

André Gide phrased his reaction to the performance in a letter to Henri Thomas.

> Artaud's lecture was more extraordinary than one could have supposed: it's something which has never been heard before, never seen and which one will never again see. My memory of it is indelible—atrocious, painful, almost sublime at moments, revolting also and quasi-intolerable.[20]

After the performance was over, Artaud admitted feeling more solitary than ever—alienated from everyone. Despite this sensation, with which he was well acquainted since he had experienced it in *all* of its ramifications, he kept right on creating: drawing, writing, reciting. On July 19th, Artaud, together with three of his friends, read poems which were accompanied by his own sound effects: for the most part, screams and cries. He wrote new poems: "Alienation and Black Magic" (*Aliénation et Magie Noire*) in which he attacked mental institutions, describing them as "receptacles" for the practice of black magic; areas where *death* is brewed and hatched; where doctors foment sickness, slowly killing their patients by sucking forth their living cells through electric shock and insulin treatment. Though Artaud dwelled on the horror and terror of past experiences, it did not prevent him from working without respite: constructively. Frequently, when writing in a notebook or on separate sheets of paper, alone or among friends, he would hum in rhythm to certain words which he seemed to be making up as he went along. These words, for the listener, were meaningless, but for Artaud they were as meaningful as plant language to plants and animal talk to animals. Artaud also continued the breathing exercises he had invented and which had now become an intrinsic part of his Theatre of Cruelty. As he scanned rhythms, panting out each beat, he was in the habit of using an enormous hammer or knife and hitting a block of wood at the same time. Dr. Delmas understood Artaud's need to express his inner tensions in whatever way he could, and it was he, therefore, who had the "imposing piece of wood, a barely squared tree trunk", brought into Artaud's room. By practising his special breathing system, Artaud had become master of both his voice and his intonations. And when he read verses to his friends, there was something electrifying in his presentation.

About poetry, Artaud wrote:

But they can only be read scanned, and only in rhythm the reader himself must find in order to understand and to think; . . . but this is only valid if it gushes forth at once; to search syllable by syllable is worthless and when written here and in this way it becomes meaningless and is nothing but ashes; another element which has been lost . . . is needed if the written word is to live.[21]

Mme. Paule Thévenin, who was studying poems by Baudelaire and Gérard de Nerval with Artaud at the time, described her endeavors as follows:

> I had to invent a melody and sing the verse. I could, in this way, understand the importance of the words in general and also sense the relationship between one word and another. I tried to read a poem after having practised this technique for a while. I did not always succeed in satisfying Artaud. I had to begin all over again and work until he was satisfied. . . . I had to learn to scream, to let this scream die out only when it had reached the point of annihilation, to go from the over-shrill to the deep tones, to prolong a syllable until my breath was exhausted. I believe I understood during the course of those sessions that the 'theatre of cruel purgation' really was.[22]

Artaud's breathing exercises were designed not merely to improve acting techniques; they were meant to be a *way of life*. Like the practice of yoga, which puts one into contact with universal forces altering organisms and vision, so *breathing* can also function in this domain, enlarging and rounding out each being's vision. Such a point of view was to lead Artaud one step further in his philosophical search. Through exercise, he claimed, extreme upheavals are experienced within the psyche and soma of man, after which the double and conflicting forces within unite and become one. The cataclysm and rebirth Artaud had predicted for the world at large in "The New Revelations of Being", could be achieved within the single being through such exercises.

For modern man to seek, much less attain, a state of unity is a difficult task and for many an unnecessary undertaking. For Artaud, however, it was essential; as it is for all those whose psychological equilibrium is deficient; whose conscious outlook is essentially unrelated to his unconscious instinctual side. As we have seen, Artaud believed that to achieve unity, destruction of matter in man must first take place. At this point in his life he went a step further. Now, the "Lord of Matter"—that is the Spirit, had to be annihilated too. The spirit, from which the material universe emanates, is flesh, according to certain mystics. Spirit is the essence of matter, the vibratory force emanating from God, that pervades all and eventually manifests itself as matter (or flesh).

Artaud was driven to this self-destructive activity perhaps unconsciously. For years, as we have seen, he had reviled the flesh, considering it base and dirty, believing it to be the source of sexuality, the great leveler, the delimiter. Renouncing sensuality on every level, rejecting any affiliation with his mother or father, any consideration of sexual birth—he had made the realm of the spirit his natural habitat. But now, he wanted to destroy the spirit.

In the poem "Shit to the Spirit", Artaud, therefore, rejects the spirit, its pseudo loftiness, its usurped pride. He labels it a "parasite", a "ringworm", a force which chooses to lord it over everything and so crush all in its wake. Such an aggressive and destructive attitude toward the spirit is also strongly voiced in Artaud's "Letter Against the Kabbala". Indeed, he calls these books of Jewish mysticism the "cock-and-ball-stew."[23] In his letter, Artaud asserts:

> If God is above all innumerable and unfathomable, and nobody ever could or did have God's number, then why not cease and desist from incessantly measuring and enumerating all these shadows of non-being into which, according to the Kabbala, he is in the process of withdrawing, beyond any possible return or recourse, from the innumerable numbers of creation.[24]

Artaud also turned on numerical symbolism in which he had formerly believed so strongly. Number "3", for example, Artaud declares to be "just as idiotic as the sign of the cross."[25]

Perhaps one of the reasons for Artaud's renunciation of the spirit as well as of numerical symbolism, was his extreme desire to reach his soul and his inability to do so. There were momen:s, however, when he almost broke through to the soul; with a sudden expansion of consciousness, he saw the universe from a different height. During these seconds of cosmic consciousness the mystics have said that the *all* can be seen; but these moments do not last, nor does the memory of them. All that remains is a feeling of nostalgia, a desire to relive this experience.

Artaud had said that he was searching for his soul through a cosmic experience, but he could not achieve this end permanently because he was always Antonin Artaud, a victim of his agonized body. To gain liberation from his body, he would have to destroy it, or else use the force of the soul to raise the level of his body (matter); to change the body from gross matter to *light*.[26] Artaud waged this battle until the very end and all of his poems indicate this huge conflict of forces.

Artaud's last poems pulsated with anger and love, vigor and pain. They were studded with moving and macabre refrains, repetitions, and neologisms. In the poems entitled: "Here I stand", "You have to begin with a will to live", "I hate and renounce as a coward", "Fragmentations", "Here lies", he confesses the differences which exist between himself and others: affirming that he is made neither of spirit nor of flesh; he is his own creation in this Godless world. "I am not of your world," he writes (in "Here where I stand") "mine is on the other side of all that is. . . ."[27]

The great torture which resulted from the struggle which was Artaud's life had permitted him to experience what few men have known—or rather, what few men have been able to express in verbal form: the vision of inner phenomena, *inner sight* which penetrates all barriers—even that of death. To achieve this sight within the abyss, that is, the experiencing of the wonders and horrors of an undifferentiated unconscious world, one must be willing to suffer torture, which is tantamount to agreeing to *act*. To act, by Artaud's definition, is in itself a *cruelty*, but essential for the creative *life*.

People content with a peripheral existence, who retreat into their external environments, who adhere to all the proper intellectual rules and regulations, eating what is fed to them, have never known the meaning of life. They are, therefore, dead. In "The Mistake is in the fact", Artaud declared that today "there are no live men, the whole earth having passed over to the dead." Man is dead because he simply never learned how to live: how to create himself by breathing life into his inner being, by fusing his disparate parts into one active organism. To live meant to Artaud

—to act, to hurt and be hurt, to experience fully joy and pain, and in so doing, to mould, *create*—and *recreate* oneself in the process.

Artaud created himself as had the Medieval alchemist who brought forth the homunculus: that sexless being whose expanded consciousness and whose concept of time and space permitted him new insights and deeper vision. And, Artaud affirmed that it is each being's obligation to create himself. No one must rely upon God, who does not exist, to accomplish this task. In Artaud's poem "I hate and renounce as a coward", God is dead because Artaud has himself assumed the role of creator.

> I hate and renounce as a coward every being who consents to having been created and does not wish to have recreated himself,
> i.e., who agrees with the idea of a god, at the origin of his being as at the origin of his thought.[28]

Man is his own creation, Artaud asserts over and over again in this same poem.

> I do not consent to not having created my body myself, and I hate and renounce as a coward every being who consents to live without first having created himself.[29]

Artaud's creation—himself—is a being where mind and body are *one; a* creature no longer tormented by sickly matter (body-spirit). And he goes one step further. Since man is his own creator he is forever in the process of recreating himself and is, therefore, immortal. The human body is immortal and perishes only "because we have forgotten how to transform it and change it". If one is acquainted with the secrets of physical transformation, one does not die nor is one turned into dust nor entombed, Artaud maintained. "I shall never cease being," he wrote in his poem "You have to begin with a will to Live" because

>   ... the human body is imperishable and immortal
>   and it changes,
>   it changes physically and materially
>   anatomically and manifestly,
>   and it changes visibly and on the spot, provided

You are really willing to take the material trouble
to make it change.[30]

Each time the organism is reborn it dwells in a "Superior
Body" in "those high brilliantly lighted planes";[31] higher, and
still higher, to "all the impassioned or psychic states that consciousness can evoke".[32] But with each birth and rebirth comes
agony.

In Artaud's "Letter to Pierre Loeb" (April 23, 1947), he attacks
those who are unwilling to go through birth pangs in order to
recreate themselves from themselves. It is only through change,
that is, destruction of past phases, annihilation of former attitudes, and physical aspects, that man can recreate himself. Otherwise, people spend their lives "counterfeiting being human". As
Shakespeare wrote in *Hamlet* (Act III, ii)

> . . . that I have thought some of Nature's journeymen had made men
> and not made them well, they imitated humanity so abominably.

If man, according to Artaud, tries to escape his individual ordeal,
his drama will have "passed into fable", and instead of experiencing perpetual creation he will know perpetual "cremation".
Until man becomes aware of his destiny and of his role in the
cosmos he will suffer over and over again.

For Artaud then the circle of existence was eternal: destruction
and rebirth—perpetual creation. This was as true for all phases
of existence as it was for any field of endeavor. The theatre was
certainly no exception. Ever since Artaud had founded the Alfred
Jarry Theatre, he had maintained that the theatre was *not* meant
to be a form of entertainment, but rather "the exercise of a dangerous and terrible act" practised over and over again *ad infinitum*. In the poem "Theatre and Science", Artaud pursues this
same idea of perpetual metamorphosis; indicating that to experience life in its myriad aspects within the framework of the theatre,
can literally bring about an "organic and physical transformation
of the body". The theatre then is a "crucible", Artaud writes, "of
fire and real meat". By annihilating mental and physical attitudes, by cracking the totality of man's organism, one paves the
way for renewal—on to lighter and more profound planes.

During the theatrical ceremony "all the dramatic, driven-under and fugitive forces of the human body," are lashed.[33] Whipping them up in this manner gives them the necessary momentum to burst forth with a crash. The forces within, like an ocean, can then surge forth turbulently or calmly—bring experience and then rebirth. To refuse such activity is to abdicate life—to degenerate and to die—for at that moment of rejection "the body is keeping its breath in irons".[34]

The same type of struggle is again depicted by Artaud in his poem "To End God's Judgment" (*Pour en finir avec le jugement de Dieu*) which is also in many ways a summing up of Artaud's philosophy. While he enveighs venomously against modern society, American militarism, scientific materialism, and God, the spreader of false forms, a "monkey" who must be eradicated once and for all, he accords an important place to the conflict between what he terms "bone" and "flesh". The "bone" as used by Artaud in this work symbolizes the hard fight each individual must wage with himself, between *being* and *living*. Only the latter force paves the way for rebirth into a more profound realm.

Artaud warns his readers and listeners that each person who *knows* conflict and seeks to grow, must expect a shearing of flesh and a letting of blood in the act of life which is a *cruelty.*

> To be you can let yourself go until you just exist,
> but to live,
> you must be someone,
> to be someone,
> you must have a Bone,
> not be afraid to show the bone,
> and to lose the meat by the wayside.[35]

As the fight for living progresses and daily existence becomes a more dynamic phenomenon, there ensues a broadening of vision and with it, further questioning and weightier hazards.

> And what is infinity?
>
> We do not know exactly.
>
> It is a word
> which we use

to indicate
WIDENING
of our consciousness
towards an inordinate,
inexhaustible and inordinate
feasibility.[36]

With an increase in consciousness or *sight* or *light,* there comes a corresponding diminution of matter, including physical pain. For Artaud, the torture of his body so obsessed him that it motivated nearly every action and thought, particularly at this period when his physical torments were nearly ceaseless.

but there is one thing
which is something,
only one thing
which is something,
that I feel
wants to
COME OUT:
the presence
of my bodily
pain,

the menacing
never increasing
presence
of my
body [37]

Artaud was the center of his universe and everything radiated outward.

As the days struggled on, still Artaud refused to stifle his creative breath, still his pains grew worse. Frequently, he was even forced to remain in bed. In fact, Artaud was experiencing such torment that his friends implored him to see a doctor. But he could not agree to consult a physician since he felt such contempt for both doctors and medicine. But when Artaud began hemorrhaging from the rectum, he finally agreed, thanks to Mme. Paule

Thévenin's intercession, to a complete physical examination and a series of X-Rays. Dr. Mondor concluded that Artaud was suffering from an advanced case of cancer of the rectum. The verdict: inoperable.

Though the prognosis was carefully concealed from Artaud he knew his own body too well to think for one moment that he was suffering from some passing ailment. In fact, Mme. Thévenin reported that Artaud frequently spoke of the "animal which was gnawing at his anus." As his pain increased, so did his intake of chloral, since opium was no longer effective. The doses of chloral put him into comatose states.

Artaud's will, however, was almost indomitable; so when Fernand Pouey of the *Radio-Diffusion Française* invited him to present a poem, to be broadcast on February 2, 1948, Artaud accepted with pleasure and it was for this occasion that he wrote "To End God's Judgment". Artaud worked arduously on the production of his radio poem, traveling almost daily back and forth from Ivry to Paris to direct the actors[38] who were performing in it, and to create the sound effects.

Artaud's great hopes for the success of "To End God's Judgment" were dashed on the eve of the scheduled radio production, when Wladimir Porché of the *Radio-Diffusion Française* forbad the performance. A press war ensued. On February 5, Fernand Pouey scheduled a private studio broadcast of the poem. Among the fifty spectators were Raymond Queneau, Roger Vitrac, Louis Jouvet, Paul Éluard, and Jean-Louis Barrault.

The banning of "To End God's Judgment" was a severe blow to Artaud. He seemed to wane quickly now. There were days when he walked with difficulty, when his right arm became paralyzed. Mme. Paule Thévenin reports that he frequently repeated, "I have nothing more to say, I have said everything I had to say."

Then on March 4, 1948, when the gardener at Ivry brought Artaud his breakfast, as he did each morning, he found him seated at the foot of his bed—dead.

CONCLUSION

"I KNOW ANTONIN ARTAUD only through his trajectory in me which is endless."[1] So wrote Roger Blin, the well known French director who had known Artaud and had played the part of one of the assassins in "The Cenci". As M. Blin indicated, to assess Artaud's precise contributions and the resonating influence of his works is like attempting steady footing on quicksand or rendering fluid static.

Artaud was like a torrent that burst forth upon a Paris already replete with currents and cross-currents: Symbolism, Dadaism, Surrealism, etc. The impact of Artaud's ideas upon the already virile artistic forces generated a whole new series of thought-waves which, in turn, gathered momentum, slowly at first then with volcanic power, culminating in the works of another generation of writers: Genet, Beckett, Ionesco, et al.

Although influenced by the Greeks, Romans and Orientals; by such thinkers as Nietzsche, Wagner, Jarry, Appia, and Strindberg, Artaud's *unique* theatrical invention was a direct result of his malady. His physical and mental torment was so acute as to make it impossible for him to see the world except through the dark prism of his tortured *Self*. Unable to master his titanic inner force he became its slave. His dramatic aesthetics not only reflect an awareness of this state of affairs, but also a painfully urgent need to restore harmony and balance to a discordant and unsteady personality.

Artaud's theatrical concepts were in many ways similar to that of the ancients, looking upon the dramatic spectacle as a ritual, a Myth, capable of evoking a numinous or religious experience within the spectators. Just as collective Myths (that is, man's living religion) had been dramatized by Aeschylus, Sophocles, Seneca, and others, so must modern authors, he felt, write from their own numinous experiences to create new myths. To make the spectators' theatrical experience meaningful, these up-to-date myths must be enacted on stage in modern terms to suit man's present day needs.

The religious (enactment of a Myth) or metaphysical drama advocated by Artaud would deal with the eternal conflict between man and natural forces. Artaud rejected the Occidental theatre's stress on intellectual understanding, on psychology (character study), on didacticism. He looked to the Oriental theatre for guidance. To evoke that which is profoundest within man and endemic to him, the Orientals combined formalized gestures, evocative sound effects, rhythmic movements, physical attitudes, words used as symbols and a whole metaphysical breathing technique. Artaud wished to use the same elements to express the contents of modern man's unconscious.

The Theatre of Cruelty which Artaud invented sought visceral reactions from the audience through the use of a new theatrical language. This language would be capable of expressing aurally and plastically the equivalent of the inner non-material world of man and the cosmos. Artaud conceived of a concrete theatrical language that would appeal to the senses rather than to the intellect; for he did not believe that the rational approach was the most effective way to reach into man's being. After all, Artaud wrote, a serpent does not react to music because of the "intellectual" notion he brings to it. As it slithers along the ground, it comes into contact with the musical vibrations which act upon the serpent like a "subtle massage". So the theatre must act upon the spectators and "charm the viewers through their organism" or shock them into a more profound state of awareness. With this deepened insight, audiences would be able to project their own torments on to the stage happenings and by means of such objectification, hopefully, become aware of their problem, making catharsis possible.

Artaud's ideas may be outlined very briefly in the following manner:

1. Rejection of psychological, literary, and didactic theatre:
2. Return to a theatre of myth (a metaphysical theatre) as known to the ancients and to the Orientals;
3. Founding of a Theatre of Cruelty (action), in order to create a new optic;
4. The invention of a new theatrical spacial language (the importance accorded to gesture, movements, masks, etc.)
5. The pre-eminence of the dream world or of the unconscious which explains the archetypal nature of the characters in Artaudian theatre;
6. The intent to touch, stir, shock the spectator for *therapeutic* reasons by eliciting sharp visceral effects;
7. The use of new breathing techniques by actors as a basis for their portrayals;
8. Each theatrical performance should be a fresh experience for the participants;
9. The role played by the audience as a contributing factor to the dynamism of the spectacle;
10. Theatrical performance as a microcosm in the cosmic whole.

Why are Artaud's ideas—violently rejected by his contemporaries—so acceptable today?

One reason for his failure during his lifetime may have been that the fulgurating insights of his genius were frequently obscured by a chaotic and repetitious writing style. But the fundamental cause of this phenomenon is more likely that what had been Artaud's individual situation in the 1920's and 1930's had become a collective malady a generation later. In his time, he was a man alienated from his society, divided within himself, a victim of inner and outer forces beyond his control—and he remained isolated in an indifferent world. The tidal force of his imagination and the urgency of his therapeutic quest were disregarded and cast aside as the ravings of a madman. Today, things have changed.

Increasingly aware of the forces of dissolution that threaten to overwhelm society; faced with the very real possibility of extinction; modern man's psyche has been altered. Fearfully aware of the threat of dissociation and of a growing lack of identity, modern man seeks frenetically for a solution to his plight. This quest, whether on a conscious or unconscious level, has brought today's sentient beings to a fuller awareness of the precarious nature of their situation. In a word, modern man can respond to Artaud now because they share so many psychological similarities and affinities.

Artaud was a seminal force: a man who helped create an intellectual climate. One may talk of Artaud's direct or indirect influence upon writers, directors, actors and spectators, but more important than this is the role he played in setting the stage for an entirely different point of view: namely, a therapeutic theatre that is the meeting ground for visceral and spiritual actions and reactions. His work has achieved acceptance because it answers a need in man today.

It is difficult to define the *precise* influence Artaud had on modern authors and directors (whether acknowledged or not). The following paragraphs will make the attempt, but only in the briefest manner and on the most superficial levels.

In Jean Genet's theatre, for example (*The Blacks, The Balcony*), religious atmosphere and ritual are of primary importance. In Beckett's drama (*Waiting for Godot, End Game*) archetypal characters use the densest language and all action is symbolic. Eugene Ionesco's plays (*The Bald Soprano, The Chairs*) are, for the most part, allegories in which a shattering of language patterns gives words the force and presence of concrete objects: the words become characters in themselves. Fernando Arrabal's spectacles (*Fando and Lis, The Automobile Graveyard*) reveal the most secret fantasies as a series of grotesque creatures emerge full grown from his dream world or from his unconscious. Jean

Vauthier uses (*Captain Bada, The Character Against Himself*) a spacial language very similar to what Artaud had advocated: sound effects, objects, accessories, and lighting are given volatile personalities of their own, in order to arouse and disturb the spectator. Harold Pinter (*The Homecoming, The Birthday Party*) pays particular attention to verbal patterns which he uses to intensify the tensions of his instinctual fractured characters. Arnold Wesker (*The Kitchen*), drawn to fables, employs Artaud-like sound effects extensively. Edward Albee (*The Zoo Story, Who's Afraid of Virginia Woolf*) has a penchant for shocking language and situations as advocated by Artaud. The more socially oriented Günter Grass (*The Tin Drum, The Wicked Cooks*) is drawn to elliptical stage happenings, jarring sounds and bizarre visual patterns to shake the spectators' complacency as does Peter Weiss (*Marat-Sade, The Investigation*). Peter Schaffer's *The Royal Hunt of the Sun* is, in my opinion, a virtual transposition of Artaud's metaphysical drama *The Conquest of Mexico*.

Directors also have been affected by Artaud's aura—directly and indirectly. Roger Blin, for example, who directed plays by Genet and Beckett, is prone to emphasize sets, lights, gestures as well as the metaphysical aspects of a work. Michael Cacoyannis (*Iphigenia* and the opera *Mourning Becomes Electra*) accords extreme importance to stylized acting, choreography and sound effects. When Peter Hall directed *The Homecoming* he underscored the mystery and horror of the drama by creating a series of mobile stage images, by using gestures and words as the repositories of arcane contents. *Marat-Sade* as directed by Peter Brook, became a horrendous drama—a dance—in which all theatrical forces (visual, aural, intellectual) were mustered in order to arouse a visceral reaction in the spectator. In fact, Peter Brook and Charles Marowitz founded a Theatre of Cruelty (1963), an experimental group affiliated with the Royal Shakespeare Company which produced works by Artaud, Robbe-Grillet, Brook, Genet, Arden, etc. Realistic, naturalistic, psychological approaches to the theatre were banished, as the twelve actors and actresses chosen to participate in this adventure, were plunged "into the swirling waters of Artaudian theory."[2]

Today, plans are afoot for productions of Euripides' *The Bacchae* and Seneca's *Thyestes,* works that Artaud desperately wished to stage, but for which he failed to find backing. In these dramas—essentially Theatre of Cruelty plays—elemental life patterns emerge and clash with cosmic spiritual forces, revealing the eternal Mystery of existence—brittle, beautiful, and brilliant as a black diamond encircled by flames.

Artaud knew, prophetically, that the world would adopt his optic eventually. Though the Theatre of Cruelty remained only a vision during his lifetime, the seed he perceived and planted took root in the creative arts with the passage of time. Today, in the theatre, in music, the pictorial arts—*cruelty,* as envisioned by Artaud has become a living reality, part of everyday jargon. The theatre of the Absurd and the theatre of happenings, op, pop, and psychedelic art, electronic, serial and *musique concrête* are all designed to arouse, disturb, and evoke bizarre and powerful sensations within man, visceral reactions capable of transforming or distorting man's conceptions of the world and himself. It is even conceivable that man's new perceptions will indeed change his ideas concerning time and space, that consciousness will expand to include the infinite cosmic abysses, that individual identity will vanish amid the swirling collective forces which threaten to overpower man today.

Perhaps what Artaud feared so desperately—inner and outer Cataclysm—may yet come to pass!

NOTES

CHAPTER I

1. *Artaud Anthology* (Translated by David Ossman), p. 33.
2. Paule Thévenin, "1896-1948," *Antonin Artaud et le théâtre de notre temps,* mai 1958, p. 17.
3. *Ibid.*
4. Antonin Artaud, *Oeuvres complètes,* III, p. 118.
5. *Ibid.,* II, p. 153.
6. *Ibid.,* p. 154.
7. On March 22, 1922 Artaud played the part of a Moorish King in *Moriana et Galvan,* a three-tableaux play drawn from the *Romancero Moresque* (Moorish Romance) by Alexandre Arnoux. He designed the costumes for the interlude *Les Olives* (The Olives) by Lope de Rueda, and played the part of Sottinet in Regnard's work *Le Divorce* (The Divorce). On April 1, 1922, Artaud portrayed the blind man for the interlude *L'Hotellerie* (Hostlery) by Francesco de Castro, and he created the costumes for this interlude as well. On the same evening, he played Don Luis in Calderon's work, *Visites de condoléances* (Condolence Calls). Two months later, in Calderon's *La Vie est un songe,* (Life is a Dream) for which Artaud had designed the costumes, he played the role of Basile—a role whose breadth fascinated him. He wrote:

> ... my role has prodigeous sweep, it has something
> of the King Lear type about it, as if I myself were
> playing the part of King Lear.

Dullin admired Artaud's Basile very much and wrote that it was "astonishing." In October 1922, *Life is a Dream* was revived, and in November of that same year Artaud performed the role of Apoplexie in *La Mort de Souper* (Diner's Death), a morality play in verse by Nicole de la Chesnaye. But Dullin was disappointed in Artaud's portrayal of a member of the Administrative Counseil in Pirandello's *La Volupté de l'Honneur* (The Voluptuousness of Honor). Dullin wrote that Artaud appeared, for the part of this bourgeois, in make-up inspired by the little masks which Chinese actors use as models. Such make-up in Dullin's opinion was completely out of place in this modern tragedy. Though there were differences of opinion between Dullin and Artaud concerning the interpretation of various roles, Artaud remained in the troupe.

A novel event took place in November: a free adaptation of Sophocles' *Antigone* by Jean Cocteau, with music by Honegger and decors by Picasso. Artaud portrayed the blind seer, Tiresias, a visionary character for whom he probably felt great affinity. In 1923 Artaud portrayed Pedro Urdemalas in *Monsieur de Pygmalion,* a tragi-comic farce by Jacinto Grau. He seemed to incarnate the spirit of evil perfectly and Dullin wrote that he created quite a stir each time he cracked his whip and pronounced "Urdemala."

8. Jean Hort, *Antonin Artaud*, p. 69.
9. Marie-Ange Mallausséna, "Antonin Artaud," *La Tour de Feu,* decembre 1959, p. 44.
10. Paule Thévenin, "1896-1948," *Antonin Artaud et le théâtre de notre temps,* mai 1958, p. 17.
11. With the Pitoëff troupe, Artaud played the part of the First Mystique in *La petite baraque* (The Small Hut) by Alexandre Block (November 22, 1923), the role of Jackson in *Celui qui reçoit les gifles* (He Who Gets Slapped) by Leonid Andreyeff, and the Prompter in *Six personnages en quête d'auteur* (Six Characters in Search of an Author) by Luigi Pirandello. Artaud was impressed by Pitoeff's directing and by his insight into the characters he portrayed. Writing about the production of *Six Characters in Search of an Author,* Artaud declared:

Thus, by successive gliding, reality and spirit penetrate
each other so thoroughly, that we no longer know, we spectators,
when one begins and the other ends.

Antonin Artaud, *Oeuvres complètes,* II, p. 161.
12. The poems included in *Tric Trac du Ciel* are the following: *Orgue*

allemand, Neige, Prière, Amour, La Trappe, Romance, L'orgue et le vitriol, Lune.

13. *Antonin Artaud Anthology* (Translated by Bernard Frechtman), p. 9.
14. *Ibid.*, p. 7.
15. *Ibid.*, p. 10.
16. *Ibid.*
17. *Ibid.*, p. 13.
18. *Ibid.*, p. 14.
19. *Ibid.*, p. 21.
20. One might compare this feeling to those of Jean Genet's characters in *Our Lady of the Flowers.*
21. *Op. cit.*, p. 20.
22. *Ibid.*, p. 20.
23. *Ibid.*, p. 21.
24. *Ibid.*, p. 24.
25. *Ibid.*, p. 25.

CHAPTER II

1. *Artaud Anthology* (Translated by Bernard Frechtman), p. 8.
2. *Tric Trac du Ciel* featured woodcuts by Elie Lascaux.
3. C. G. Jung, *Symbols of Transformation*, p. 293.
4. *Artaud Anthology* (Trans. Marc Estrin), p. 27.
5. Like the physicists who seek to understand and control energy, Artaud tried to discover and understand the nature and function of thought processes, so that he might gain control over his own thinking. As any scientist might, he used the experimental material at hand. He tried to dissect his own thought patterns, to capture and examine that moment *before* the *idea* took shape and rooted itself within the word. Artaud wanted to feel thought ever present and strong within him, but the *word* Artaud sought to extract from the mass of mysterious forces within him, either through the drug or naturally, seemed either to lose its force or else to elude him constantly.

The loss of the word (thought), the inability to express the inner world via language, or to express the infinite by using finite forms, was a problem that had troubled not only Artaud, but which has preoccupied mystics from time immemorial. In the *Zohar*, "The Book of Splendor", a work which fascinated Artaud, *speech* was said to have been a product of divine emanation. Thought, the inner unheard word and voice, was considered a differentiated expression of the deity within the Self.

The Kabbalist mystics tried to translate these emanations into an esoteric language made up of mysterious series of letters and words with no apparent connection. They "revealed" words that are formed within the void and emerge from it and about which Artaud speaks, actually arise, according to the Mystics, from a state of Nothingness or Chaos, and are transmuted into Being and Something. Gershom Sholom, *Jewish Mysticism*, pp. 52-67.

6. *Artaud Anthology* (Translated by Jack Hirshman) , p. 26.
7. *Op. cit.,* p. 218.
8. *Ibid.*
9. *Ibid.,* pp. 52-67.
10. *Ibid.*
11. Antonin Artaud, *Oeuvres complètes*, I, p. 60.
12. *Ibid.,* p. 32.
13. *Ibid.,* p. 33.
14. *Ibid.,* p. 64.
15. C. G. Jung, *Symbols of Transformation,* p. 99.
It must be recalled that the mouth and the tongue are active and rhythmic organs of pleasure, Jung stated. The mouth also represents the organ of speech and as such is an expression of a concentration of emotional forces. Images such as *fire* (energy) are associated by him with *Spirit*, which is in turn allied to *Speech*. Such associations are evident in many religious works. The Holy Ghost, for example in the *New Testament,* was said to have appeared to the Apostles in the form of flames. In the Bible, mouth, speech, and fire are also frequently related, as witnessed in *Jeremiah* (23:29) :
> Is not my word like as a fire? saith the Lord; and like a hammer that breaketh the rock in pieces?
In *Psalm 29:* "The voice of the Lord divideth the flames of fire."
16. Antonin Artaud, *Oeuvres complètes,* I, p. 55.
17. Concerning the scorpions, for example, one read in *Revelations*: (9:30 and 9:10) :
> And there came out of the smoke locusts upon the earth;

and unto them was given power, as the scorpions of the earth have power.

And they had tails like unto scorpions, and there were stings in their tails: and their power was to hurt men five months.

18. *Op. cit.,* p. 287.

19. This article was not signed, but attributed to Artaud by Maurice Nadeau in his *Histoire du Surréalisme.*

20. Maurice Nadeau, *Histories du Surréalisme,* pp. 740-6.

21. *Artaud Anthology* (Translated by David Rattray), p. 117.

22. This same expression is used by Northern Buddhists in a similar fashion. Hidden forces live and function within man's body in a fragmented state and are imprisoned there. When liberated or when the "knots" are "untied", these forces are released and returned to their original unity.

23. To try to understand more adequately Artaud's obsession with his "thought processes" or the mechanics of his mind, it might be fitting here to examine a similar kind of preoccupation on the part of a man whose disposition and nature are diametrically opposed to Artaud's: Paul Valéry.

Paul Valéry advocated a rational and intellectual control over irrational inspiration and passion. Such a decision, however, had been made only after having experienced an agonizing crisis of despair at the age of twenty-one. For over twenty years thereafter, Valéry stopped publishing because he had come to the conclusion that writing was a mere game. He chose, instead, to spend his time studying mathematics, meditating on abstract problems and trying to understand the mechanism of thought.

By a complete and total act of Valéry's conscious mind, he sought to focus his attention not on what had already been created by him, but on *creation itself,* that is, to exercise consciously his powers as creator. His aim was to see the world in one *intuitive vision,* to discover its continuity, the link between things, the analogies (the faculty of combining images) —to know the secret of all creation. One of the functions of man's supreme instrument, the mind, was to create: creating was an ordering, a construction or reconstruction of the world's unity, a translation of feeling and ideas into a universal language of metaphors.

Valéry, master of his faculties, knew that inspiration was nothing without attention, judgment, reflection, and discernment. To him, ideas and sensations, those "Mysterious favors" that surged forth during a moment of "illumination" from the unconscious, helter-skelter, were not all worthy of being included in the work of art. Valéry captured his ideas, isolated them and adjusted them through the ordered use of his mind. He could, therefore, express the joy he felt during those moments of inspiration.

24. Antonin Artaud, *Oeuvres complètes*, I, p. 108.

CHAPTER III

1. Antonin Artaud, *Oeuvres complètes*, II, p. 14.
2. *Ibid.*, I, p. 217.
3. *Ibid.*, II, p. 12.
4. *Ibid.*, p. 31.
5. *Ibid.*, I, p. 215.
6. *Ibid.*, II, p. 12.
7. *Ibid.*, II, p. 13.
8. *Ibid.*, I, p. 201.
9. *Ibid.*, I, p. 215.
10. Anaïs Nin, *The Diary of Anaïs Nin*, p. 163.
11. Artaud had first thought that the program for the 1926-1927 season would be the following: *La Peur c'est l'Amour* (*Le peur chez l'amour*, Dialogue No. 8, in *L'Amour en visites* by Alfred Jarry) : *Le Vieux sur la Montagne*. (last or 10th part of *L'Amour en visites* by Alfred Jarry) : and *Les Mystères de l'Amour*.

    The three plays Artaud did direct were produced under the most trying conditions. Rehearsals began in May 1927, in the small rehearsal hall in the Théâtre de l'Atelier lent to them When the Théâtre de Grenelle was finally available, only rehearsal was possible before opening night, and that took May 31st. The cast for *Les Mystères de l'Amour* was ma the following: Génica Athanasiou, Jacqueline Hopstei. Mamy, Edmond Beauchamp, Raymond Rouleau, René Le.
12. Antonin Artaud, *Oeuvres complètes*, II, p. 267.
13. *Ibid.*, III, p. 317.

    Much of Claudel's theatre bears the theme of an impossible love which always comes into conflict with his Catholic faith.

Le Partage de Midi was not produced until 1948 and then, by Jean-Louis Barrault, and with Claudel's permission.

In Artaud's production of *Break of Noon*, the cast consisted of the following: Génica Athanasiou, André Berley, Henri Crémieux, etc., and was directed by Artaud.

14. Antonin Artaud, *Oeuvres complètes*, II, p. 272.

The cast for *A Dream Play* consisted of Tania Balachova, Yvonne Save, Ghita Luchaire, Raymond Rouleau, Strarem, Maxime Fabert, Boverio, Decroux, Beauchamp; Artaud played the part of the Dean of Theology.

15. *Ibid.*
16. *Ibid.*, p. 262.
17. *Ibid.*
18. *Ibid.*, III, p. 141.
19. The cast for *Victor* included Elisabeth Lannay, Edith Farnese, Jeanner Bernard, Germaine Osler, Domenica Blazy, Marc Darnault, Robert Le Flon, Auguste Bovério, Maxime Fabert, Max Dalban.
20. *Op. cit.*, II, p. 363.
21. *Ibid.*, II, p. 17.
22. *Ibid.*, I, p. 213.
23. *Ibid.*, II, p. 23.
24. *Ibid.*, II, p. 23.
25. *Ibid.*, II, p. 77.
26. Henri Béhar, "Lettres d'Antonin Artaud à Roger Vitrac," *Nouvelle Revue Française,* April 1, 1964.

CHAPTER IV

1. Antonin Artaud, *Oeuvres complètes*, III, p. 23.
2. *Ibid.*, III, p. 80.
3. *Ibid.*, III, p. 74.
4. *Ibid.*, III, p. 151.
5. *Ibid.*, III, p. 164.
6. Jean Cocteau, *Oeuvres complètes*, X, p. 260.
7. Maurice Bardèche and Robert Brasillach, *Histoire du Cinéma,* p. 9.
8. Eileen Bowser, *The Films of Carl Dreyer.*
9. Artaud acted in the following movies: *Mater Dolorosa* (Abel Gance,

speaking version, 1933); *Napoléon* (Gance, part of Marat, 1926);
Lucrèce Borgia (Gance, part of the monk Savanarola, 1935);
Jeanne d'Arc (Carl Dreyer, Monk Massieur, 1928); *L'Argent*
(Marcel L'Herbier, Mahaud, 1928); *La Femme d'une nuit* (Marcel
L'Herbier, 1930); *Tarakanova* (Raymond Bernard, Young Gypsy,
1929); *Les Croix de Bois* (1931); *Faubourg Montmartre* (1931);
L'Opéra de Quat'Sous (Georg Wilhelm Pabst, 1931); *Verdun,
Visions, d'histoire* (Léon Poirier, a Young Intellectual, 1930); *Fait
Divers* (Claude-Autant-Lara, Monsieur 2, 1925); *Entr'acte* (René
Clair, the Joueur, 1924); *Sourcouf* (Louis Morat, 1922); *Le Juif
Errant* (1926); *Graziella* (Marcel Vandal, Cecco, 1926); *Coup de
Feu à l'aube* (Alliance Cinématographique, made in Berlin); Serge
de Poligny, 1932); *Sidonie Panache, L'Enfant ma soeur* (Louis
Nalpas); *Liliom* (Fritz Lang, 1934).

10. Antonin Artaud, *Oeuvres complètes*, III, p. 74.
11. *Ibid.*, III, p. 21-24. ("The Surrealist Film", *Art Forum*, translated by Toby Mussman, September, 1966).
12. Paule Thévenin, "1896-1948," *Cahiers de la Compagnie Madeleine Renaud Jean-Louis Barrault,* mai 1958.
13. *Ibid.*
14. Antonin Artaud, *Oeuvres complètes*, III, p. 20.
15. *Ibid.,* VI, p. 407.
16. *Ibid.,* VI, p. 417.
17. To make certain that *The Monk* would become the persuasive agent Artaud had hoped it would be, he built up the episodes of the Bloody Nun, the Wandering Jew, the fall and disaster at the convent, the pursuit through the catacombs, the apparition of the magic statue. These hypertense adventures aroused Artaud's senses and evoked image upon image in his imagination.
18. *Op. cit.,* III, p. 73.
Artaud and Bernard Steel translated *Crime passionnel* by Ludwig Lewisohn. It was published by Denoël and Steel in June, 1932.

CHAPTER V

1. The Orientals had made a Temple of their theatre. Indeed, the Hindus felt that Brahma had created drama. It is said that the

No drama in Japan developed out of the dance which had been invented by the Gods.

Sheldon Cheney, *The Theatre Three Thousand Years of Drama Acting and Stagecraft,* p. 106.

2. Antonin Artaud, *Oeuvres complètes,* III, p. 218.

3. Antonin Artaud, *The Theatre and its Double* (translated by Caroline Richards) , p. 71.

4. *Ibid.,* p. 67.

5. Oriental theatre is *presentational* and Occidental is *representational.* The former, therefore, does not consider that the actor should be "believed" as a "real person" he is portraying, but rather an actor acting a role. Nor is the stage area considered the "real place" where the play is being enacted but simply a platform for acting. The Orientals do not reproduce nature realistically on stage nor does the Oriental actor reproduce reality, that is, by acting realistically. He transmutes what appeals to him into rhythmic and visual patterns. Only when he has created his own image or his concrete conception of reality, does his work have any artistic value. In the Oriental theatre, the actor, the audience, and the performance exist on one plane, that of actuality. No one "pretends" to "believe". Therefore, direct communication exists.

Earle Ernst, *The Kabuki Theatre,* p. 18.

6. Antonin Artaud, *The Theatre and its Double* (translated by Caroline Richards) , p. 65.

7. The metaphysical element is particularly evident in the Balinese "trance dances," the most exciting of which is the "fire dance." Here, two girl performers, after reciting prayers, pouring libations, and drawing mandalas, plunge into real flames, where they remain stamping about, until they have extinguished the last ember. Neither costumes nor feet are burned. During their frantic dance they have reached a deeper level of consciousness—they exist in a transcendental world. Their dance, therefore, no longer belongs to man who lives but a transitory existence, but to a superior intelligence; Brahma, Vishnu, Krishna, Siva. Acting or dancing for the Balinese is a sacred, transcendental rite.

Faubion Bowers, *The Theatre in the East,* p. 247.

8. C. G. Jung, *Psychology and Religion*: West and East, p. 560.

9. Antonin Artaud, *The Theatre and its Double* (translated by Caroline Richards) , p. 116.

10. C. G. Jung, *The Archetypes and the Collective Unconscious*, p. 6.

11. Antonin Artaud, *The Theatre and its Double* (translated by Caroline Richards), p. 102.

12. *Ibid.*, p. 104.

13. C. G. Jung, *The Archetypes and the Collective Unconscious*, p. 96.

15. Antonin Artaud, *The Theatre and its Double* (translated by Caroline Richards), p. 85.

16. *Ibid.*, p. 85.

17. Antonin Artaud, *Oeuvres complètes*, IV, p. 112.

18. *Ibid.*, III, p. 232.

19. Antonin Artaud, *The Theatre and its Double* (translated by Caroline Richards), p. 134.

20. They can be seen as "objects of inner perception and sensed as external phenomena." C. J. Jung, *The Archetypes and the Collective Unconscious*, p. 33.

21. Antonin Artaud, *The Theatre and its Double* (translated by Caroline Richards), p. 135.

22. *Ibid.*

23. *Ibid.*, p. 136.

25. Antonin Artaud, *The Theatre and its Double* (translated by Caroline Richards), p. 139.

26. *Ibid.*, p. 135.

27. Artaud goes into a detailed discussion concerning the six possible breathing combinations: neuter, masculine and feminine. And into further detail in "Le Théâtre de Seraphin."

28. Antonin Artaud, *The Theatre and its Double* (translated by Caroline Richards), pp. 133-141.

29. *Ibid.*, p. 140.

30. *Ibid.*, p. 140.

31. C. G. Jung, *Psychology and Religion*: West and East, p. 560.

32. Both alchemy and the theatre consist of both the virtual and the material: both are reflections and externalizations of unconscious and primordial dramas within man. Both actor and alchemist create their realities by means of symbols and through illusion. The actor, for example, takes an amorphous and inanimate entity (his role) and tries to transform it into a lifelike creation. In doing so, he reveals mysterious and powerful elements within man's psyche through projection. These unknown forces or this "psychic energy" is, according to C. G. Jung, comparable to the alchemists' "secret fire,"

to Heraclitus' "ever living fire", to the "primal warmth" of the Stoics. It means an all-pervading vital force which lives within man —and the cosmos and which is necessary to the actor's art.

33. Antonin Artaud, *The Theatre and its Double* (translated by Caroline Richards), p. 110.

34. *Ibid.*, p. 46.

35. Artaud sought "diffused action" as did the Orientals in certain respects and perhaps for similar reasons. It must be noted that there are few visual centers in Oriental, and particularly in Kubuki, theatre. According to Earle Ernst, in his excellent work, *The Kabuki Theatre,* interest on stage is widely dispersed. One actor may be performing on one side of the stage while someone else may be gesturing on another. A performance consists of a series of "parts" of a play isolated in space. These parts of images are usually not bound together according to a so-called rational pattern as they are in the West. There are no situations created to develop progression, suspense or depth of character, as the Westerners think of it.

36. Such spatial isolation had been intrinsic to Buddhist culture and philosophy from time immemorial. For the Buddhist, existence consists of a series of fleeting moments. Mind, matter, and time, as conceived by the Westerner as something tangible, is *unreal* for the Buddhist. Nothing is permanent for the Buddhist because "continuity" and "duration" do not exist. Life is not a whole, but a series of agglomerations. Time, for the Oriental, is a concept devoid of meaning. It is a figment of the mind. There is no past and no future. The only concrete reality is the *moment* or *actuality*.

37. Antonin Artaud, *Oeuvres complètes,* V, p. 234.

38. The plays Artaud saw produced in Paris and elsewhere in France at that time, were mere "mechanical" exercises and held little or no interest for him. In a letter to Jean Paulhan (January 22, 1933), he declared that the outline and *mise en scène,* so far, of what he intended for the theatre.

> .... one sees in a concrete, lucid fashion, well couched in words, exactly what I want to do, and my plastic, palpable and spatial theatrical conceptions appear in their most perfect form in it.— *Oeuvres complètes,* V, p. 197.

39. Antonin Artaud, *The Theatre and its Double* (translated by Caroline Richards), p. 126.

40. *Ibid.*
41. The historical facts concerning Mexican colonization were as follows. Montezuma II (1466-1520) was ruler of Mexico when Fernando Cortez (1599), chafing for gold and conquest, arrived on his shores. Certain tribes, dissatisfied with Montezuma's rule, rebelled against him and joined forces with the invader. Aware of his precarious situation, Montezuma sent his Ambassador, laden with gifts, to Cortez. He also gave orders to prevent the invaders from gaining access to his capital. Montezuma's men, however, were unable to stop Cortez. The Spanish conqueror not only dethroned Montezuma, but took him as hostage. In despair, Montezuma let himself die.
42. Antonin Artaud, *The Theatre and its Double* (translated by Marie Richards), p. 129.
43. *Ibid.,* p. 130.
44. Antonin Artaud, *Oeuvres complètes,* III, p. 229.
45. Erich Neumann, *The Origins and History of Consciousness,* p. 195.
46. This drama is unfinished. It was designed to be an opera for which Edgard Varèse was to write the music. Only four of the six movements were written. (Pauline Thévenin, "The stage Music for the Cenci").
47. Antonin Artaud, *Oeuvres complètes,* II, p. 101.
48. *Ibid.,* III, p. 207.
49. *Ibid.,* III, p. 291.
50. *Ibid.,* p. 296.
51. *Ibid.,* p. 303.

Artaud considered Seneca the greatest of tragic authors, even more profound in certain respects than Aeschylus. Seneca's plays had all the qualities needed for what Artaud termed a "Theatre of Cruelty". Artaud wrote: "In Seneca the echo of the primordial forces is heard in the spasmodic vibrations of the words."

Seneca had spent most of his life studying, writing, and instructing his disciple Nero in the stoic philosophy. He was a man in complete control of himself. Indeed, when ordered by his former pupil to kill himself, he opened his veins and bled to death, always with the greatest of Stoic control. Yet, it was Seneca who brought instinctuality to the stage, he who created creatures motivated by what was deepest within them—their bestiality. The monstrous creatures that Seneca created were those "buds" which lived within him and which he forever sought to destroy or to dominate.

52. To raise funds for *The Cenci,* Artaud decided to give a reading of *Richard II* and of a theatrical scenario *La Conquête du Mexique* (The Conquest of Mexico) at the home of his friend Lise Deharme, a writer. His hopes of raising the desired funds failed. Artaud felt he had been "betrayed" by his hosts. They had promised him 30,000 francs. They rewarded his efforts with merely a pittance. In a pitiful letter to Jean Paulhan, Artaud asks him to collect the needed 15,000 francs to make the production of *The Cenci* a reality. By February 1935, miraculously enough, Artaud succeeded in raising the necessary funds for his production.

Princess George of Greece, Princess Edmond de Polignac, Count E. de Beaumont were present, among others, at the gala opening of *The Cenci.*

In Shelly's preface to *The Cenci,* he tells his readers that he had been given a copy of a certain document stored in the archives of the Cenci palace in Rome. From it, he learned about the hideous Cenci incident in history. Francesco Cenci, murderer and vice-ridden creature that he was, Shelley indicated, had been pardoned several times by the Pope for his capital crimes after having paid the Pontiff considerable sums of money. The Pope was incensed by Count Cenci's murder, since his treasury would then be deprived of "copious sources of revenue." Shelley further stated that he increased the "ideal" and diminished the "actual horror of the events . . ." He substituted, therefore, Count Cenci's nail-hammering death for one by strangulation, which he considered less offensive to his sensibilities. He had been led to feel great compassion for Beatrice Cenci after he had seen the painting Guido Reni had made of her while she was in prison awaiting execution. For Shelley, Beatrice was an ideal loveliness.

When Stendhal went to Italy in 1923 he was struck by Guido Reni's "admirable portrait" of Beatrice Cenci. He was touched by her beauty, her large and tender eyes. He was also impressed by the painting of Lucretia Petroni, Beatrice's step-mother, a matronly type of woman, possessed of a proud natural beauty. According to Stendhal's translation of an eye-witness account of the Cenci incident, the Count had sent his three older sons to study at the University of Salamanca in Spain. Once there, however, the Count sent no money for living expenses and his sons were forced to beg their way back to Rome. After indulging in a series of "infamous loves" and murders, Count Cenci was sent to prison. His three sons begged the Pope to sentence their father to death. The Pope was unwilling to do so and after receiving large sums of money from the Count, freed him. At liberty once again, Count Cenci had his two older sons murdered. It has been said, wrote Stendhal, that this Italian nobleman used to parade around his castle in the nude with his daughter Beatrice beside him. Then he took her to his wife's bed and by the light of the lamp forced his wife to witness his antics. When Beatrice would resist him he would beat her. Two assassins were hired to murder the Count, by hammering a nail into one of his eyes, and another, into his throat as he slept. After the trial, Lucretia, Beatrice, and her brother, Giacomo were put to death.

53. Antonin Artaud, *Oeuvres complètes,* V, p. 303.
54. *Ibid.,* V, p. 45.
55. This exchange is reminiscent of the Faustian myth.
56. Antonin Artaud, *Oeuvres complètes,* IV, p. 188.
57. Lucifer came to be regarded as Satan before his downfall.
58. For a further discussion of God as *One* see C. G. Jung, *Symbols of Transformation* and *The Archetypes and the Collective Unconscious.* For an excellent discussion of man's relationship with God and with himself in ancient times see William Barret, *Irrational Man,* pp. 69-91.

In ancient times such a situation did not exist. *God* was *One.* He incorporated within himself both Good and Evil. In Egypt, for example, Ra, the Sun God, spent half of his life in light (Good) and about the earth, and the other half in darkness (Evil), when he passed beneath the earth during his "night journey". In Greece Gods were close to man and were forever performing Good and Evil deeds. They were amoral, that is, all forces co-existed within their beings. God, for the Hebrew was *One.* We read in *Deutero-Isaiah* (40-55) or the Second Isaiah, the following:

> I form the light, and create darkness;
> I make peace, and create evil; I the Lord do all these
> things.

With the coming of the Persians who believed in the Zoroastrian concept of the principle of Good in the form of Ahuramazda, and the principle of Evil in the form of Ahriman, the *One God* of the past was transformed into a *Double God.* After Nebuchadnezzar had destroyed Jerusalem (586 B.C.) and carried away the Hebrews to

Babylonia, the Hebrews had a Persian ruler. The Persians influenced their way of thinking, to a certain extent, in connection with the dual forces of Good and Evil, preparing the way perhaps for the split subsequently introduced by Christianity. (For an excellent study concerning this question see Salo W. Baron, *A Social and Religious History of the Jews,* I and II.)

Christian ascetics taught man to abhor his "lowly" or "instinctual" half and worship his "spiritual" or "god-like" aspect. The Saint, a creation of Christianity, which supplanted the old Wise Man of ancient religions, introduced the "inhuman condition" of rejecting permanently everything which was connected to man's physical side, that is, to man himself. Bodily pleasures were considered Evil. But the more one-sided man's conscious attitude became, the more it activated its counterpole in the unconscious. Each half of man was now at war with the other. One of the many interesting examples of such splits occurred to St. Anthony. As a hermit, trying to destroy his physical or manly half in order to become the all-spiritual being he idealized, St. Anthony had vision upon vision of sensual and earthly pleasures. Nietzsche expressed the change over from pre-Christian to Christian thought in *The Dawn*

The passions become evil and insidious when they are considered evil and insidious. Thus Christianity had succeeded in turning Eros and Aphrodite—great powers, capable of idealization—into hellish goblins . . .

. . . . gradually the "devil" Eros became more interesting to men than all the angels and saints, thanks to the whispering and the secret-mongering of the Church in all erotic matters: this has had the effect, right into our own times, of making the love-story the only real interest shared by all circles—in an exaggeration which would have been incomprehensible in antiquity and which will yet be laughed at someday . . . .

The Portable Nietzsche (translated by Walter Kaufman) , p. 79.

59. Antonin Artaud, *Oeuvres complètes,* IV, p. 191.
60. *Ibid.,* V, p. 46.
   Paule Thévenin, "A propos de la musique de scène des Cenci".
61. *Ibid.,* IV, p. 200.
   Notice how this theme is used in Jean Genet's *The Balcony.*
62. Similar feeling is achieved by Victor Hugo in his poem *La Rose de*

l'Infante when he contrasts the whiteness of the Infanta to the Blackness of the Spanish monarch Philip II.

63. Antonin Artaud, *Oeuvres complètes,* IV, p. 204.

64. Paule Thévenin, *A propos de la musique de scène des Cenci.*

65. Antonin Artaud, *Oeuvres complètes,* IV, p. 250.

66. The wheel was a popular form of torture during the Middle Ages.

67. Antonin Artaud, *Oeuvres complètes,* V, p. 41.

68. *Ibid.,* p. 327.

69. *Ibid.,* p. 54.

70. Iya Abdy played the part of Beatrice Cenci and possessed tremendous strength and power according to Artaud. Roger Blin portrayed one of the mute assassins as well as one of the guests at the banquet. Antonin Artaud acted the part of Count Cenci.

71. Antonin Artaud, *Oeuvres complètes,* IV, p. 169.

72. Perhaps it was his attraction to fire and energy which prompted Artaud to write *Héliogabale.* It is a documented, philosophical, and metaphysical study of the Roman Emperor (204-222), Marcus Aurelius Antonius, a member of a sun-worshipping cult. As a youth he had been made the great priest of this adored God who appeared to his worshippers in the form of a black stone, the Heliogabalus. Marcus Aurelius Antonius identified himself, Artaud wrote, with this God who embodied all opposing principles, forgetting both family and name. Slowly however, the Emperor gave himself over so completely to debauchery that his mother was obliged to attend to the affairs of state. The situation became so critical that Marcus Aurelius Antonius was killed by a Prætorian Guard.

CHAPTER VI

1. *Artaud Anthology* (translated by David Rattray), p. 83.

2. The published articles by Artaud are the following: "L'homme contre le Destin" (April 26 to May 24, 1936 *El Nacional*).

"Premier Contact avec la Révolution Mexicain" (June 3, 1936, *El Nacional*).

"Une Médée sans Feu" (June 7, 1936, *El Nacional*).

"La Jeune Peinture française et la tradition" (June 17, 1936).

"Pourquoi je suis venu au Mexique" (July 5, 1936, *El Nacional*) .

"La Culture Eternelle au Mexique" (July 13, 1936, *El Nacional*) .

"La Fausse Supériorité des Elites" (July 25, 1936, *El Nacional*) .

"Secrets Eternels de la Culture" (August 1, 1936, *El Nacional*) .

"Les Forces Occultes du Mexique" (August 9, 1936, *El Nacional*).

"L'Anarchie Sociale de l'Art" (August 18, 1936, *El Nacional*) .

"La Montagne des Signes" (Oct. 14, 1936, *El Nacional*) .

"Le Pays des Rois-Mages" (Oct. 24, 1936, *El Nacional*) .

"Le Rite des Rois de l'Atlantide" (Nov. 9, 1936, *El Nacional*) .

"Un Race—Principe" (November 17, 1936, *El Nacional*) .

"Le Théâtre de l'après-guerre à Paris" (June 1936, *Revista de la Universidad Nacional Autonoma de Mexico*) .

"Franz Hals" (July 1936, *Boletin Mensual Carta Blanca*) .

"La Peinture de Maria Izquierdo" (August 1936, *Revista de Revistas*) .

3. Antonin Artaud, *Les Tarahumaras,* p. 182.

4. *Ibid.,* p. 202.

5. *Ibid.,* p. 204.

6. Eric Bentley, *In Search of Theatre,* pp. 126, 186.

7. *Op. cit.,* p. 148.

8. *Artaud Anthology* (translated by David Rattray), p. 77.

9. Antonin Artaud, *Les Tarahumaras,* p. 128.

10. *Artaud Anthology* (translated by David Rattray) , p. 71.

11. *Ibid.,* p. 73.

12. Marie Seton, *Sergei M. Eisenstein,* pp. 205-213.

13. *Artaud Anthology* (translated by David Rattray) , p. 73.

14. *Saint Matthew* II, 1-17.

15. C. G. Jung, *Symbols of Transformation,* pp. 98-107.

16. Antonin Artaud, *Les Tarahumaras,* p. 61.

17. *Ibid.,* p. 212.

18. C. G. Jung, *Symbols of Transformation,* p. 178.

19. Antonin Artaud, *Les Tarahumaras,* p. 159.

20. *Ibid.,* p. 159-166.

21. C. G. Jung, *The Archetypes and the Collective Unconscious,* pp. 174-175.

22. Sir James George Frazer, *The New Golden Bough* (Edited by Theodor H. Gaster) , p. 466.

23. Antonin Artaud, *Les Tarahumaras,* p. 14.

24. *Ibid.,* p. 17.

25. *Ibid.,* p. 12.
26. *Ibid.,* p. 31.
27. LSD: *The Consciousness-Expanding Drug* (Edited by David Solomon).
28. *Artaud Anthology* (Translated by David Rattray), p. 78.
29. *Ibid.,* p. 77.
30. *Ibid.,* p .80.
31. *Ibid.,* p. 79.
32. Antonin Artaud, *Les Tarahumaras,* p. 25.
33. *Artaud Anthology* (translated by David Rattray), p. 83.
34. *Ibid.,* p. 83.

CHAPTER VII

1. Antonin Artaud, *Oeuvres complètes,* VII, p. 199.
2. *Ibid.,* p. 202.
3. *Ibid.,* p. 194.
4. *Ibid.,* p. 439.
5. *Ibid.,* p. 224.
6. *Ibid.,* p. 233.
7. *Ibid.,* p. 240.
8. *Ibid.,* p. 250.
9. *Artaud Anthology* (translated by David Rattray), p. 98.
10. Antonin Artaud, *Oeuvres complètes,* VII, p. 151.
11. Paule Thévenin, "A Letter on Artaud," *Tulane Drama Review,* Spring, 1965.
12. *Ibid.*
13. *Ibid.*
14. Antonin Artaud, *Oeuvres complètes,* VII, p. 282.
15. Paule Thévenin, "1896-1948", *Cahiers de la Compagnie Madeleine Renaud Jean-Louis Barrault,* May 1958, p. 38.
16. Antonin Artaud, *Oeuvres complètes,* VII, p. 284.
17. *Ibid.,* p. 286.
18. *Ibid.,* p. 289.
19. Antonin Artaud, *Lettres de Rodez,* p. 24.
20. There are certain people who feel that Artaud did not want to recognize his mother.

21. Dr. Armand-Laroche, *Artaud et son Double,* p. 28.
22. Paule Thévenin, "1898-1948", *Cahiers de la Compagnie Madeleine Renaud Jean-Louis Barrault,* May 1958, p. 40.
23. Gaston Ferdière, "J'ai soigné Antonin Artaud," *La Tour de feu,* December, 1959.
24. Dr. Armand-Laroche, *Artaud et son Double,* p. 58.
25. *Op. cit.*
26. Maurice Saillet, "Close to Artaud," *Evergreen Review,* May-June, 1960.
27. *Lettres d'Antonin Artaud à Jean-Louis Barrault,* p. 117.
28. Antonin Artaud, *Les Tarahumaras,* p. 99.
29. *Ibid.,* p. 102-103.
30. *Ibid.,* p. 103.
31. *Ibid.,* p. 104-109.
32. C. G. Jung, *Symbols of Transformation,* pp. 85-96.
33. Honoré de Balzac, *Louis Lambert,* p. 447.
34. Antonin Artaud, *Les Tarahumaras,* p. 113.
35. Antonin Artaud, *Letters from Rodez,* p. 14.
36. *Ibid.,* p. 15.
37. *Ibid.,* p. 15-16.
    Fragments of Artaud's adaptation of Jabberwocky were published in an article on Lewis Carroll in *L'Arbalète.*
38. *Ibid.,* pp. 18-19.
39. *Ibid.,* pp. 18, 39.
40. *Ibid.,* p. 27.
41. *Ibid.,* p. 17.
42. Erich Neumann, *The Origins and History of Consciousness,* p. 26.
43. Antonin Artaud, *Les Tarahumaras,* p. 114.
44. Paule Thévenin, "Letter on Artaud," *Tulane Drama Review,* Spring, 1965, p. 101.
45. Gaston Ferdière, "J'ai soigné Antonin Artaud," *La Tour de feu,* December, 1959.

CHAPTER VIII

1. Paule Thévenin, "A Letter on Antonin Artaud," *Tulane Drama Review,* May-June, 1965.

2. *Ibid.*, p. 42-43.
3. *Artaud Anthology* (translated by Jack Hirshman), p. 128.
4. Maud Bodkin, *Archetypal Patterns in Poetry*, 1963.
5. *Artaud Anthology*, (translated by David Rattray), p. 127.
6. *Ibid.*, p. 128.
7. Antonin Artaud, *Oeuvres complètes*, I, pp. 178-186.
8. *Ibid.*, II, pp. 197-206.
9. Pierre Loeb, "Dessinateur et Critique," *Cahiers de la Compagnie Madeleine Renaud Jean-Louis Barrault*, Mai, 1958.
10. *Ibid.*, p. 48.
11. *Artaud Anthology* (translated by Mary Beach), p. 146.
12. *Ibid.*, p. 146.
13. *Ibid.*, p. 156.
14. *Ibid.*
15. *Ibid.*, p. 160.
16. *Ibid.*, (translated by Jack Hirschman), p. 231.
17. *Ibid.*, p. 232.
18. Antonin Artaud, *Oeuvres complètes*, I, p. 236.
19. Maurice Saillet, "Close to Artaud," *Evergreen Review*, May-June, 1960.
20. J. L. Armand-Laroche, *Antonin Artaud et son Double*, p. 31.
21. Paule Thévenin, "A Letter on Antonin Artaud," *Tulane Drama Review*, Spring, 1965, p. 106.
22. *Ibid.*, p. 107.
23. *Artaud Anthology*, "Letter Against the Kabbala," (translated by David Rattray), p. 113.
24. *Ibid.*
25. *Ibid.*, p. 120.
26. Light is a word used by the mystics and by Artaud as far back as his essay on Abélard in *Art and Death*, and means the regions of the soul.
27. *Artaud Anthology* (translated by Jack Hirshman), p. 201.
28. *Ibid.*, (translated by David Rattray), p. 222.
29. *Ibid.*, p. 222.
30. *Ibid.*, (translated by Daniel Moore), p. 170.
31. *Ibid.*, p. 172.
32. *Ibid.*, p. 173.
33. *Ibid.*, p. 170.
34. *Ibid.*, p. 173.

35. "To End God's Judgment," *Tulane Drama Review*, Spring, 1965, p. 66.
36. *Ibid.*, p. 69.
37. *Ibid.*, p. 72.
38. The actors were: Roger Blin, Maria Casares, Paule Thévenin.

CHAPTER VIII (Conclusion)

1. *Critique,* July, 1948.
2. *Tulane Drama Review,* Winter, 1966, p. 154.

SELECTIVE BIBLIOGRAPHY

WORKS BY ANTONIN ARTAUD

Oeuvres complètes, Paris, Gallimard, I-XIV, 1956-1980.

Translation of *Crime Passionel* by Ludwig Lewisohn in collaboration with Bernard Steele, Paris, Denoël et Steele, 1932.

L'Arve et l'aume tentative anti-grammaticale contre Lewis Carroll.

Xylophonie contre la grande presse et son petit public (in collaboration with Henri Pichette, "Historie entre le Groume et Dieu," Paris, 1946.

Lettres de Rodez, Henri Parisot, Paris, 1946.

Ci-gît, précédé de la culture indienne, Paris, K., 1947.

"Portraits et dessins par Antonin Artaud," (containing the poem "Le Visage Humain"), Paris, Galerie Pierre, July 4-20, 1947.

Artaud le Momo, Paris, September 15, 1947.

"Le Chevalier mate tapis" (Ye Carpette Knygts poem by Lewis Carroll adapted by Antonin Artaud), *Les Cahiers du Sud*, No. 287, 1948.

Supplément aux Lettres de Rodez suivi de Coleridge le traître, Paris, G. L. M., 1949.

Lettre contre la Cabbale adressée à Jacques Prével, Paris, J. Haumont, 1949.

Suppôts et Supplications, (extracts) *Temps modernes*, No. 40, February, 1949.

Suppôts et Supplications, (extracts) *La Nef*, December 1950-January, 1951.

Lettres d'Antonin Artaud à Jean-Louis Barrault, Paris, Bordas, 1952.

La Bouche ouverte, Paris, 1952.

Vie et Mort de Satan le feu (Serge Bernar) Paris, Arcane, 1953.

"Lettres à André Breton," *L'Ephémère*, 8, 1954.

Les Tarahumaras, Decines (Isere), l'Arbalète, 1963.

Lettres d'Antonin Artaud à Roger Vitrac (Henri Béhar), *Nouvelle Revue Francqise, April 1, 1964.*

To End God's Judgment (Victor Corti translation), *Tulane Drama Review*, Spring, 1965.

Artaud Anthology (edited by Jack Hirshman), San Francisco, City Lights Books, 1965.

The Theatre and its Double (Mary C. Richards translation), New York, Grove Press, 1958.

SECONDARY SOURCES

Armand-Laroche, J. H., *Antonin Artaud et son Double*, Perigueux, Pierre-Franlac, 1964.

Baron, Salo, *A Social and Religious History of the Jews*, N.Y. Columbia University Press, I & II, 1952.

Barrett, William, *Irrational Man*, New York, Doubleday Anchor Book, 1962.

Bardèche, Maurice, Brasillach, Robert, *Histoire du Cinéma*, Paris, Les 7 Couleurs, I, 1964.

Barrault, Jean Louis, *The Theatre of Jean-Louis Barrault*, New York, Hill and Wang, 1961.

————. *Réflexions sur le théâtre*, Paris, Vautrain, 1949.

Balakian, Anna, *Literary Origins of Surrealism*, New York, King's Crown Press, 1964.

Bays, Gwendolyn, *The Orphic Vision*, Lincoln, University of Nebraska Press, 1964.

Benedikt, Michael and Wellwarth, George E., *Modern French Theatre*, New York, E. P. Dutton and Co., 1966.

Bentley, Eric, *In Search of Theater*, Vintage Book, 1953.

Bodkin, Maud, *Archetypal Patterns in Poetry*, Oxford University Press, 1963.

Bowers, Faubion, *Theatre in the East. A Survey of Asian Dance and Drama*, New York, Grove Press, 1960.

Bowser, Eileen, *The Films of Carl Dreyer*, New York, Museum of Modern Art, 1964.

Brau, Jean-Louis, *Antonin Artaud*, Paris, La Table Ronde, 1971.

Breton, André, *Manifeste du Surréalisme*, Paris Gallimard "Idées", 1963.

————. *La Clé des Champs*, Paris, Les Editions Sagittaire, 1953.

Cahiers de la Compagnie Madeleine Renaud Jean-Louis Barrault, "Antonin Artaud et le Théâtre de notre temps," Paris, Julliard, mai, 1958.

Charbonnier, Georges, *Antonin Artaud*, Paris, Seghers, 1959.

Cheney, Sheldon, *The Theatre: Three Thousand Years of Drama Acting and Stagecraft*, New York, Tudor Publishing Co., 1947.

Collomp, Alain, *Antonin Artaud: De la Maladie a l'oeuvre* (medical doctoral dissertation), Paris, Editions A.G.E.M.P., 1963.

Duplessis, Yves, *Le Surréalisme*, Paris, Presses Universitaires, 1961.

Ernst, Max, *La Femme 100 Têtes*, Paris, Editions du Carrefour, 1929.

Ernst, Earle, *The Kabuki Theatre*, New York, Oxford University Press, 1956.

Ferdière, Gaston, "J'ai soigné Antonin Artaud," *La Tour de feu*, December, 1959.

Fowlie, Wallace, *Age of Surrealism*, Bloomington, Indiana University Press, 1960.

Frazer, James George, *The New Golden Bough*, New York, Criterion Books (edited by Dr. Theodor H. Gaster), 1959.

Gide, André, *Journal*, Paris, Pléiade, 1954.

—————. "Hommage à Antonin Artaud," *Combat*, May 19, 1948.

Gouhier, Henri, *Antonin Artaud et l'essence du théâtre*, Paris, Vrin, 1974.

Greene, Naomi, *Antonin Artaud: Poet Without Words*, New York, Simon and Schuster, 1970.

Hort, Jean, *Antonin Artaud*, Genève, Editions connaître, 1960.

Joski, Daniel, *Artaud*, Paris, Editions Universitaires, 1970.

Jung, C. G., *Psychology and Religion: West and East*, New York, Pantheon, 1958.

—————. *Symbols of Transformation*, New York, Pantheon, 1952.

—————. *The Archetypes and the Collective Unconscious*, New York, Pantheon, 1959.

La Tour de feu, "Antonin Artaud ou la Santé des poètes," December, 1959.

Lemaître, Georges, *From Cubism to Surrealism in French Literature*, Cambridge, Mass., Harvard University Press, 1945.

MacKensie, Norman, *Dreams and Dreaming*, New York, Vanguard Press, 1965.

Mallausssena, Marie-Ange, "Antonin Artaud," *Revue théâtrale*, No. 23, Annee 8, 1953.

—————. "Affaire Antonin Artaud ce qu'l faut savoir," *La Tour de feu*, December 1959.

Mangeot, Guy, *Histoire du Surréalisme*, Bruxelles, René Henriquez, 1934.

Mussman, Toby, "The Surrealist Film," *Art Forum*, September, 1966.

Nadeau, Maurice, *Historie du Surréalisme*, Paris, Seuil, 1945.

The Diary of Anaïs Nin, New York, Harcourt Brace, 1966.

Neumann, Erich, *The Origin and History of Consciousness,* New York, Pantheon Books, 1954.

Plottel-Parisier, Jeanine, *Les Dialogues de Paul Valéry,* Paris, Presses Universitaires de France, 1960.

Sadoul, Georges, *Dictionnaire des cinéastes,* Paris, Seuil, 1965.

————. *Dictionnaire des films,* Paris, Seuil, 1965.

Saillet, Maurice, "Close to Antonin Artaud," *Evergreen Review,* May-June, 1960.

Scott, A. C., *An Introduction to the Chinese Theatre,* Singapore, Moore, 1958.

Sellin, Eric, *The Dramatic Concepts of Antonin Artaud,* Chicago, University of Chicago Press, 1968.

Sholem, Gershom G., *Major Trends in Jewish Mysticism,* New York, Schocken Books, 1961.

————. *Zohar the Book of Splendor,* New York, Schocken Books, 1949.

Seton, Marie, *Sergei Eisenstein,* A. A. Wyn, 1952, New York.

Sollers, Philippe, ed. *Artaud,* Colloque de Cérisy, Union Générale d'Editions, 1973.

Théâtre Populaire, "Relire Artaud," No. 18, mai, 1956.

Thévenin, Paule, "1896-1948", *Cahiers de la Compagnie Madeleine Renaud et Jean-Louis Barrault,* Paris, Julliard, mai, 1958.

————. "A Letter on Artaud," *Tulane Drama Review,* Spring, 1965.

Virmaux, Alain, *Antonin Artaud et le théâtre, Paris,* Paris, Seghers, 1970.

Zoete, Beryle de and Spies, Walter, *Dance and Drama in Bali,* London, Faber and Faber, Ltd., 1938.

INDEX